It's All In The Stars

Zolar is the leading astrologer of the United States. His interpretations of the heavens and their effect upon the individual are read by more millions than those of any rival in his craft.

Whether or not you believe that the conjunctions of the planets can really affect personality or influence the course of events, you must believe in the uncanny accuracy of his characterisations. To look oneself up under the proper birth date is to be confronted by a pen portrait which can startle the non-believer, and reveal tendencies which inevitably follow from the sort of person you are.

As an explanation of the science and an exercise in the casting of horoscopes, to those of great or little faith, this book, in its gripping personal application, stands supreme.

It's All In The Stars

Zolar

TANDEM
14 Gloucester Road, London SW7

First published in Great Britain by Allan Wingate
(Publishers) Ltd., 1970

Published by Universal-Tandem Publishing Co. Ltd., 1973

I dedicate this book to Pythagoras, Hippocrates, Manilius, Ptolemy, Copernicus, Galen, Tyche, Brahe, Kepler, Newton, Dryden, Bacon, Lilly, Raphael, and Alan Leo – without whose wisdom this work would have been impossible.

Made and printed in Great Britain by
Hunt Barnard Printing Ltd., Aylesbury, Bucks.

ARIES
HEAD

TAURUS
NECK

GEMINI
ARMS

CANCER
BREAST

LEO
HEART

VIRGO
BOWELS

LIBRA
REINS

SCORPIO
SECRETS

CONTENTS

PREFACE

Astrology itself is a combination of two sciences: Astronomy and Correspondences. These two are related to each other as hand and glove. The former deals with Suns, Moons, Planets, and Stars, and strictly confines its researches to a knowledge of their size, distance, and motion. The latter deals with the spiritual and physical influences of the same bodies—first upon each other, then upon the earth, and, lastly, upon the organism of man. Astronomy is the external lifeless glove; Astrology the living hand within.

It was from the mystical land of Chaldea that the Egyptians derived their knowledge of Astronomy and Astrology. This knowledge was, fortunately, transplanted to fertile soil and flourished for untold ages under the fostering care of a mighty priesthood and colossal sacerdotalism.

From the fertile valley of the Nile, long ages before Abraham and his herdsmen wandered over the desert of Arabia, this sublime science of the starry heavens, with its priestly devotees, was carried by tidal emigrations over the Caucasus, across the arid steppes of Asia, through the wild mountain passes of Afghanistan and Tibet, to the burning plains of Hindustan, and thence spread by Indian's dusky sons among the Mongol and Tartar races of the still more remote East.

From the magical schools of lost Atlantis the sacred stream of learning flowed towards the rising sun into the regions of Central Africa, and from there to the coast, up the Persian Gulf to Chaldea. Then from the banks of the sacred Euphrates and the plains of Shinar the stream flowed backwards (as though weary and seeking rest) towards its native home in the Western seas. It was detained upon its journey and found a temporary resting place in the wondrous valley of the Nile; but after changing its personal appearance somewhat and adopting the dress of its gifted patrons, it was again projected onwards by the restless impulse of Egyptian enterprise, along the shores of the Mediterranean and Black Seas to the Caucasus, and thence eastward, as before mentioned, to the dreamy skies of India.

When we come to think of the imposing vastness and inconceivable beauty of the glittering worlds which stud, like jewels, the dark canopy of our midnight skies, we must admit that the contemplation of the shining heavens, with its myriad galaxies of starry systems and stretches of fathomless space, forms a sublime area of luminous study. There, alone, can we see something of the unbounded unity of the universe. But to the Occult student of Urania's blazing firmament, the shining constellations, with their cabalistic names and weird mythological histories, the glittering suns of these far-off astral systems, and the shining planets which belong to the same solar family as ourselves possess a deeper interest. Everything around us, save it, is in a state of transition. Besides the fleeting changes which the return of the seasons brings, the landscape around us changes its aspect every year. In fact, all around us is change.

But the gorgeous creations in the sky are still there: undimmed in brightness, unchanged in grandeur, performing, with unflagging pace and unvarying precision, their daily, annual, and mighty cyclic rounds.

Upon the same heavens, just as we see them now, bespangled with the same planets and with the same familiar stars, gazed the first parents of our race when they began and ended their pilgrimage upon this mundane sphere. The same constellations, Arcturus, Orion, and the Pleiades, sang together with the morning stars when the fiery foundations of our earth were laid, and they rolled in the fabled darkness over Calvary when the gentle Nazarene was slain. They are truly the only objects which all nations have witnessed, and all people admired. They are truly the only objects in the universe which have so far remained unpolluted by the finger of man. They presided at the Horoscope of our birth; they will sing the funeral requiem when we die, and cast their pale radiance over the cold, silent tombs beneath which we are ultimately destined to repose.

Before the aspirant can become an Astrologer he must make himself familiar with the general principles of

Astronomy, and learn how to trace the external symbo. physical life, which are the phenomenal results, back into the stellar worlds of cause.

One must not expect the revelation of some divine, mysterious secret that will instantly convey the power of reading the past, realizing the influence of the present, and foreseeing the momentous events within the sphere of the future. On the contrary, one must expect nothing but a clear and concise statement of nature's immutable laws, which require both study and application to master. The principles involved and the ultimates evolved as the natural outcome of cause and effect can only be mastered and understood by devoting time and unprejudiced thought: first in learning the theory, and then in reducing that theory to practice.

Astrology does not imply fatality. On the contrary, probably two-thirds of man's so-called misfortunes are the result of his ignorance. Man, when ignorant of the laws of nature which control his existence and destiny, is somewhat like a lifeless log floating with the stream. It may be that the various currents of the river will carry him safely to the river's mouth, and launch him uninjured upon the great Ocean of Eternity. But it is far more likely that the winding course of the river of life will land him into a mud bank of trouble where he may stick fast for the remainder of his days; or, liberated by some stronger current, may again take his chances, either on future safety or on floating into some whirlpool of destruction.

When man understands the laws of his being, he is then safe on board a strong boat. He sees the whirlpools and mud banks of life ahead, and skilfully, by the use of his steering apparatus (the will), avoids collision. But it often happens that with all his knowledge and skill he cannot successfully battle against the mighty currents that oppose his way, simply because there are, in these days, too many lifeless logs of human lumber that are constantly throwing themselves with the swell of the current across his path. It must be at once apparent how infinitely superior the one is to the other, and how enormous the chances of success are upon the side of the one who has attained this wisdom—who, by study, knows himself.

"The heavenly bodies urge, predispose and influence to a

great extent, but they do not compel." When we are ignorant of their power, we decide our actions to the best of our worldly knowledge, and we think we have free will in the matter. If we could only see the influences at work moulding our actions, we would realize that we are obeying the stellar powers with slave-like servility—not always wisely, but blindly and too well.

Under such a state of bondage the planetary influence would, indeed, be fatality. Knowledge alone is the great liberator of human suffering and social inharmony. Our self-control increases exactly in proportion to the extent of our knowledge. "It is the Wise Man who rules his stars, and the fool who blindly obeys them." Consequently, this Chaldean science of the stars, in order to be practically utilized, must be thoroughly realized; but when realized it will repay a hundredfold for the time and labour bestowed. It will give the student a tangible foundation whereon he may safely stand amid the wild and conflicting opinions of unbalanced mystics. In it he will find the key to the sacred sanctuary wherewith he may eventually unlock the doors of the temple and penetrate the mystic veil of Isis, there to behold the lovely form of the Goddess and to read the glowing verities of nature inscribed upon the imperishable scrolls of time and, if he have the will to seek further and deeper, the truths of eternity itself.

Astrology, in its purity, though forming a system of divination, is totally unconnected with either fortune-telling or insensitive, irresponsible mediumship. It is a divine science of Correspondences, in the study and application of which the intellect and intuition become blended in a natural, harmonious manner. They commence to vibrate in unison. When this union becomes complete, the ignorant man becomes the prophetic sage.

The Chaldean sages, when constructing their mighty system of sidereal Astrology, held to one idea throughout the whole of their philosophy. In order to penetrate the mysteries of God, they first sought out the mysteries of man, and then formulated a complete science of Correspondences. The human organism, so complex in its wonderful mechanism and so beautifully harmonious in all its parts, became their architectural design upon which they constructed the Grand

Man of the Starry Heavens. The twelve Signs of the celestial Zodiac were divided into sections of the human frame, so that the entire Zodiacal belt was symbolized as a man bent round in the form of a circle, the soles of the feet placed against the back of the head. Each of the twelve Signs contains 30 degrees of space, the whole making 360 degrees of a circle. The number 360, therefore, is the symbol of completion. When the 3 and 6 are added together they make 9, which is the highest unit we possess, and as such is held to be the sacred number of Deity. It is a triune trinity—3 times 3.

The mystical symbolism relating to the twelve Signs of the Zodiac and the human organism hold an important position in our system. In this connection, they form the body of the musical instrument, as it were, while the Sun, Moon and Planets constitute the strings. Our bodies then, when astrologically considered, are merely sounding boards for the celestial notes, struck by the starry musicians during the performance of their celestial opera. It will be noticed that the Sun and Moon, through mediumship of their Signs, Leo and Cancer, govern the two principal organs: the heart and stomach. When these are in harmony within the body the whole system is healthy.

More depends upon the position, aspect and power of the Sun and Moon at birth than upon all the planets of our solar system combined. For this reason, the Sun and Moon are, to us, the transmitters of the stellar forces. They act in the capacity of astral mediums and cast their gathered or reflected potencies into our magnetic atmosphere, harmoniously or discordantly, according to how they are aspected by the malefic or benefic rays of the major planets.

Man has five positive points of projection and four positive centres of energy, thus making up the mystical nine, symbol of Deity. The head, hands, and feet are the five points of projection from which streams of vital force are constantly radiating. These are symbolized by the five-pointed star.

The positive centres of energy within the odylic sphere are the brain, the spleen, the heart, and the generative organs, while the great centre of reception is the solar plexus.

When trouble of anxiety of mind crosses our path the first

place we feel its influence is that part of the body called the pit of the stomach. This sensitive region is within the solar plexus. How many times do forebodings of coming trouble impress themselves upon this delicate centre? As a rule, when we are in trouble we have no appetite. This calls forth inharmony in the various secretions of the body. Mental and psychic liberty depend, to an extent hitherto undreamed, upon the perfect freedom of the physical organism. Therefore, that which cramps, binds, and warps the body out of its natural proportion is fatal to any real spiritual progress, because it correspondingly inharmonizes the action of the odylic sphere. For this reason alone, India, Chaldea, and Egypt adopted the loose flowing robe, and the dress of all priesthoods is loose and ample to give them the very fullest measure of physical freedom.

When we regard the astral structure of man and closely examine his organism, we see that he forms a beautiful oval or egg-shaped figure, the narrow end being the feet, the broad end being the brain. This oval form constitutes the magnetic atmosphere, or the odylic sphere of the person, and consists of seven concentric rays of force, each of which has a direct affinity with the seven creative principles of nature, and therefore corresponds in colour to the seven prismatic rays of the solar spectrum. Each zone or ring exercises a peculiar power of its own, and is pure or impure according to its state of luminosity. When mediumistic clairvoyants assert that such and such a particular colour denotes a pure and benevolent person or one who is depraved and sinful, they assert that which is untrue, for each colour has a special quality of its own—purity and impurity depending entirely upon the brightness of its tint. For this reason, the animal passions, when exercised, dull and becloud the soul sphere, while the exercise of the spiritual faculties illuminate. The brain centre is represented by a Sun, the feet by a crescent Moon, and the three secondary centres of force by stars.

From these colours are formed every conceivable shade and tint in the infinite variety of combinations found in the infinite variety of human beings; each and all depend upon the ever-changing positions of the stars, and also upon the corresponding magnetic states of our atmosphere at their respective moments of birth. The colour and magnetic polarity of this odylic sphere are fixed, quick as lightning's flash, at the first moment of our separate material existence. This true moment is, generally, when the umbilical cord is severed and the child exists as a separate being, independent of its mother. Until that time the body is polarized by the soul force of its parent, and the planets can only influence it by reflex action from the mother's organism. But when the tie is severed, the lungs become inflated with the magnetic atmosphere, charged with the stellar influx, and in an instant the whole organism thrills with the vibrations of celestial power. These vibrations produce, in each of the concentric rings of the sphere, the exact tint and shade of colour corresponding to the harmonious or discordant rays of the heavens at that time.

The vibrations, once in action, retain their special polarity for the whole tenor of earthly existence. They form the keynote of the musical instrument which is ever sounding forth the harmony or discord of its material destiny. This keynote is either high or low according to the particular influences which may be operating upon it at the time. At one time the life forces may be so low that the note will be too faint for the most sensitive to detect; at other times the throbbing pulsations of life will be so strong with the physical vitality that it will swell into the highest octave, and launch forth such potent health-giving vibrations as to affect other bodies near it, and draw from them responsive vibrations, thus giving life and health to others in harmony with, but weaker than, itself. But should the bodies with which it comes in contact be naturally antagonistic to it, in temperament and magnetic polarity, then, instead of responsive harmony, their contact will produce fierce jarring commotions of discord to the detriment of both, the weaker being the greater sufferer.

The action and interaction of planetary influx upon the human being after birth is determined upon the same lines. When a planet, by its progressive motion, reaches a point on the sphere where it forms an inharmonious angle with the angular vibrations set in motion at birth, magnetic discord is produced. When this magnetic storm awakens and sets in motion the cosmic and other elementals corresponding in their nature to the primary cause, external misfortune and trouble are the material results, and vice versa should the planets form benefic rays. This is the true secret of planetary influence as concerns good and bad luck. It is planetary harmony or discord.

It is utterly impossible for antagonistic natures to benefit each other mentally, no matter how good or pure they as individuals may be. To attempt to do this is like trying to make oil and water harmonize. This is the true secret of the Astrologer's lack of success with certain individuals.

For example, any person born under and controlled by the planet Mars, which corresponds to the element of fire, will prove antagonistic by nature to anybody and everybody who is governed by the planet Saturn. Their personalities will not blend and mingle. The most gentle and loving spirit that it is possible for the Astrologer to exercise under such circumstances will recoil from the odylic sphere of the other like a thunderbolt.

At this stage it is necessary to explain several matters of great importance in forming a true conception of astral law. One must not suppose that the planets are the sole cause of the fortunes and misfortunes which fall to the lot of mankind generally. This is by no means the case, for the primary cause has its origin within the soul sphere of the parents. The sexual relationship between man and woman has its laws, its harmonies and discords. It is man's duty to investigate and know these laws, especially when we bear in mind the fact that there is neither morality nor sentiment in the cold inflexible justice of nature.

It is equally in accordance with the same immutable laws that every species of crime is born into the world. When inflamed passions and cruel thoughts are latent within the parents, and remain uncontrolled by the higher self during the conjugal union, we must not be surprised if a child with a similar nature is conceived. When such is the case there is no benevolent God to graciously interfere and prevent a criminal from being launched upon society. Only when the matters are harmonious can that which we term good become manifest upon the earth.

The stars and planets are the magnetic instruments of the nine creative principles. They influence externally, by their attractive sympathies and repulsive antipathies, the cosmic life forces and physical organisms of precisely the same objects, which, in the realm of spirits, are controlled by their celestial progenitors. By this we mean that the various physical orbs called planets, stars, etc., act as so many magnetic centres. They are magnetic by solar induction.

The Sun itself is not magnetic but electrically positive. This mighty force acts upon the planets in precisely the way an electric current acts upon iron. When a piece of iron is charged with electricity it becomes at once a magnet, its power depending first upon its mass and secondly upon the strength of intensity of the electric current. Without this current the iron ceases to be a magnet. Remove the Sun from our system and the planets would immediately lose their peculiar physical influence.

The sum total of those powers which we term "planetary influence" is contained within the potentiality of the Solar Ray. But when so united, as primal cosmic force, the action of this Solar Ray upon the human organism and its material destiny is neither harmonious nor discordant, fortunate nor unfortunate. To become potent in special directions, it is necessary for this solar force to become refracted and resolved into its active attributes. There are nine of them, to which each is allotted a single attribute or principle, each according to its peculiar nature and affinity. While the solar orb itself retains but one active energy whose potency is embraced within the orange ray of the spectrum; these planetary bodies, having become magnetically charged with their own special energy, are powerful radiators of the same attribute they have received from their solar parent. These energies possess a distinctive motion and potency, each peculiar to itself, which when externalized upon man's internal nature, produce a marked contrast in his mental and physical characteristics.

It is an ancient theory that the shepherds during the silent watches of the night, having no other objects to contemplate than the view which the heavens above presented, soon began to divide the firmament of stars into particular constellations, according to how they adjoined each other. They filled the heavens with symbolical subjects.

By this division, the stars were easily distinguished from each other; and by the help of the celestial globe on which the constellations are delineated, any particular star could easily be found in the heavens; and the most outstanding stars were placed in such parts of the constellations as are most readily distinguished.

The heavens were thus divided into three parts:

1. The Zodiac, which is a great circle extending around the heavens, nearly 16 degrees broad, so as to take in the different orbits of the planets, as well as that of the earth's satellite, the Moon, in the middle of which is the Ecliptic or Path of the Sun.

2. All that region of the heavens which is on the north side of the Zodiac, containing twenty-one constellations.

3. The whole region on the south side, which contains fifteen constellations.

Astrologers, however, confine their observations to only twelve, which are denominated by the twelve Signs of the Zodiac. These Signs answer to twelve periods of the year. Astrologers further divide each Sign into three parts of ten degrees each, and for closer observation, each degree or birthdate is delineated as to character and destiny.

We shall now consider the influence of the Sun's apparent passage through the twelve Signs of the Zodiac, caused by the earth's movements around the Sun. From the Sun's position each day we may judge the contrast between those born from December to June, and those born between July and the end of November. We should find that the longest livers are born in March, April, and May, so a great majority will be found to have their natal day in these months. On the other hand, a majority of the short-lived population will be found to be born during the months of August, September, and October. This is only true on general principles and does not apply to any one individual Horoscope; in fact, the remarks in reference to the four Triplicities will also apply here. The increase of the Solar Light simply governs the vitalizing capacity of the race and not the individual.

Everything in nature, though constituting a Trinity in itself, possesses a fourfold application when viewed from the external plane. At least, we find this fourfoldness a truth so far as "the things of Earth" are concerned and, therefore, by the laws of Correspondences, the same application must hold true in regard to the Celestial objects in the heavens. The Hermetic rule is a very precise rule upon this: "As on earth, so in the sky."

In the following pages I am going to delineate the twelve Signs of the Zodiac, based upon the Sun's apparent progression through the 360 degrees of the Zodiac. These are the most comprehensive astrological readings possible when the time, day, year, and place of birth are not known.

They should not be confused with a personal Horoscope, which can only be prepared when the time, day, month, year, and place of birth is known.

The wise men of Chaldea inspected the beautiful constellations of heaven, and learned therefrom the mighty secrets of the soul's origin and destiny, as well as the material details of their physical lives. The same book of nature is open now as then, but only the pure in heart can read its pages and trace the mystical chain of life from nature through the stars.

—Zolar

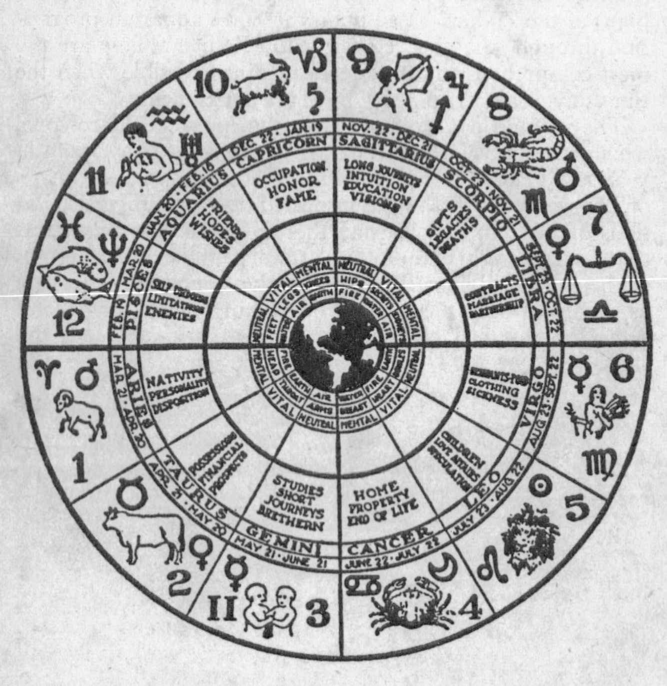

10
9
8
7
6
5
4
3
2
1
12
11
DEC. 22 · JAN 19
CAPRICORN
NOV. 22 · DEC 21
SAGITTARIUS
OCT. 23 · NOV. 21
SCORPIO
SEPT. 23 · OCT. 22
LIBRA
AUG 23 · SEPT. 22
VIRGO
JULY 23 · AUG 22
LEO
JUNE 22 · JULY 22
CANCER
MAY 21 · JUNE 21
GEMINI
APR. 21 · MAY 20
TAURUS
MAR 21 · APR. 20
ARIES
MAR 20
PISCES
JAN 20 · FEB. 16
AQUARIUS
OCCUPATION HONOR FAME
LONG JOURNEYS INTUITION EDUCATION VISIONS
GIFTS LEGACIES DEATHS
CONTRACTS MARRIAGE PARTNERSHIP
SERVANTS-FOOD CLOTHING SICKNESS
CHILDREN LOVE AFFAIRS SPECULATION
HOME PROPERTY END OF LIFE
STUDIES SHORT JOURNEYS BRETHERN
POSSESSIONS FINANCIAL PROSPECTS
NATIVITY PERSONALITY DISPOSITION
SELF UNDOING LIMITATIONS ENEMIES
FRIENDS HOPES WISHES
MENTAL
NEUTRAL
VITAL
KNEES
HIPS
LEGS
FEET
HEAD
THROAT
ARMS
BREAST
HEART
EARTH
FIRE
AIR
WATER

I

ARIES

March 21st–April 20th

The sign Aries in its symbolical aspect represents the sacrifice. The flocks and herds bring forth their young during the portion of the year that the Sun occupies this Sign. The symbol of the Sign is the Ram.

The Ram also symbolizes Spring, when light and love, symbolized by the Sun, are bestowed upon the sons of the Earth. The Sun once more has gained victory over the realms of winter. The Sign Aries represents the head and brains of the Grand Man of the Cosmos.

The gems of this Sign are the amethyst and diamond.

The fortunate day is Tuesday.

Fortunate numbers are seven and six.

The colours are shades of bright red.

Best locations for success are large cities.

Aries is the first and highest emanation of the fiery Triplicity, and is located in the constellation of the Planet Mars. It radiates an influence which is sharp, energetic, thoughtless, intrepid, and fierce. It is without either fear or timidity—an influence which is free with everything and everybody.

Addressing an Aries, I would say: You have an active and dynamic personality. The expression which you give to your mind and emotions determines the actual degree of personal, social, and economic progress and success you will experience in life. You have natural, charming manners and good mental power; you are fond of having others look up to you. You have the happy faculty of exercising diplomacy to swing others towards interesting themselves in you or acting upon your ideas and suggestions. Courageous to the point of daring, you possess an active spirit of adventure and enterprise. By nature you are restless and fond of all sorts of activity. You will do well to cultivate an understanding of your adventuresome nature. Avoid engaging in unwise and risky or hazardous ventures. Under ordinary circumstances, you display an affectionate, courteous, and generous disposition. You are often inclined to be too generous for your own good, particularly when your personal feelings and emotions are aroused. This disposition may lead you to be quite generous to people who may not be deserving while you neglect those who should receive more consideration.

You are quite sensitive emotionally. You have a quick temper and can be easily angered at little things that could be straightened out with a few seconds of logical thinking. *It is one thing to have a quick temper and another to let it rule you.*

You are inclined to hold a grudge. By nature you are aggressive, self-willed and determined. You have the type of personality and temperament that can make or break your own destiny. Many of your personal misunderstandings and difficulties arise because you have an impulsive tendency to hurry and be impatient. *Learn to be more patient with yourself and with others.*

You love action, and you will be wise if you will apply some thought to your own interesting nature. You are an independent thinker, but this does not mean that you are always right or logical in your thinking. The most important thing for you to guard against is a tendency to judge matters according to your personal feelings and emotions, especially when you are upset. If you will adhere to the principles of sound reasoning, you will overcome intolerance and prejudiced attitudes.

You are capable of mentally grasping and understanding the minute details of a proposition before the average individual has given the matter much thought. The only drawback to such quick perception is that you are apt, at times, to become over-confident and neglect important details. Quick perception is essential to your particular type of personality. Your thought and action shows good co-ordination between mind and body and is essential to your progress. Your restless and aspiring mentality shows an active imagination. For you to accomplish anything, you must learn to use your imagination. You are capable of thinking up original ideas, and have the ability to carry them to practical conclusions. You have the ability to make some of your daydreams a reality. You are naturally very studious of things that interest you. Your particular type of personality is dependent upon a good memory, since your venturesome nature inclines you to face many and varying situations in life.

You are capable of acquiring and retaining a great amount of knowledge without applying much effort. This capacity is an asset and it will aid you to increase the power and influence of your personality. It helps to make you an interesting and witty conversationalist and will prove valuable in whatever line of work or business you choose to follow.

Your greatest difficulty is an inclination to act on impulse. You must carefully investigate your impulsive ideas before acting on them. Do your best to determine the logical outcome of an impulsive idea before you act. Thus, you may not act at all and so wisely save yourself from financial loss or personal disillusionment.

You have within yourself the Voice of Intuition

It will give you foresight and help you master many difficult problems and obstacles in the course of life. Intuition can provide you with the happy faculty of divining the causes of your failures and help you eliminate them, thus enabling you to live a progressively more successful life

You also have the Power of Inspiration within you

There are times when you are inspired to do certain things. Your difficulty will be discriminating between ordinary impulses and an inspired idea.

Very few persons really understand the true intensity of the mental activity of those born under Aries. There are times when you may be called rash and impetuous. These charges, if you are honest with yourself, must be, at times, admitted as true. It is also true that you cannot stifle your individuality which is manifest in everything you do. You can, by an effort of will, express, direct and apply your mental efforts and energy in a wise and progressive manner. Because of the intensity of your mental, emotional, and physical activities, give thought to your diet and your health. You are inclined to burn up more mental and physical energy than the average individual. *Fresh air, sunshine, good home surroundings, proper diet, relaxation, and rest should enable you to avoid many ailments common to persons of your temperament.*

Your Sign presides over the head and face—common head colds should be guarded against in order to avoid serious complications. The eyes should receive attention and should not be overworked. The teeth should be looked after carefully at all times. Colds are more apt to affect the sinuses and throat than the chest. Exercise moderation in drinking and eating, as the kidneys may become affected. Most of your ailments will be of an acute, rather than a chronic nature. Chronic ailments with Aries people are usually the result of sheer neglect. Avoid mental, emotional, nervous, and physical strain after the middle years of your life. *Aries are generally born with a good physical constitution and good recuperative powers.*

It appears that there will be more than one outstanding love affair in your life. *Emotionally, you are affectionate, tender, and inclined to passion.* You are unusually sensitive in love matters; you must guard against unreasonable jealousy. Avoid too great a mental and emotional domination over the object of your affections, and your love life will be much happier and more harmonious. Disappointments in love are indicated during the early twenties and at about the thirtieth year. Uncertainty and instability in your home life and domestic affairs are also indicated during the first half of your life, because of your adventuresome nature. You love and respect your relatives, but you desire that they recognize your individuality. In the later years of life you will become more settled in matters that pertain to home life and family affairs. You desire to have your home in a prominent location.

Indications point to considerable love of pleasure, which is expressed in games, sports, adventures, and travels. You have a great appreciation of the beauties of nature. You enjoy reading and the theatre.

You are aggressive, energetic, and have a determined nature with qualities that will enable you to follow several vocations. Your rise in life will be gradual and deliberate rather than spontaneous. The personality and mental make-up to the average Aries qualifies you for medicine, law, teaching, construction work, electrical engineering, aviation, mechanics, stage and screen work, accounting, merchandising—in fact, for most types of work you might desire to do, because you have natural organizing and executive ability, and can be trusted with important commissions and responsibilities. You are loyal to your work. Your independent nature does not qualify you for partnership ventures unless you have full freedom to work things out in your own way. *Enter into business for yourself*. Remember, there will be times in the beginning when you must guard against becoming discouraged too easily.

There are indications that you can be fairly successful in money matters. Your earning capacity should be good, but you are inclined to be a generous spender. You desire to have the best money can buy, and to spend money more for temporary than for permanent benefit. *Your money, like your mind, needs careful handling*. During favourable financial periods of your life you will find it to your advantage to make conservative investments. Your adventuresome nature inclines you towards speculation and gambling. You may not be aware of it, but in such matters you are inclined to "stack the cards against yourself" because of your impulsiveness. You will obtain true wisdom when you cease taking chances and spending to suit your personal whims, fancies, and impulses. Be conservative in financial matters and your money will take care of you. There is no other road to travel in order to attain financial security and success. If and when you make investments, avoid speculative issues and get-rich-quick schemes.

You are exceedingly loyal to those you consider close friends, and will stand up for them forcefully if necessary. You are inclined to be generous with close friends and associates, and will aid them in every manner possible when they are in difficulties. Your general attitude in social matters, aside from friendships, is variable. There are times when you enjoy being with a great number of people, but in the main you prefer the companionship of a few loyal friends. In society you are capable of commanding the respect and good will of many, and have the ability to lead in your own set.

You have all the essential mental, emotional, and physical faculties and qualities which should enable you to make a reasonable success of your life. Understand these faculties in order that you may apply them with wisdom. It is up to you to direct yourself and your energy for progress. Pay attention to your shortcomings. Do not be afraid of them. Learn to know them and seek to use your energy constructively, in order to be the master of your own destiny and the captain of your own soul, and you will know the true meaning of happiness, success, and security in life.

The Aries Child

The Aries infant will turn out to be aggressive and pioneering; he will not like to be ruled by other people. The parents of the Aries child must use discretion, lest he become stubborn, and leave home at an early age. Much heartbreak can be avoided if the parents will notice this inclination, and accept the idea that he can be more easily handled if not "driven". Children of Aries often tend to impulsive action—at times rather fiery. They are ready to take the initiative in any movement that appeals to them, regardless of danger, yet they sometimes lack the necessary persistence to sustain their efforts over serious obstacles. Therefore, we must teach them consistency of purpose, so that success and happiness will be attained later in life.

Prominent leaders, explorers, and pioneers are often born under this sign. The child can grow up to become successful in government work, work connected with tools and sharp instruments, or occupations that require wearing a uniform, such as fireman, policeman, or soldier. If you watch a group of children at play, you can depend upon it that the Aries child will usually be "on top of the heap"—always telling the others what to do. This "leadership complex" may be a splendid thing but it has to be developed in a balanced manner. Otherwise, the child will grow up into a domineering individual, disliked and avoided by others. These children will be courageous, which will often take them into hazardous work. All of this should be taken into consideration in their education and upbringing. Generally speaking, children who are born between April 10th and 20th are likely to be more fortunate and successful as their life progresses than those born earlier in the sign.

The Aries Wife

The Aries woman personifies one of the highest feminine developments of the Zodiac. These women make wonderful wives for ambitious men. They like to spend their spare time in constructive self-improvement. They are witty, clever conversationalists, with wonderful social presence. Either they are willing to help the husband in business or they have some lucrative side line of their own that adds to the family fortunes.

The appearance of the Aries wife is very smart, for she is usually a good-looking woman who takes great pride in the way she looks. Pride is one of her outstanding qualities. She has such a superior opinion of her own family that it shows quite plainly in her behaviour and sometimes causes others to be resentful.

Jealousy and a desire for a competitive social life are two of her worst faults. She is apt to be jealous of her husband's attentions, and may have a vivid imagination when she feels she might have been wronged. She knows her worth and wants her husband to concentrate upon her with great intensity. This type of woman should marry a passionate, possessive man—one who makes her own sense of possession seem fragile by comparison. She should not have reason to seek grievances, for she is at her best when making self-sacrifices for her family.

When family life rolls along smoothly the Arien wife can become rather extravagant. She is also generous, so much so that she frequently goes overboard for family and friends. She likes people to be obligated to her and is hesitant to accept repayment for her generosity.

She loves only the man she can greatly admire; his ability to control her is an important part of her devotion to him. If his hold over her is dominant, and his constitution is virile, she is his for life.

The Aries Husband

The Aries husband is a distinguished, desirable sort of man. He is the kind of man that all girls aspire to own, but who is by appearance and temperament a little hard to acquire. This is because he is exacting. He has a romantic mental picture of what he wants in a wife, and this image is his idea of perfection. The lady must be beautiful, clever, and most understanding.

Such men are conventional in thought and do not generally go in for Bohemian types of romance. They demand a high moral code in the women of their choice, regardless of their own leanings—usually an isolated adventurous fling. As a matter of fact, the Aries man dislikes clandestine affairs. He is outspoken to a fault, and refuses to hide or lie about his activities. He would consider it a personal affront that he might have to look outside of his home for affection. He is rather demanding sexually, and if not gratified at home, he may look elsewhere.

The Aries man is ardent and proud; all through life, he has an appeal for the woman he married. About the most difficult problem in his married life is to satisfy his romantic conception of physical love. He has a voracious appetite which he will not sublimate. No substitute devotion satisfies him, but a wife can gain his everlasting faithfulness if she harmonizes with him physically and mentally.

The Cusps of Aries

(If your birthday is not within the cusp of your Sign, the following does not apply to you.)

If your birthday is from March 21st through March 23rd

You are an Aries with Pisces tendencies. Your ruling planets are Mars and Neptune. This gives you unusual intelligence, understanding, and originality. You are cautious, studious, amiable, and thorough in whatever you do. You are extremely ambitious and painstaking, but want to carry out your plans in your own way. You resent being forced or interfered with. You should be interested in the mechanical and electrical sciences. You like to direct the activities of others. To some extent you will disagree with general public opinion and have the urge to introduce new ideas. While many will regard these ideas as radical, others will respect them because you show courage. *To get the most out of life, curb your tendency to be impatient and irritable.* You are fond of adventure, and delight in entertaining your friends to whom you are loyal. You are destined to succeed in some outstanding way through a career quite different than the one you started to follow early in life.

If your birthday is from April 17th through April 20th

You are an Aries with Taurus tendencies. Your ruling planets are Mars and Venus. You have all the indications of Aries and a few of Taurus. This makes you fiery, romantic, and determined. You will succeed regardless of hazards but you will not trample the rights of others. You possess an impatient and nervous temperament. You are endowed with wonderful talents that may not at first be apparent. You attend to one thing at a time and are likely to become annoyed when things around you are disorderly. You have a high moral sense and are almost immune to unchaste thoughts. You do everything in your power to excel in whatever you may undertake. You can achieve success, while holding the respect of your relatives, friends, and business associates.

The Decanates of Aries

If the birthday is between March 21st and March 31st

Your personal and ruling planet is Mars, which is doubly forceful in this aspect. Mars will tend to bring out the more dominant dictatorial and positive side of your nature. There is a tendency to become impatient and irritable with others because they may not have the ability to think and act as quickly as you do. It is highly important to practice tolerance, patience, and understanding. An active body and an impetuous, spirited nature is shown by the double aspect of the planet Mars in your chart. You are capable of acquiring and retaining a great amount of knowledge without much effort. Your personality will always be aggressive, independent, temperamental, and persevering. Avoid a tendency to talk too much and monopolize conversation. While you may have many original ideas, you prefer to have others execute them for you. Your best results will be obtained when you are permitted to assume leadership.

If the birthday is between April 1st and April 10th

Your personal planet is the Sun, known as the Ruler of the Day. As the giver of life it is the centre of the Solar System. The Sun stands for dignity, honour, and ambition. The Sun in this decanate causes great love of change and a desire for reform. The Sun governs pride and personal ambitions. It will confer good fortune and assist greatly in offsetting some of the negative aspects of your ruling planet Mars.

If the birthday is between April 10th and April 20th

Your personal planet is Jupiter, which is known as the God of Fortune. It influences the intellectual, moral, and sympathetic tendencies. Jupiter will greatly aid the aspects of your ruling planet Mars, since it stands for sincerity and honesty, and inclines its subjects to become genuinely warm-hearted. A noble nature, ever grateful and courteous to all, is one of the favourable aspects of this planet. It is well said that Jupiter is the most fortunate and beneficent of all planets. It brings good fortune and success.

The Degrees of Aries

March 21st

You possess an ambitious and determined personality. You show a marked aptitude for dealing in financial matters, and should obtain a position pertaining to monetary pursuits. Intense concentration will aid you materially, providing you overcome a tendency to display your strong likes and dislikes. One aspect in this Horoscope indicates the possibility of a military career or fame in the art world. You are positive and forceful.

March 22nd

You possess an independent personality and splendid intuitive powers. You should train your impetuous nature and overcome a rash temperament. Because of your highly practical mind, you are a good organizer. Your fertile mind will help develop your ability as a scientist and a mathematician. Persons born on this day are enterprising, practical, and charitable.

March 23rd

You possess a good sense of humour. Your versatile mind and marked social instincts indicate that you would be successful in some form of public service. One aspect of your Horoscope shows that you may become successful in the literary field. You are ardent, refined, and ambitious. You should avoid overindulgence in both food and drink.

March 24th

You possess a highly magnetic personality. A strong and healthy body coupled with good recuperative powers will enable you to overcome most physical dangers. Your loyal disposition will bring many sincere friendships into your life. One aspect in this Horoscope indicates a passionate nature with a good degree of vanity. You will meet with good fortune sometime during your life. Although impulsive and sensuous, you are capable of great attachments.

March 25th

You possess great creative ability. You can become a patron of the fine arts. Keen interest in literature endows you with the qualities of an intellectual personality. You accomplish your purpose through your marked sympathies and sense of fair play. You will attain the greatest measure of success and happiness in life by catering to the public.

March 26th

You possess a discerning personality. Your restless nature may cause you to become involved in some unfortunate undertakings during your lifetime. A sense of purpose should be developed in order to overcome unsatisfied longings. You are fond of animals. You could be successful as a trainer or owner of race horses.

March 27th

You possess lofty ideals and great intensity and sincerity of purpose, which tend to make you over-critical when your plans and ambitions are interrupted. You can avoid the development of this aspect by carefully analysing inevitable difficulties and their consequences. You are fond of outdoor activities. Mother Nature will help you relax. A spiritual nature with high ideals indicates an ideal marriage.

March 28th

You possess the qualities of an orator. You can be cutting and sarcastic in your manner of speech. A fondness for mysteries is indicated, along with a love of argument and debate. These qualities add greatly to your store of knowledge and can be prime factors in the development of your mental faculties and social background. While you may be affectionate and magnanimous to your immediate family, you show a tendency to be somewhat inconsiderate towards others. You can be turbulent and vengeful where outsiders are concerned.

March 29th

You possess a courageous and aggressive disposition. You are independent and have the ability to carry out your objectives without much assistance from outside influences. Do not attempt to force yourself into a vocation, but permit your natural foresight to hold full sway. Your great desire to travel may be satisfied by a military career. A career in the law enforcement field should be considered.

March 30th

You may rise to great heights of success with the aid of influential friends. Because you possess a natural, aristocratic bearing and a flair for social recognition, you may have a tendency to attach too much significance to appearances. There are times when you become quite intolerant and vindictive. Curb this tendency.

March 31st

You possess a resourceful and capable nature. You have a scientific mind, and possess the energy and ability to understand situations and command the respect of your friends and associates. Hopes and ambitions are sometimes realized through sheer genius by many natives of this degree. Follow your hunches; they are usually right.

April 1st

You possess great intuition. You will only succeed in life through your own merit and natural capabilities. You are clever with details and will achieve success in any position or business where intelligent application of detailed knowledge is essential. Certain aspects in your Horoscope indicate many trials and tribulations. There is also a tendency to day-dream.

April 2nd

You possess an imaginative and intuitive mind. One aspect in this Horoscope indicates the ability to achieve fame in the humanitarian fields of medicine, philosophy, and psychology. It is necessary to overcome the tendency to be lustful and destructive when you are forced to yield in your ambitions.

April 3rd

You possess a violent temper and a brooding nature. Unless you are in congenial surroundings, your sensitive disposition can easily develop into an inferiority complex. You are markedly introspective and have an inclination to become moody and despondent at the slightest provocation. You are vehement in your desires and should temper your aspirations with logic. Fame may come through athletic prowess.

April 4th

You possess a bright, literary mind. Great generosity and kindness of heart are also indicated. One aspect in this Horoscope shows a marked tendency towards daydreaming and timidity, yet you are always well disposed. You must learn concentration and the importance of completing one task before starting another. Great sex appeal will bring popularity in love. You have a flair for speculation.

April 5th

You possess an appealing and persuasive personality. You have ability as an orator. One aspect in this Horoscope shows a judicial and perceptive mentality coupled with a high-strung nervous system. You are extremely fond of your family and friends. You may be more fortunate in business and vocational affairs than in personal and intimate matters. You are artistically inclined.

April 6th

You are fond of children and will experience much happiness through them. An artistic temperament and lovable nature brings the desire for better things in life. One aspect in this Horoscope indicates a marked tendency to consult occult and mystical literary works. You have the ability to sense the thoughts and feelings of others.

April 7th

You are emotional and romantic. You can develop an excellent literary career. One aspect in your Horoscope indicates a tendency to find fault with others. This failing is perhaps due to a highly sensitive and emotional nature. Nevertheless, many natives of this degree will devote their lives to scientific research.

April 8th

You possess a fertile mind and a noble disposition. You display unusual prowess in outdoor sports and all physical activities. There are indications of possible fame in athletic games. Your strong will power and well-defined course of action will enable you to overcome many obstacles in life. You have the natural ability to make friends readily, because of your ardent personality and ability as a lover.

April 9th

You possess a resourceful and shrewd mind. Executive traits and natural charm will bring many profitable friendships. You show great enterprise in acquiring the good things in life, and success will be attained mostly through your own efforts. One negative aspect is a tendency to become unscrupulous when pressed.

April 10th

You possess an active and impressionable mind. There is a tendency to become irritable and impatient when your plans and desires are not easily fulfilled. There is a strong liking for the sea. One aspect in your Horoscope shows that you will make any sacrifice to help those you love.

April 11th

You possess a profound but melancholy disposition. A magnanimous personality and desire to help those who are in less fortunate straits will lead you into many strange experiences during your life. Studies of a scientific nature, which can be used for the good of humanity and the alleviation of sorrow and suffering, may be your life's ambition. Just rewards in the form of honour and success will be the result of such undertakings. One aspect here shows instability under certain circumstances.

April 12th

You possess a strong personality and a pleasing, honest disposition. You are fond of music and art, and enjoy the beautiful, refined, and aesthetic things in life. One aspect of this Horoscope indicates a tendency towards self-indulgence which should not be encouraged. You are a seeker after strange and unusual places; this curiosity leads to a desire to travel in foreign lands.

April 13th

You possess a silent, philosophical, yet flexible nature, and a methodical, prudent, but gentle disposition. Marked capability in dealing with the masses and success through association with influential and prosperous friends are indicated. An education which will equip you for a life of public service will bring greater happiness and success. You are not receptive to any proposition that does not coincide with your own inherent sense of justice and fair play. You have great patience and forebearance, and are a born optimist.

April 14th

You possess a restless and aspiring nature. Because you are somewhat hasty emotionally, you should practice self-discipline and restraint. Develop consistency of purpose and your natural ability, intuition, and keen foresight will assure success. One aspect in this Horoscope indicates that you should exercise caution while travelling. Foreign lands intrigue you.

April 15th

You possess an inspirational and creative genius. You are fond of social activity. You show a marked aptitude for organization, and are always ready to accept responsibility. You possess versatility and an artistic temperament; you can best serve yourself by developing latent talents.

April 16th

You possess a bold imagination and a keen mind. These characteristics will aid in the attainment of success in the business world. A bold nature and a decided flair for leading others assures your success as an executive in the field of your choice. At times you can be very wilful and obstinate.

April 17th

You possess a meditative and somewhat gloomy disposition. You are gentle and prudent but lack confidence. You are considerate and obedient to the wishes of your loved ones and usually bear the brunt of family responsibility. You are thoughtful but lack tenacity of purpose and are inclined to be something of a recluse.

April 18th

You possess lofty ideals and great intuition, but also have a decided tendency to be contrary and mischievous. Good business ability and commercial foresight will greatly aid you in the attainment of success in the business world. Trouble through relatives is shown at various intervals in your life; however, children will bring much satisfaction, and possibly honour.

April 19th

You possess a well-balanced mind, good intuition, and a kind, affectionate nature. You have a magnetic personality, and the gift of foresight. You may have a delicate constitution and should not over-exercise or go to extremes in mental or physical exertion. Enlightenment through personal efforts and past experiences is indicated.

April 20th
You possess a profound mind alternately swayed by principle and ambition. You show a great deal of adaptability and unusual aptitude for imitation. One aspect in this Horoscope indicates a tendency to become extremely temperamental and excitable when anyone interferes with your plans and ambitions. You are a born leader and want to have your own way in all matters. Develop tact and diplomacy.

Compatible and Incompatible Signs of Aries

Much heartbreak and disappointment might be avoided if one takes the advice and absorbs the knowledge offered by the dependable impartial adviser—Astrology.

Aries is a rash, impetuous, and headstrong Sign. People born under this Sign tend to be impulsive in love and marriage, as in everything else. As befits a martial sign, it is passionate, but there is also a great amount of idealism. Sexual indulgence is more a matter of sudden impulse than of deliberate seeking. Aries generates a positive type which does not harmonize well with a positive partner; an Arien tends to seek someone of a weaker nature on whom he can impress his sexual qualities.

A man with Aries rising is attracted by beauty and apparent helplessness. He needs a wife who will be content to remain in the background and duly admire his prowess and ability. Normally Aries is a better Sign for a man than for a woman.

The Aries woman is apt to be too masterful, too much of a whirlwind in the house for anyone who is not of a quiet and passive type. She is capable and generous, but can easily become loud, self-opinionated, shrewish, and "bossy" under affliction; i.e., when born with adverse planetary aspects.

The Aries nature is intense, capable of sudden violence and great jealousy. With certain afflictions, especially from Mars or Uranus, a sadistic tendency can easily develop, though by itself it is too direct, simple, and primitive a Sign to lend itself readily to perversion. Aries must always strive for leadership, however, whether in man or woman, and unless the partner is content to be led, constant friction may develop. For this reason, Aries marriages are often unhappy, though other factors also contribute to cause disharmony. One of them is a tendency to physical or psychic sex weakness, which is sometimes present in the Aries man, or sometimes to sexual indifference in the Aries woman; and another is the propensity of the Aries man—and sometimes in the Aries woman also—to indulge in promiscuous flirtations and love affairs. The underlying reason for such affairs is usually that they flatter the Aries vanity, but in the man there is also the additional search for the ideal, often the cause for matrimonial infidelity.

Arien and Arien

If one partner will permit the other "to rule the roost", there should be much compatibility between two persons born in the same Sign. Although there is a lack of contrasting personalities, there will be a sympathetic understanding on the part of both regarding the qualities and shortcomings of the other.

A note of warning, however, must be sounded here. If both Ariens have dominant and forceful aspects in their Horoscopes, much conflict will arise because of the unflinching desire of both partners to be the head of the house and family.

Arien and Taurus

This combination should make an excellent match. The Taurean nature is ruled by Venus, the Goddess of Love, the one thing an Arien always seeks in a mate. Though the slow-moving Taurus may find the going a bit hectic, the excitement may help to stimulate the courtship. One thing the Arien must avoid is temperamental outbursts, for while Taurus is not highly emotional on the surface, he can become obstinate and ferocious as a bull when it sees red!

Arien and Gemini

This alliance usually results in a great deal of bickering due to strong differences about sex. Gemini is a mercurial Sign where the mind plays an important part in all love-making.

The emotional Martian Arien may prove too much for the conventional nature of the Gemini.

Above all, Gemini respects the refined, intellectual approach to connubial bliss. The impatient Arien may find this frustrating, and after a time seek a less difficult companion.

Arien and Cancer

This is usually a hard combination to match. Cancerians are ruled by the moon and are moody, sentimental, and secretive. They have a tendency to live in the past, and rarely forget serious quarrels or family disagreements which occur early in marriage. What might be an unimportant breach to Aries could become a traumatic block to Cancer. Though the Cancerian holds on with the tenacity of a crab, he has a tendency to back away from situations which have been hurtful in the past.

Arien and Leo

This is usually a splendid combination. While both Signs are emotional in their make-up, Leo will lionize an Aries mate. This is particularly true if Aries will allow Leo to hold the centre of the floor on occasions. The impetuous Aries lover will find a welcome home in the lion's den. Leo admires the aggressive tendencies of fiery contempories.

Arien and Virgo

This combination is similar to the Aries-Gemini combination. Virgo is ruled by Mercury and does not blend well astrologically with the Martian tendencies of Aries. Virgoans are usually too precise and fault-finding for the Arien personality. Virgo wants a well-ordered existence and will not be happy under Arien dictatorship. The prissy Virgo will, certainly, not condone the bossy Aries.

Arien and Libra

An excellent combination of Mars and Venus. The warm and passionate Libran will make a welcome home for the fiery, impetuous Aries. This will be particularly true if both persons are on the same cultural and intellectual plane. Libra's refined and artistic temperament yearns for reciprocal attachments.

Arien and Scorpio

Since there is never room for two heads in one family, this combination would not make an ideal partnership. Both Signs are strongly dominated by the planet Mars, which makes for very positive temperaments unless there are several benign natal planetary aspects.

While Scorpio may adore the Aries from a sexual standpoint, their more mundane interests would be constantly at odds.

Arien and Sagittarius

This combination of the first and third sign of the fiery Trinity usually makes an ideal partnership. The Mars-Jupiter duo are an ideal match for each other. Both are creatures of impulse. They can both have outside interests without causing personal conflict and friction. The Sagittarian banner is "liberty, and the pursuit of happiness"; Aries is usually willing to subscribe to this theory.

Arien and Capricorn

A doubtful combination. Saturn, represented by old Father Time, is the Capricorn standard bearer. Ariens are too impatient to cope with the slow, methodical plodding of the Capricornian nature. The Capricornian goat will butt up against the Martian will and an impasse is bound to occur.

In matters of sex there is an affinity; however, their inherent personalities clash.

Arien and Aquarius

The unpredictable Aquarian may tax an Arien mate's patience while the instability of the Arien temperament will surely provoke the Sign of good will and self-sacrifice. Such are the bones of contention that make this partnership a gamble. The planet Uranus, which rules Aquarius, is unpredictable in its actions; therefore, Aquarians have a tendency to procrastinate too much to please the Arien "up and at 'em" characteristics.

Arien and Pisces

The sentimental Pisces nature finds little comfort in the Arien's aggressiveness. Pisceans are romantic, but they desire the delicate approach that the Arien lacks. Neptune, the planet of the higher mind, gives Pisces an ethereal quality. Unless the Arien mate is willing to take a trip to the clouds now and then, the partnership will prove incompatible.

Some Famous Persons Born in the Sign of Aries

Marlon Brando—Actor
John Burroughs—Author
Charles Chaplin—Actor
Joan Crawford—Actress
Thomas E. Dewey—NY Governor
Robert Frost—Poet
Bernard F. Gimbel—Merchant
Shirley MacLaine—Actress
J. Pierpont Morgan—Financier
Mary Pickford—Actress
Joseph Pulitzer—Publisher
Leopold Stokowski—Musical Conductor
Alec Guinness—Actor
Thomas Jefferson—US President
Nikita S. Khrushchev—Soviet Premier
Clare Booth Luce—Authoress and Ambassador
Henry R. Luce—Publisher
Gloria Swanson—Actress
Arturo Toscanini—Musical Conductor
Tennessee Williams—Author
F. W. Woolworth—Merchant
Wilbur Wright—Inventor

2

TAURUS

April 21st–May 20th

The Taurean is born under the rulership of Venus, the planet of love and beauty. This planet absorbs an energy entirely different from the energy absorbed by other planets. The internal influence is warm and impulsive. A pliable, receptive, clinging, and feminine nature results. This energy yields to a nature more positive than its own loving submission, hence the myths of friendship between Mars and Venus.

The Sign of Taurus, in its symbolical aspect, represents the procreative forces in all departments of nature. Its genius is symbolized as Aphrodite, who was generally represented as wearing two horns upon her head in imitation of the bull. Many mythologists have been deceived by this symbol and have taken it to represent a figure of the crescent Moon upon the head of Isis. Apis, the sacred bull of the Egyptians, is another conception of Taurus. Since the Sun passed through this Sign during the ploughing month of the Egyptians, we find this symbol used as that of husbandry.

The Sign Taurus represents the ears, neck and throat of the Grand Old Man of the Skies, hence it is the Sign of the silent, patient, and listening principles of humanity. It rules the lymphatic system of the organism.

The gem of this Sign is the sapphire, and this stone is the natural talisman for those born under Taurus.

The fortunate day is Friday.

Fortunate numbers are one and nine.

The colour for this Sign is blue.

Best locations for success are quiet places.

Taurus is the highest emanation of the earthly Trinity, and is the constellation of the planet Venus.

Addressing a Taurus, I would say: You have a natural, magnetic, and attractive personality, which, if properly cultivated and expressed, will enable you to go far in life and progress beyond the circumstances of your birth. The cultured Taurus personality radiates mental and physical beauty. His other characteristics include a charming and unaffected refinement and an interesting enjoyable wit. The uncultured Taurus personality is apt to be somewhat gruff, manifesting a peculiar self-willed, obstinate and self-important attitude, which often proves to be boring, dull, and antagonizing—the "I am for myself" type of personality.

The true and unspoiled Taurus character and temperament is just like the season of the year the Sign represents. There is beauty, culture, grace, honesty, depth of feeling, affection, and an understanding sympathy in the Taurus personality. However, behind all this lies a great power that can be abused. The power of determination, when it is wisely directed and applied, can do great good. The average Taurus individual is easy-going until crossed; but once crossed, rightly or wrongly, he or she can be the most obstinate and headstrong of people. This reaction takes place because these natives have an unusual emotional sensitivity. However, the great beauty of the Taurus nature lies in the deep sympathy and understanding manifested towards those they love. It will pay you many dividends in personal happiness to investigate thoroughly your nature and disposition and to seek to make wise corrections and adjustments if you find them necessary.

There will be much good in your life if you will but naturally allow yourself to blossom forth in all your radiant and latent potentialities of mind and character. Honesty, sincerity of purpose, and reliability are attributes of your nature. Others can depend upon you. You are inclined to be methodical in your way of doing things; whatever you do, you desire to do it well. You have courage, patience, and fortitude. There are times when you must guard against being influenced too much by the opinions, feelings, and emotions of others. It will be advisable for you to think things out alone, in the sacred freedom of your own mind. You will do well to learn to subscribe to the principles of logic and reasoning to avoid erroneous and prejudiced conclusions.

You do not investigate things hurriedly. You are inclined to be methodical and sure, and are not given to haphazard ways of doing things. You have a reflective imagination. In fact, your daydreaming often affords you great mental relaxation and private pleasure. However, do not indulge in this practice to excess as it may make you impractical. Daydreaming may cause you to lay foundations for disillusionment. *Endeavour to control your imagination; do not let it control you.* You are inclined to pay close attention to what you are studying or doing. You seldom overlook details that others forget.

In your education you pay close attention to what you study (which often makes you take longer than others do), because you want to be sure of yourself and your knowledge. Some people may think you are a little slow in learning, but do not let this alarm you in any way. You remember what you have learned much longer than others. You are determined, which enables you to learn anything in which you take an interest. You have sufficient imagination and power of original thought to improve, which will help you succeed in business, in professional life, or your chosen work. You are fond of the good things of life—rich foods and other luxuries.

You have the type of mind that receives inspired ideas from time to time—inspired ideas which present opportunities for your welfare and progress. If you do not act upon them, the fault is yours alone. It is the exercise and application of your mental powers that determines the degree of success you will enjoy in life. Use your intuition which is the faculty that gives you instantaneous knowledge. Intuition often warns you about something that is to take place. It gives you an unusually deep insight into the character of people you meet in the course of your life.

You are apt to be sensitive in the region of the neck, throat, and ears. Do your best to avoid exposure to common colds for they have a tendency to affect the throat. Also avoid straining the voice. You are born with a fairly good constitution and are capable of withstanding the ordinary rigours of life. Learn to cultivate rational control over what you eat and drink. Avoid overeating and curb any tendency towards excess of rich foods. Be rational in your diet and you will do much to avoid the common ailments of the digestive system.

Your affectionate, sympathetic, and passionate nature requires expression. You are sincere and intense where romance in concerned. You desire the love, affection, companionship, interest, and attention of the object of your affection. You are faithful in your devotion as long as conditions remain reasonably harmonious. Once you have cared, you always care. Coolness and lack of attention or indifference from your loved one can darken your life, and it takes you a long time to forget. There are times when adverse conditions and circumstances affect your loved one, but you lack understanding because you are thinking of yourself then. It is not natural for those born under Taurus to live alone. You will love children and make a tender and affectionate parent. You are fond of a quiet and harmonious atmosphere at home. As you are somewhat fixed in nature, you want to be master or mistress in your own home; within this limit you desire a certain amount of independence. Without freedom you are inclined to become cross. You want the best that money can buy around you at home. You have a deep appreciation of the artistic and the beautiful aspects of life and nature.

People of your Sign make good executives, whether in business for themselves or in the employ of others; even the Taurus housewife will manage her home and its affairs with firmness. Taurus is the Sign of finance and favours bankers, merchants, brokers, salesmen, farmers, lawyers, as well as doctors and teachers.

The artistic qualities of the Taurus nature lead many under this Sign to the theatre and screen. People born under Taurus also go into commercial art and interior decoration. When in business, they often manage department stores or specialty shops.

Experience will enable you to develop a keen insight into your work and the affairs and motives of others. In matters of partnership, it is advisable for you to use good judgment, particularly because you are, at times, stubborn, headstrong, and set in your ways. Others may try to shift more than your share of responsibility upon you. But if you are given a definite amount of work to handle and are not imposed upon in partnership affairs, you will do well. Your fondness for the good things of life makes you somewhat whimsical in your expenditures, so it is advisable that you develop a modicum of horse sense. During favourable financial periods, invest in practical propositions, such as real estate, but not in any speculative or get-rich-quick schemes. Success in gambling and speculation is not indicated for most Taurus people.

Although your Sign is known as a Fixed Sign, indications show there will be some travel in your life. You derive a certain amount of pleasure from travel as it affords you an opportunity for a change of perspective. The indications point to active social life. Your personality attracts many friends, and acquaintances. You are loyal to your friends, and enjoy extending hospitality to them. You are thoughtful of your friends, and many will rely on you in times of stress for advice, courage, hope and consolation. You have, under ordinary circumstances, a soothing influence upon them.

Study your interesting mind and personality, but do not permit your sensitivity to rule your life. The unwise use of your remarkable determination can hinder you and cause much sorrow. It is well within your ability to curb or control a tendency to be obstinate, and you must do it if you ever wish to become a success. Because of your sensitive, emotional nature, it is advisable for you to exercise your best judgment in love and marriage. Your impulsiveness appears to be emotional rather than mental; herein lies your greatest difficulty. Understand this impulsiveness and do your best to direct both your mental and emotional energies wisely.

Success will come primarily as the result of applying your efforts in the right direction. You are a born builder and worker, so work out your own destiny. You will succeed because of patience, thoughtfulness, and determination. While you may not be as aggressive as some people, you have fortitude, and will go forward in the face of obstacles when many others would give up. The necessity for well-planned application of your mental and physical energies cannot be overstated. Good planning serves to eliminate enemies and obstacles and attracts to you friends, love, respect, and success.

The Taurus Child

This child will have a persistent, steadfast, self-reliant nature. He will be able to carry to a successful completion any idea that he might develop. The parents of children born under this Sign will be wise to handle them carefully because sometimes they turn out to be stubborn and unyielding. It follows that a great deal of tact is necessary to keep this child from turning against the parent. When provoked, the children of Taurus are quick to anger. Once the Taurus child has made up his mind, he will be found very difficult to influence. Taurus is known as a Fixed Sign and has a tendency to be very steady in ideas and opinions.

Taurus children have a basically amicable and kind disposition, but they resent contradiction. When one has once succeeded in showing them they are wrong, their inherent love of justice and truth will prompt them to acknowledge their mistakes. The parent should prevent the offspring from becoming obstinate, as this unhealthy quality may lead to a desire to leave home.

The Taurus vitality is naturally strong, but may be readily exhausted by a quick temper and over-indulgence in rich foods. The child is prone to discomfort due to the latter. Diseases peculiar to the Taurus-born include abscesses, impure blood, and tonsillitis. The Sign is ruled by the planet Venus, and influences the throat. Care should be taken to avoid strain of the throat.

The following are a few of the natural vocational tendencies: actor, artisan, clothing dealer, dancer, designer, farmer, jeweller, miner, musician, singer, painter, maker or seller of toilet accessories. The Venus rulership influences the artistic tendencies as outlined above.

The Taurus Wife

The Taurus wife is, perhaps, the most dependable wife in the whole range of Zodiacal types. She seldom resorts to divorce; she will endure extreme hardships rather than desert her mate. The Taurus wife is naturally adapted to domestic life. She is a perfect homemaker, a devoted mother, and a loving mate. She is usually quite ambitious, for Taurus women are domineering in their own quiet way. They appear to be calm, reserved, and friendly, yet underneath they are jealous, and covet the material things in life.

The Taurus wife never questions her husband's devotion because she, herself, seldom strays. She is a most affectionate, demonstrative woman, wholly engrossed in her home and family. She watches her family with a personal attention that occasionally exacts service from them. Beneath the goodness of a Taurus wife there is a streak of determination that pushes her husband to meet her demands. She covers her determination by seeming to be dependent.

The devotion of these women can best be held by a man who is important in the business world and can afford to give his wife a luxurious home where she may show off her housekeeping ability and her social charm. A positive Taurus woman with good planetary influences possesses well-directed determination; a negatively influenced woman is obstinate and stubborn. The great redeeming feature of the Taurean wife is a deep understanding and sympathy manifested towards those she loves.

The Taurus Husband

The Taurus male has one of the finest qualities of all for attaining success as a husband. It would appear from previous descriptions of the Taurus-born that the man is rather stern. It is true there is a bullish tendency to satisfy the intense physical urge latent in him. But the Taurus man is so dependable, kind, generous, and faithful to his trust as a home builder that any violence in his emotional nature must be overlooked. He seldom neglects his home for an outside interest. Any such diversion is usually transitory and fleeting.

This type of husband adores his wife and children, and takes pains to give them the best home, education, clothes, and amusements that this world provides. These men often marry above their station in life, partly because they are so ambitious to establish themselves, and partly because their search for success leads them to high social goals.

The rulership of Venus in the Sign gives them great appreciation of beauty. In order to hold a Taurus husband throughout life, the wife must constantly look her best and behave lovingly. The husbands adore independence and like to feel they are the sole providers of their families' happiness. Domestic life, tiresome to so many of the other Zodiacal types, is never tiresome to the Taurus husband. Once married, he never regrets his lost bachelor existence nor does he even think of the liberty that others count as precious.

The negative type of Taurus husband is apt to be somewhat gruff, manifesting a peculiar, self-willed and obstinate attitude. He represents the "I am for myself" type of personality.

The Cusps of Taurus

(If your birthday is not within the cusp of your Sign, the following does not apply to you.)

If the birthday is from April 21st through April 24th

You were born in Taurus with Aries tendencies. Your ruling planets are Venus and Mars. This denotes an impulsiveness too strong for your own good. You are broadminded, intellectual, clever, and practical. You have a dominating nature, strong powers of persuasion, self-confidence, and you are a good mixer. At times you may be headstrong, stubborn, and self-sufficient. When you have made up your mind about something, it is very difficult to make you change it, regardless of consequences. No one's judgment is infallible—consider all things well before you take a definite stand. You can be too generous for your own good; often you go to extremes to be a good fellow. You make a delightful companion and a dependable friend. You dislike criticism, but you will only harm yourself if you take a stubborn attitude to constructive criticism.

If your birthday is from May 18th through May 20th

You were born in Taurus with Gemini tendencies. Your ruling planets are Venus and Mercury. With negative influences you may be sarcastic, self-willed, and indifferent to the feelings of others, but positive influences will make you confident, serious, and a good mixer. This Sign gives you talent and ambition, but there are times when your imagination runs away with reality. In this case, it becomes difficult for you to concentrate upon any one thing. Your firm and straightforward tendencies can bring about success in spite of any opposition. Your magnetic personality has the power to attract friends. You must not be too hasty in choosing a mate because many people born between these dates contract unhappy marriages. By exercising prudence in important matters and overcoming your impulsive nature, you can become a successful and happy person.

The Decanates of Taurus

If the birthday is between April 21st and April 30th

You have the double aspect of the benevolent planet Venus in your chart. You possess perseverance, will power, and vitality. Your personal planet, Venus, which is the symbol of love and beauty, gives constancy to your affections and denotes a fixed nature. Both likes and dislikes will be maintained tenaciously. You share things freely and are charitable, especially to those who are near and dear. A truly magnanimous spirit is indicated by the double aspect of Venus in your Horoscope.

If the birthday is between May 1st and May 10th

Your personal planet is Mercury, the symbol of knowledge. It rules the more rational part of the soul and mind. You are deliberate, conservative, and constructive with an unusually active mind. Mercury in its favourable aspect indicates an alert, perceptive, studious, and forceful personality. On the negative side, it inclines towards an inquisitive, meddlesome, careless, radical, forgetful, and effusive nature. This planet is the great mental ruler. Without Mercury's influence, we lack memory and the powers of speech and expression.

If the birthday is between May 11th and May 20th

Your personal planet is Saturn, which is the symbol of Time. This planet is restrictive in its influences, governs the thoughtful and meditative tendencies which incline to make its subjects careful, patient, and considerate. Its powers lie in the realms of stability, endurance, tenacity, and perseverance. Gain through thrift and careful investment is indicated. You possess a truly magnanimous spirit and a kind, benevolent, and sympathetic nature.

The Degrees of Taurus

April 21st

You possess a masterful, thoughtful, and persevering disposition. You display unusual ability in the arts. Your strong will power brings you into contact with many important people. You have the natural ability to make friends readily because of your pleasing personality. This is the degree of the dictator, so curb any tendency you may have in this direction.

April 22nd

You possess a magnetic, determined, and generous nature. You will succeed in life through your own merits and natural capabilities. Your loyalty and inherent ability will help you find marked success in any profession of a scientific nature where intelligent application of detailed knowledge is essential. You should be surrounded by love, affection, and understanding, since certain aspects in this Horoscope indicate the possibility of developing a grasping, selfish, and materialistic outlook.

April 23rd

You possess a well-balanced philosophical mind coupled with a kind and affectionate disposition. You have a generous nature, but at times may be somewhat temperamental and headstrong. You may have a delicate constitution and should not go to extremes in mental or physical exertion.

April 24th

You possess a refined, artistic, and charitable nature. You are gentle and prudent, but lack confidence. Learn to concentrate upon your problems in order to develop the ability to assert yourself with confidence. You are considerate and obedient to the wishes of others. Beware of people who are likely to take advantage of you and cause you to bear the brunt of responsibility.

April 25th

You possess a practical and reserved nature. You will succeed best in a position of authority. Learn to be considerate of other people's feelings by using more tact. You show great enterprise in acquiring the good things in life; success will be attained mostly through your own efforts. You are a natural leader. One aspect in your Horoscope indicates the possibility of success as an officer of the law.

April 26th

You possess a bold imagination and a keen mind, which will aid in the attainment of success in an academic career. An extravagant nature and a decided flair for fine clothes and expensive possessions is shown. You should curb your tendency to gamble, as it may cause you financial embarrassment.

April 27th

You possess a diplomatic and a kind nature. You are intuitive and show unusual aptitude in the culinary arts. You are fond of good food. You also display a marked tendency to prefer your own company to that of others. You are, however, affectionate and magnanimous to your immediate family. You have a tendency to indulge yourself in both food and drink.

April 28th

You have a keen and perceptive mind and possess the ability to learn quickly. A magnetic temperament and lovable nature bring the desire for better things in life. One aspect in this Horoscope indicates a marked wish to have your own way, and to get it with the least possible personal effort, thereby creating enemies. Do not permit yourself to become self-indulgent; try to overcome a tendency to pamper your whims and fancies.

April 29th

You possess a stubborn nature coupled with a resourceful and a determined mind. Resolution combined with the ability to express yourself clearly are your outstanding characteristics. You show a tendency to become obstinate and reckless. A disregard for convention and an inherent desire to express radical views may cause you to become an influential person in the lunatic fringe.

April 30th

You possess initiative, originality, and perception. You also show a decided tendency to be contrary in a mischievous manner. Good conversational ability and profound foresight will aid you in the attainment of success in the business world. Gains through relatives are shown at various intervals in your life. Careful training and a good education will materially aid in developing the more positive aspects in this Horoscope.

May 1st

You possess a bright, cheerful, and affectionate nature. Generosity, kindness of heart, and a desire to help others are also indicated. One aspect in this Horoscope shows a great love for domestic life. You possess great powers of persuasion and can be successful in any career where master salesmanship is necessary. You gain through life at the expense of your enemies.

May 2nd

You possess an artistic, ardent, and generous nature. A versatile mind coupled with marked social instincts will enable you to gain success and recognition in public service. One aspect in your Horoscope indicates a tendency to be too apprehensive where the welfare of your loved ones is concerned. Learn moderation of this golden virtue, as it is apt to cause unnecessary strain on the heart. Remember, it is foolish to worry about things that you cannot control.

May 3rd

You possess a resourceful, scientific, and practical mind. You are inventive, and interested in all phases of scientific endeavour. You are painstaking and honest, and command the respect of your friends and associates. One aspect in this

Horoscope indicates danger through misplaced friendships. Talent is shown for those who desire a political career.

May 4th

You possess a refined and artistic nature. You have a tendency to be irritable and impatient when your plans and desires are not readily fulfilled. Because you possess an unusually progressive mind and a vivid imagination, you could become a good executive. You have a great deal of literary talent and could gain success as an author or politician.

May 5th

You possess an ethereal mind, remarkable intellect, and a keen sense of judgment. Great fixity of purpose and skill in the art of salesmanship will bring success in business endeavours. Unhappiness is indicated in personal life due to misfortune in affairs of the heart. Misplaced affection may be the main source of trouble.

May 6th

You possess a clever, subtle mind, and a sympathetic nature. Keen interest in literature, art, and writing endow you with the qualities of a successful author. Your sense of fair play will help to develop the practical side of your nature. Influential friends will be helpful throughout your life.

May 7th

You possess an original mind; this will have great influence upon your friends and associates. You possess a natural aristocratic bearing and a flair for social recognition; this may cause you to attach too much significance to outward appearances. You desire to impress outsiders; this may cause you to neglect your family and those who are most interested in your welfare.

May 8th

You possess a sympathethic nature and an intellectual mind. Unless you are in congenial surroundings and have the proper friends, your sensitive disposition can easily develop into an inferiority complex. A tendency to become introspective should be curbed. One aspect in this Horoscope shows a strong desire to help those in less fortunate circumstances than yourself.

May 9th

You possess a resourceful, determined, and forceful nature. Self-discipline will prevent tantrums. One aspect in this Horoscope shows a judicial and perceptive mind coupled with a high-strung nervous system. This is the degree of a born leader, the man who pulls himself up by his bootstraps.

May 10th

You possess a profound mind alternately swayed by principle and ambition. You show a great deal of adaptability combined with an unusual aptitude at reproducing and imitating. One aspect in this Horoscope indicates a tendency to become a great artist in the entertainment world. You will want your way in all matters. It is essential that you bear in mind that the desire to achieve personal satisfaction at all costs may bring with it the animosity of others.

May 11th

You possess an aspiring nature and keen mental powers. You are quite versatile; however, a political career holds great charm for you. Your natural ability, intuition, and keen foresight also favour a legal career. One aspect in this Horoscope indicates that you should use caution while handling medicines. There are certain astrological influences that show danger due to carelessness or temporary depressive moods.

May 12th

You possess an adventurous spirit and a strong desire to travel and visit strange places. You are fond of company and social activity. You show a marked aptitude for organizing and controlling others, and are always ready to accept responsibility. You have a determined nature and should gain fame in your chosen profession.

May 13th

You possess an aspiring, passionate, and sensitive nature. You are independent and have the ability to carry out your objectives in life without much assistance from outside influences. When choosing your vocation, permit your foresight to have full sway . . . by so doing, you will decide your own course in life. You are impressionable; you will readily react to your environment.

May 14th

You possess a humble spirit and a good sense of humour. A great love for travel upon the sea is also indicated. A magnanimous personality and a desire to help those who are in less fortunate straits will lead you into many strange experiences during your life. The alleviation of sorrow and suffering will be your great ambition. Just rewards in the form of honour and success will result from such undertakings.

May 15th

You possess an imaginative and intuitive nature. An experimental and poetic mind coupled with a leaning towards mystic and occult sciences is also indicated. You should seek the company of understanding companions to avoid loneliness. One aspect in this Horoscope indicates the ability to achieve fame in humanitarian pursuits. Your magnetic personality will make you popular with the opposite sex.

May 16th

You possess an ambitious and determined personality. You show a marked aptitude for dealing in financial matters, and should study and prepare for a position pertaining to monetary pursuits. Intense concentration of purpose will aid you materially, providing you overcome a tendency to display your strong likes and dislikes regardless of consequences. An aspect in this Horoscope indicates the possible development of an inferiority complex due to confusion of purpose.

May 17th

You possess an eloquent and persuasive personality. You are fond of music and art. You enjoy the beautiful, refined, and aesthetic things in life. This Horoscope in one aspect indicates good fortune in marriage. You are well adapted to a business or a professional career, with the ability to patiently bide your time until a real opportunity presents itself.

May 18th
You possess a steadfast and persevering personality. A strong healthy body coupled with good recuperative powers will enable you to overcome most of your physical dangers. A charming, winsome disposition will bring many sincere friendships into your life. One aspect in this Horoscope indicates much good fortune through a career. You can depend upon your good powers of organization to bring you success.

May 19th
You possess will power and a prudent disposition. Capability in dealing with the masses and an ability to obtain the confidence of influential and prosperous friends will insure success. Financial gains from investments in land are under strong aspect. You will be unreceptive to any proposition that does not coincide with your sense of justice.

May 20th
You possess a clever, perceptive mind, which coupled with intensity of purpose will influence others to co-operate with your plans and desires. Much talent in literary matters may bring substantial recognition in this field.

Compatible and Incompatible Signs of Taurus

The Sign of Taurus has a strongly physical sex nature. The Taurus man is often inclined to lust; this may frequently drive him to excesses. The tendencies toward self-indulgence are comparable to the equally strong inclinations to overeat. The Taurus possesses strong animal instincts. He is not one to search for the ideal. At heart, Taurus is faithful, good-natured, easily satisfied, and patient. As a husband, he is the "stick-in-the-mud" type who is happy and contented if his slippers are properly warmed and his dinner is plentiful and to his liking. Of course, if he has an aggressive Sign rising at birth, these virtues may be somewhat lessened.

The obstinacy of the Taurean has been stressed in the former sections for this Sign, but it is well to mention here that neither the man nor woman with Taurus rising can be driven, though he or she can be very easily led by affection. People born under this Sign are not demonstrative. They are persons possessed of deep, strong feelings; they are inclined to be possessive. Money is usually a big consideration in Taurean marriages, since Taurus is the money Sign of the Zodiac. Money need not necessarily be considered, for, by the law of polarity, the exact opposite may occur and the marriage may be one in which lack of money gives rise to critical situations.

Another Taurean characteristic of importance is a natural soothing and healing power, which makes this native a good partner for one with a high-strung nervous system. Taureans have an eminently practical nature; the limitations which this practical outlook imposes upon their otherwise passionate nature will, of course, yield observable effects. They are less impulsive than calculating, but when they have made their final selection and are resolved upon a course, they are firm in decision.

Taureans have a dominant, obstinate nature and are imbued with the idea that what they say must go. Once they have made up their minds, they leave no stone unturned until they accomplish their own desires. They are conservative in their mannerisms and habits. Strangely enough, despite this conservative trait, they often promise more than they can deliver. At times, they make such promises without having the slightest real intention of fulfilling them. This idiosyncrasy frequently makes them unpopular because people resent being let down. The Taurean will find the compatible and incompatible Signs in the following:

Taurus and Aries

Although Aries is an impatient, energetic Sign, rather domineering, Taurus should not have any difficulty finding compatibility with this Sign. The slower-moving Taurus may find the going a bit hectic, but the excitement may help stimulate the courtship since Taurus is a highly emotional Sign, though very obstinate when dictated to. The Taurean, ruled by Venus, Goddess of Love, will usually show the Mars-ruled Aries the error of his ways when they meet on a common level.

Taurus and Taurus

This appears to be a compatible combination from a purely physical standpoint. There could be trouble on the mental plane due to tendencies towards jealousy and stubbornness. Unless one or the other is willing to give way when tempers flare and accusations fly, serious difficulties could arise to mar the nuptial bliss. One point in favour is that both understand the little quirks of the other, and if deeply in love, they will readily forgive in the privacy of the love nest.

Taurus and Gemini

The Gemini personality may prove too restless for the Taurean nature. Emotionally these two Signs are at odds. The Mercurian outlook on intimate matters does not sit well with a son or daughter of Venus. The Gemini loves variety of thought, and delights in all mental pursuits, while the Taurean is mostly interested in the material things of life. The great sex drive of the Taurean could overpower the more docile Gemini.

Taurus and Cancer

This usually makes a good combination. Cancer likes a good home and much affection. This is what every Taurean hopes to find when undertaking connubial responsibilities. From an emotional point of view, there is nothing in the stars that bars the prospect of a happy married life between these two partners. One thing the Taurean must remember is that Cancer is exceedingly sensitive, and will crawl into a shell if unhappy emotionally.

Taurus and Leo

Venus and the Sun make a good combination, especially when each understands his companion's shortcomings. Both have great sex appeal and excellent physical qualities. Magnanimous Leo is just what the doctor ordered for the Taurean's love of the finer things in life. If the Taurean curbs the tendency towards jealousy and gives Leo a little leeway to show off, all is fine and will go well with this combination.

Taurus and Virgo

Taurus should avoid the attractiveness of the Virgonian if a love-at-first-sight predicament is to be avoided. Taurus will certainly not get his own way here. The Taurean does not like criticism, the sharpest weapon of Virgo. Unless you are willing to take a lot of nagging, it would be well to think twice before taking a Virgo mate.

Taurus and Libra

This is a Venus and Venus combination. It should prove compatible, except under negative aspects from other planets. There will be common interests and a meeting of the mind and body. The Goddess of Love will continue to shine on these lovebirds until one gets out of line. If this occurs, beware, for the feathers will fly! Generally speaking, however, this is usually a good marital combination.

Taurus and Scorpio

This combination belongs to the mutual admiration society. The strong sexual urge in both of these Signs will find much in common. Jealousy is the big bad wolf that keeps hovering at the door. Taurus must be very careful to keep faith with the Scorpio mate, or the roof will cave in without warning. Woe to the one who crosses the Scorpion's path—the sting is considered deadly.

Taurus and Sagittarius

The possessive Taurean may find the freedom-loving Sagittarian hard to cope with. The Sagittarius natives are frank and generous; this Jupiterian trait can clash with the Taurean jealousy. The Taurus who marries a Sagittarius will find that no amount of arguing or berating is going to change the reckless Sagittarian.

Taurus and Capricorn

With mutual understanding of each other's idiosyncrasies this can be a compatible marriage. Venus blends well with Saturn from an emotional point of view. Both need a certain amount of encouragement and flattery, but Taurus will be the one who must take the lead in this direction. While Capricorn may seem a little cold and aloof at first, the warm rays of Venus will soon melt the exterior of caution and prudence that is inherent in all Capricorns.

Taurus and Aquarius

This combination usually runs into many difficulties. The unpredictable Aquarian may prove too much for the easy-going Taurus nature. Conversely, the conservative habits of Taurus soon get on the dynamic Aquarius' nerves, and tempers start to flash. While both love ease and comfort, their views on how to obtain them are widely divergent. Another source of irritation for the Taurus lover is the unwillingness of Aquarius to share his secrets.

Taurus and Pisces

This is usually a very happy combination. Sentimental Pisces will find great comfort in sympathetic Taurus. Neptune, the ruler of Pisces, is the higher octave of Venus, who, in turn, rules Taurus. Pisces is impressionable, romantic, imaginative, and flexible, which is just what the Taurus native is looking for. Both have much in common from an artistic standpoint, which helps to blend their mental inclinations.

Some Famous Persons Born in the Sign of Taurus

Fred Astaire—Dancer
Irving Berlin—Song Writer
Perry Como—Singer
Gary Cooper—Actor
Oliver Cromwell—British Statesman
Bing Crosby—Actor and Singer
Salvador Dali—Painter
Elizabeth II—Queen of England
Ulysses S. Grant—Soldier and President
Henry J. Kaiser—Industrialist
Guglielmo Marconi—Inventor
Nellie Melba—Opera Star
James Monroe—US President
Henry Morgenthau—Financier
William Shakespeare—Dramatist and Poet
Bishop Fulton J. Sheen—Author
Shirley Temple—Actress
Harry Truman—US President
Rudolph Valentino—Actor
Orson Welles—Actor and Director

3

GEMINI

May 21st–June 21st

THE SIGN of Gemini symbolizes unity and the strength of united action.

The two bright stars Castor and Pollux represent the twin souls.

The Sign Gemini represents the hands and arms of the Grand Man of the Universe, and, therefore, expresses the projecting and executive forces of humanity in all mechanical departments.

Upon the esoteric planisphere, the Sign is occupied by Simeon and Levi. "They are brethren," says Jacob, "and instruments of cruelty are in their habitation"—which refers in a very unmistakable manner to the fearful, potent powers of projection that lie concealed within the magnetic constitutions of all those who are dominated by this Sign. The mystical symbol of The Twins conceals the doctrine of soul-mates and other important truths connected therewith.

Gemini is the first and highest emanation of the airy Trigon; it is the constellation of the planet Mercury.

The planet Mercury absorbs an energy which appears to be a compound of all other planets of the spectrum put together; he has been well designated as "The Messenger of the Gods".

The mystical gem of this Sign is the emerald, which is the talisman-stone for those born under this Sign.

The fortunate day is Wednesday.

Fortunate numbers are three and four.

The fortunate colours for this Sign are silver and grey.

Best locations for success are high places, well above sea level.

The specific action which this orb radiates is purely intellectual and scientific. It is quick and active, intuitional, enterprising, careless, volatile, bright, changeable, and what we call "smart".

This influence is extremely inventive and is the originator of all cunning schemes and devices. It is what men term bright and witty. It is that which makes the man of commerce. It constitutes the leading influence embodied within that sharp, clever and chameleon-like individual who makes a fortune in real estate or the stock market.

Addressing a Gemini, I would say that you have what is known as an intellectual type of personality. You are attractive, active, and magnetic upon first impression. Your manners are charming and pleasing. You are fond of being looked up to and respected. Under normal conditions you will be well liked by the majority of people you meet. There are times, however, when it will be necessary for you to take stock of yourself and your personality. You are whimsical and somewhat changeable, especially in regard to people you associate with consistently. You will find it to your advantage to exercise your interesting personality in the direction of self-control.

Do your best to avoid unwise whims and fancies. You desire to have others show you consideration; in return, you should show consideration for others. Do all within your power to exercise the more charming characteristics of your personality and you will do much towards making yourself happy and be able to make your loved ones and others happy because of you.

You have a sensitive and active mind; emotionally you are quite affectionate, generous and impulsive. These qualities often cause you to be misunderstood by others. Your procrastination is brought about by the intense activity of your mind and your reactions to your own thoughts and ideas. There are times when you are unusually generous. You have a fairly quick temper, but this amounts to unpleasant peevishness more than downright anger. Most of the time you are over it quickly. Under ordinary circumstances you are not much inclined to hold a grudge for long. Your active mind disposes you to be talkative and even to take delight in personal arguments on many subjects. You often argue for the sake of arguing. Avoid unwise or excessive indulgence in this direction and you gain by it.

Indications point to originality of thought, vivid imagination, a good sense of humour, and forcefulness of expression. You have good powers of observation and perception and can be patient if you want to be. You are able to grasp the facts of a proposition quicker than the average individual. You learn things easily.

Your imagination often causes you to desire to live a picturesque and romantic life. Herein may lie the secret of some of your greatest difficulties and disillusionments in life. You are somewhat of a dreamer and idealist; when your ideals or dreams are shattered you are deeply disillusioned and hurt. Give your imagination the proper scale and you will do much towards improving its practical value. Use imagination's energy for constructive planning and visualization of the things you wish to accomplish. You are inclined to acquire all sorts of knowledge, with the result that your memory does not always furnish you with retained facts. You will, however, readily recall such things in which you have taken an unusual interest or have paid particular attention to at some time or another. For example, you will often recall an insult much quicker than you will a kind word. The former made a deeper impression upon your mind and the latter was something you took, more or less, for granted.

Your memory functions most efficiently in matters pertaining to work and business. Your active mind ravishes acquiring all sorts of ideas and theories. This makes you an exceptionally good conversationalist. Much of your impulsiveness rises from your subconscious mind. Someone of your temperament is apt to be impulsive, more from a mental than an emotional point of view. It will help to study and understand this part of your personality. It will help you to avoid many psychological and emotional errors which could make your life uncertain and unhappy. You should curb the tendency to act upon impulse.

A person of your temperament often has inspirational ideas. How far they advance beyond the point of your imagination depends entirely upon you. If you are content to just muse and daydream about them, they will never serve a useful or practical purpose. Your inspired ideas are usually of an artistic nature. You have an active intuition which gives you the power to separate the real from the ideal. It also serves to warn you in times of danger and gives you an unusually keen insight into the characters of others.

If you give yourself the proper mental training, you will find that your subconscious mind will furnish you with all the material you require. You have the power to think up new and original ideas. Many persons born in your Sign are excellent writers, creators of new forms of art, inventors, musical composers, etc.

You are sensitive, affectionate and refined as a lover. However, your affection, tenderness, and passion depend upon your mental moods. You are capable of warmth and tenderness in one moment and coolness and indifferency in the next. If your attention is focused on mental problems, you show physical indifference and may readily be misunderstood. This capacity for detachment often helps to complicate your love affairs. When you wish, however, you can be exceedingly expressive. More than one outstanding love affair is indicated during your lifetime. Indications show that you are more likely to care for people from an intellectual, rather than from a physical, point of view. You appear to be flirtatious and flighty; in reality, you are interested in enjoying diversified mental companionship.

Your imagination plays an important part in your love life. You require a mental and physical balance in love in order to be happy and contented. You have a mind of your own and wish to exercise the independence of your own nature to a great degree; thus, it is advisable that you use exceptionally good judgment in matters of love and marriage. Your sensitive emotional nature requires an intellectual, affectionate, and refined mate. Your Sign does not give promise of many children.

Your Sign presides over the chest, lungs, hands, and arms. Always do your best to avoid exposure to common colds. It is also advisable not to overwork your body or mind, as this appears to tax your sensitive nervous system and makes you peevish and irritable. Use care in your diet and eat wholesome and nerve-building foods. Plenty of fresh air, sunshine and light exercise are essential to your physical and mental well-being. You should never confine yourself to close or stuffy quarters. Above all, endeavour to do your best to exercise rational control over a tendency to brood and worry. This habit, if you indulge in it, will upset your nervous system. Such upsets will lay the foundation for future complications in your state of health.

It appears you will be somewhat critical in matters pertaining to your home life. You desire to have things "just so", otherwise, you become a fuss-pot. You are extremely sensitive in your reactions to home surroundings. You have an aversion to monotony. Your active mind makes you bored with the sameness of things. You often become restless and nervous if you have to stay too long in one place. A certain amount of control of this tendency will go a long way to help you get along better with others. A vacation away from home surroundings will often do you much good. When this is not possible, it is up to you to curb your restlessness until conditions make it possible for you to get out and enjoy a change.

You appreciate the type of work which exercises your active mind. You possess natural qualifications for writing, merchandising, practicing law, medicine, or occupations connected with travel, printing, and aviation. Often you desire to follow several vocations at once. There may be times in life when you feel that your progress is too slow; then you become depressed. You will do well, under such circumstances, to realize that all progress is not rapid and that patience is the key to advancement. Many Gemini natures have proved to be their own stumbling block. Both men and women of this Sign have either active or latent artistic ability which can be developed. It may be in music, art, or dancing. Odd and unusual literature has proved profitable for many of your Sign.

You also have good promotional and sales ability and succeed in occupations dealing with the general public. In matters of partnership you can get along fairly well. You are apt to desire the upper hand and if you do not handle yourself wisely you will cause dissension. If you are thoughtful and co-operative you will be able to prosper in such ventures.

Your financial circumstances, like your moods, may vary

considerably during the course of your life. You are apt to spend money for little things that bring you only temporary benefit. You are fond of dress and finery. It will be advisable for you to cultivate the habit of being reasonably conservative in your personal expenditures. During favourable financial periods you will do well to make practical investments in such things as properties, large industrial organizations, government bonds, and transportation lines. It will be well for you to curb impulsiveness in your financial affairs. The secret of financial success lies in the art of making your money work for you.

Indications show that you will have many very interesting friends and acquaintances. Although you will attract a great variety of people, your choice of close friends will be the intellectual type. You will derive much pleasure from such people, as they will afford an outlet for your keen mind. You will, however, be inclined to have serious arguments with some of your best and closest friends. You have a liking for an active social life and desire to mingle with many people. You have the type of personality that leads to success in social circles. With the ability to influence others, you can set a good example by your own ideals and philosophy.

Your greatest handicap in life arises from your tendency to procrastinate. You are selfish and have little regard for the feelings and thoughts of others. Independence of will is to be commended, but should not be overdone. Any individual with true wisdom knows the value of co-operation and will always work harmoniously with others for the common good of all. Many Gemini people are apt to assert an air of independence in order to cover up feelings of inferiority. Take stock of yourself and do all within your power to eliminate or control this tendency to be peevish and irritable over little things. You will also find it to your advantage to cultivate patience and fortitude. It is up to you to improve your mind and its qualities so that you will be able to attain a rational understanding of yourself. Take advantage of your natural creative abilities. Study such subjects as will enhance your prospects of gaining greater self-confidence. You must develop consistency of action in all constructive activities.

The Gemini Child

This child has an inquiring mind; he is continually asking questions with the intent of discovering the reason why. Gemini children are usually very humane and generous in disposition. These children have the ability to be clever, and often turn out to be progressive—with an inventive genius.

They will be fond of change and diversity. It is best to keep them busy, as inactivity will cause them to become impatient, and that's when mischief starts!

They like to use their talents in their own way; if given the opportunity, there are few things they cannot master. They are readily able to adapt themselves to persons and circumstances as they grow older, and usually they make many friends.

Parents often find it hard to understand their Gemini children. These children are outwardly bold and inwardly timid. They like to use their own methods, while ignoring the suggestions or orders of others. A particular point for the parents of these children to remember is that, unless they are trained to complete each task before beginning another, they are apt to start much that they never finish.

The Gemini child's fundamental vitality is moderate; therefore, care should be taken in early life to guard his or her health. A study of the pathology of this birthsign indicates that the system may be kept under unnecessary tension by restlessness and nervousness. The Sign is ruled by the planet Mercury which has rulership over the nervous system. The child has a natural tendency to a nervous temperament and should not be frightened or left in the dark too long; neither should it listen to weird tales or see horror movies. Another point to be guarded against is the possibility of fractures of the shoulders, arms and hands. Lungs as well as diet should receive plenty of attention. Mental and bodily exercise will aid the Gemini child very much more than a lot of medicine.

The mountains, as well as upstairs rooms, are harmonious surroundings for them.

The Gemini child will possess latent conversational ability as well as creative powers. In general, the best training for this child is a liberal arts education. Their versatility will enable them to choose from a variety of occupations. The Gemini child will sometimes lack concentration, but if trained properly, the future possibilities for achievement will be greatly enhanced. There is also a tendency at times to be ungrateful, and it would be well to encourage and stimulate gratitude as well as sympathy.

The Gemini Wife

The Gemini wife is first and foremost an intellectual woman. The strongest appeal to her is mental companionship. She must be made to feel that she is a partner, and not just a housekeeper. It is natural for a woman of this type to want to maintain her outside activities after marriage. Of course, outside activities take up a lot of time, and many husbands resent this diffusion of interest. However, if there is to be harmony in the home it is better to treat this condition tactfully. Sometimes the wife, herself, discovers that two separate existences are impossible if justice is to be done to her home, and she gradually gives up her hobby or career. In many cases, the Gemini woman is so capable that her home and her work are managed smoothly.

When these natives are talented, it is usually in some well-paid line. They have been called mercenary, as they demand just compensation for their efforts. They are not the long-suffering type that works for nothing.

Gemini women are particular as to how their homes are run, even though they may not be in them as much as other wives. They are refined, meticulous women who abhor untidiness. They seldom do their own work if they can help it but direct efficiently and command obedience.

The Gemini woman shines brightly in society. She is scintillating and well informed. She is the type of woman who would make a helpful wife for a professional man. One who builds his practice on agreeable social contacts would find this kind of woman the very partner for his interests. This nativity gives a somewhat flirtatious nature, and many a husband watches his Gemini with anxiety. He would feel much better if he knew that she was just using her sharp wits to enjoy a mental battle of the sexes.

Her common sense and protective instincts are strong; she

would never sacrifice her home and husband for an extra-marital affair.

The Gemini Husband

The Gemini husband is not the type of husband for a possessive, passionate wife. While these men are talented and interesting persons, they desire frequent changes in scenery. They make good newspapermen, writers, or scientists. Their domestic life is usually sketchy. The Gemini looks for a marriage partner who can share his mental and social interests and who is not too tied to her home. She must be willing to change her environment as often as he desires. The wives of these men must suffer their husband's interest in people and other women. He is inclined to be flirtatious, but his wandering fancy should not be taken seriously.

Actually Gemini men have a great deal of common sense, and while they love to pursue the "will o' the wisp", no other man can close a romantic chapter with more finality when the heat is on. If the Gemini husband could find a wife to vitalize his interest in family life without nagging, his marriage would be more successful. These natives are apt to assert an air of arrogance to hide an inferiority complex.

They have a somewhat critical attitude when it comes to home life. They like everything to be "just so", and can become very fussy when things are not up to their standards.

These men have an aversion to monotony and usually seek some diversion when they become bored at home. Though they possess a great amount of love for their children, they are apt to be strict with them.

The Cusps of Gemini

(If your birthday is not within the cusp of your Sign, the following does not apply to you.)

If the birthday is from May 21st through May 23rd

You were born in Gemini with Taurus tendencies. The ruling planets are Mercury and Venus. This indicates a strong magnetic personality and many unusual talents. Music, art, literature, and the society of intellectual people appeal greatly to these natives.

They are good conversationalists and possess refined habits. They are full of life and energy. They always desire to excel as hosts and hostesses. They create good impressions wherever they go. The one fault they must overcome is their fear of public opinion. These natives are fond of travel and change. They possess determination and are not easily swerved from their course. They are alert, careful, progressive, and tactful.

They present a good appearance and have the ability to attract many friends, but need to cultivate the faculty of holding them. They will be popular with a wide circle of friends and are good entertainers.

If the birthday is from June 18th through June 21st

You were born in Gemini with Cancer tendencies. The ruling orbs are Mercury and the Moon. This indicates that you are subject to self-pity; you may be too sensitive for your own good. You possess foresight and have an analytical type of mind. Graceful in movement and neat in appearance, you place much importance upon dress and style. You are inclined to be affectionate.

You can adjust yourself to many talents easily, and can master almost any profession you tackle, if you work with a congenial and intelligent partner.

You seem somewhat fond of speculation and the taking of chances, but the birthdays within this cusp do not promise much success along these lines. You make a good friend, and will meet any reasonable appeal for a helping hand, and do not listen to rumours or scandal.

You are precise and can be depended upon to do exactly as you promise. You are an idealist at heart and promote these ideals whenever possible, but intelligent enough, also, to be practical.

The Decanates of Gemini

If the birthday is between May 21st and May 31st

The personal and ruling planet is Mercury. It is known as the symbol of knowledge and rules the rational part of the mind.

It imparts an alert, ingenious, perceptive, intellectual, studious, and forceful personality when in favourable aspect. In unfavourable aspect it inclines towards an inquisitive, shiftless, forgetful, and effusive nature.

This planet is said to be the great mental ruler; without Mercury's influence we would be devoid of memory and the powers of speech and expression.

If the birthday is between June 1st and June 10th

The personal planet is Venus—symbol of love and beauty. It denotes a nature not liable to easily change. Both likes and dislikes will be maintained tenaciously. There is a tendency to be fearless, domineering, and obstinate. Personal things are shared freely; there is charity with the native's earthly possessions. A truly magnanimous spirit is indicated by this aspect of Venus in the chart.

If the birthday is between June 11th and June 21st

The personal planets for this, the third decanate of Gemini, are Saturn and Uranus. These form an unusual combination with the ruling planet Mercury. The influence of these three planets is considered to be mostly mental. The native possesses an unusually brilliant mind that may verge on genius. The ideas and thoughts may be well in advance of the age in which the native lives.

The Degrees of Gemini

May 21st

You of this day possess a sensitive, idealistic nature and a friendly, kindhearted disposition. Certain planetary aspects indicate generosity too extreme for your own good. Learn to recognize the true from the false. You will always work for the common good and will be popular with co-workers and associates.

Fondness of travel by water is shown. It is probable that a long sea voyage will result in a profitable business connection or a successful marriage.

May 22nd

A practical and somewhat materialistic disposition is indicated here. There may be legal difficulties in the conversion of personal possessions to cash. You have strong convictions and ambitious goals. One aspect in this Horoscope shows excellent latent ability as a writer or orator. Your good speaking voice shows a talent for a public career.

May 23rd

Here is shown a shrewd and alert mind. You will be deeply moved by higher sympathies and become a champion of human rights. There will be a tendency to meddle in the affairs of others; and while the intentions may be most charitable, many disappointments are indicated until it is learned that life's greatest rewards come to those who learn to mind their own business first. You are very capable in an emergency and will be an ambassador of good will.

May 24th

You possess a magnetic and fanciful mind. You must learn the value of concentration in order to overcome a tendency to attempt too many things at one time. You are a fluent conversationalist and a prolific writer. One aspect in this Horoscope shows the possibility of making a financial success in some matter dealing with water or chemicals.

May 25th

You possess an artistic personality with excellent literary ability. This is the degree of the politician and statesman. You will travel to foreign lands and exert influence as a master salesman. A relative of this native may gain worldwide recognition for some outstanding accomplishment.

May 26th

You possess a sensitive and retiring disposition coupled with deep emotions. You possess an inquiring mind but may develop a tendency to become too reserved and lonely. Try to overcome a sense of insecurity. Do not hesitate to show your friends and associates the shrewd side of your nature; they will admire you more for it.

May 27th

You are courteous and affable with an obliging, perceptive

mind. A highly magnetic personality and an enterprising disposition will bring many respected and beneficial friendships in life. There will be one great love in your life. You have the force of leadership, and will make a success through some original idea of undertaking. Do not let good fortune go to your head and upset your progress.

May 28th

You possess an alert, impressionable, and often irritable nature. At times, you may become downright cantankerous and lose many friends thereby. Try to check this tendency as much as possible. One aspect in this Horoscope shows a marked degree of leadership with excellent talent for the five arts. This is the degree of the composer, the poet, and the artist.

May 29th

You possess a romantic nature and may be an idealist and dreamer. You are most truthful, and are quite candid in your opinions of others. You may show a decided preference to be in the company of sophisticates and to associate with important persons. You will go far in the social world, and as your experience and character develops, you will move up the ladder of success.

May 30th

You possess wholesome charm and great magnetism. You have an artistic temperament and show originality in your ideas and undertakings. Your lofty ideals will help you to attain considerable success in the social world. Gains through marriage and partnerships are indicated. One aspect in this Horoscope shows long journeys and many influential friends.

May 31st

You possess a bright, cheerful disposition and a kind, generous nature. You are just and righteous in both personal and social matters. You should pursue a professional career, where your mental faculties will be demonstrated to the best advantage. A strong attachment for the home and parents is also indicated.

June 1st

You possess a strong will and a commanding, energetic personality. Success in the art of dealing with the public will bring wide recognition. There is a tendency, however, towards extravagance, which should be curbed. You should learn to understand the value of personal possessions and to cherish them. An ardent, highly emotional nature, full of adventure and wild dreams, should be moderated.

June 2nd

You possess an active, strong, and sometimes domineering personality. One aspect in this Horoscope indicates that you inspire others with your ideas and plans, but become restless and are inclined to worry a great deal if you run into obstacles. Practice tolerance and patience and there will be a better chance to fulfill your hopes and desires.

June 3rd

You possess a keen mind and a calm, peaceful attitude towards life. A charming, open-minded manner, coupled with inherent humanitarian principles, will endear you to all. Gain is indicated through sentimental associations and influential friendships. One aspect in this Horoscope shows a tendency to take good fortune and successful ventures too lightly. This may result in taking things for granted.

June 4th

You possess an ingenious, active, and alert mind. An artistic temperament will bring you many lasting and influential friendships. You are generous, kind-mannered, and are charitably inclined. One aspect in this Horoscope indicates that there may be a tendency to shirk responsibility. Remember that hard work and the diligent application of your many natural talents are necessary attributes to success and happiness.

June 5th

You possess the ability to develop your mind along intellectual and scientific lines. You will display independence of thought and will possess a steady and forceful disposition. One aspect in this Horoscope indicates a desire to defy convention and become a bold innovator. An inheritance at some time in your life is indicated.

June 6th

You possess an energetic and commanding personality. Because you are an excellent conversationalist, you will be in great demand at social gatherings. An able and orderly spirit coupled with a keen sense of diplomacy and tact will help you to attain public esteem. Your fine qualities will make it rather easy for you to get what you want from your parents, friends, and associates. One aspect in this Horoscope shows many artistic relatives.

June 7th

You possess a dual personality and a very imaginative mind. Success in the business world seems to stem from lessons taught in the home. You will be fond of mimicry and will possess a liking for the stage and theatre. One aspect in this Horoscope shows a strong will and an excellent ability to organize and direct. Success in a business or a vocation catering to women is influenced by this degree.

June 8th

You possess artistic sympathies and a humane disposition. This combination of mental qualities is usually found in persons who attain success and recognition in public service. Try to curb a tendency to be impulsive, as such a characteristic, if permitted to develop, can prove detrimental.

June 9th

You possess an intuitive mind. You are able to exert great skill in the execution of your duties. Persistence and determination, even in the face of difficulties, will bring success and financial independence. You choose your friends and associates discriminately and display considerable reserve at all times. You will overcome many disagreeable obstacles. One aspect in this Horoscope indicates a sensuous nature and a hasty temper.

June 10th

You possess a quick mind and a love of travel. Success in a

material way is indicated through the ability to make and hold influential and beneficial friendships. Marked originality and a good sense of humour will make for a position of prestige in the social world. A vivid imagination, coupled with excessive energy, may cause you to become impatient at times. Learn that "haste makes waste".

June 11th

You possess a retiring, studious, and chaste nature. An envious streak, which may become apparent from time to time, should be curbed. You are fond of literature, music, and art. You should make the maximum use of your intellectual and commercial talents. Learn self-confidence and the ability to see the other person's point of view. Due to lack of emotional stability, you may be hard to understand at times. This degree shows public acclaim through artistic or literary endeavour.

June 12th

You possess an imaginative mind coupled with excellent powers of observation. Avoid a tendency to trust too much to luck. You are a natural student with excellent mathematical ability. This is the degree of the inventor and the scientist. You are very sympathetic and will do well in government work.

June 13th

You possess a serious, aspiring nature coupled with strong mental capabilities. You are profound and practical. A strong sense of independence and desire to help those in less fortunate circumstances is indicated by this degree. At times you may become too magnanimous for your own good. You should learn the value of financial conservatism. Success in life through dealing with new enterprises and large institutions catering to the public welfare is indicated.

June 14th

You possess a studious and reserved disposition with an alert, thoughtful, and intuitive mind. You are well able to concentrate upon your goal in life and will be spurred on by a desire to achieve and fulfil most of your hopes and desires.

You are industrious and self-reliant because of a highly ambitious and determined disposition.

June 15th

You possess great compassion for your fellow man. A desire to help all those who ask assistance can result in expenditures beyond your means. You are subject to flattery and can easily become the prey of designing friends and associates. One aspect in this Horoscope indicates inspirational ideas backed by a keen insight. This will be an important asset in helping you overcome periods of so-called hard luck.

June 16th

You possess a solemn and melancholy disposition. Marked sympathies for your friends and relatives will make you very popular as a consultant. The art of diplomacy is inherent in your make-up. You will show much compassion for those who come to you for advice and help.

June 17th

You possess a very impressionable character. A highly magnetic personality and an enterprising disposition will bring many respected and beneficial friendships in life. Guard against a desire to make changes without considering the consequences. You may experience fluctuating financial security unless you develop consistency of purpose.

June 18th

You possess a positive and domineering personality. Develop a sense of stability in order to check your adventurous spirit. You have good ideas and will find success in unusual undertakings. This is the degree of one who makes hay while the sun shines. Many successful inventors and scientists were born in this degree.

June 19th

You possess a good sense of direction. A strong will coupled with a desire to have your way will not hamper your success. An inquisitive, aspiring, and perceptive mind indicates success in the professional world. You will be attracted to the study of literature and music. An ability to get along well with all types of people will aid materially in attaining success as a teacher or public official.

June 20th

You possess an adaptable, versatile, and intuitive mind. The value of concentration should be learned. You may lack the desire to combat the realities of life. See that you complete one thing before turning your attention to another. A charming personality coupled with a good sense of humour will attract many friendships, but only diligent application of your many capabilities will aid in attaining success and happiness.

June 21st

You possess an expansive and genial personality. You will attain much popularity in your social life. An artistic temperament coupled with an aspiring mind will make for success in a professional rather than business career. Your enthusiastic and idealistic nature will enable you to participate in some very interesting and profitable undertakings.

Compatible and Incompatible Signs of Gemini

The Gemini outlook is purely a mental one; sex interests are quite secondary so far as these natives are concerned. Gemini is essentially a cold-blooded Sign and lacks great sensuous passion. This native is a kind of living question mark. He is forever analysing his own and other people's actions and reactions. Mental dissection is a particularly Geminian habit. Gemini wants to analyse everything, and is entirely unmindful of the effect this may have upon others.

It is, therefore, obvious that the normal attitude of Gemini to sex matters is not only experimental, but rather cool, calculating, and selfish. These natives are born under what is known as a fickle and changeable Sign. Actually the fickleness arises not from wandering sex desires, but from a hope of attaining theoretical ideals. Unfortunately this aim—for those of Gemini—is impossible to achieve, for their ideal varies according to the mood of the moment, and can swing from one extreme to the other.

Gemini is a difficult Sign for most people to understand,

as it is both more illogical in nature and more ideological in tendency than some of the others. Gemini's analytic nature produces a suspicious effort to try and read between the lines. The Geminian's imagine that other people mean much more than they say. The native's mental gymnastics brings about rapid changes of thought and desire. Slowness in others is a constant source of annoyance to Gemini. The wife or husband of a Gemini must never be mentally dull or obtuse if happiness is to be maintained. Owing to a sensitive nervous system and highly moral outlook, a Gemini person with a badly afflicted Horoscope can readily develop physical frigidity because of emotional instability.

The duality of the Sign is often evident in romantic matters. Gemini natives may often carry on two love affairs simultaneously. The great desire of Gemini's heart is to remain as free as the air, which this Sign represents. Those born under Gemini should be very careful in their choice of a lover or mate, instinctively avoiding the too-possessive or jealous type. Geminians are rather difficult to cope with because they are so unpredictable in their romantic moods. One hardly ever knows how to take them, or where one stands with them. They want someone who is capable of constantly stimulating their interest and who can offer them variety, novelty, and adulation, regardless of reciprocation. However, like many Utopian ideas, this ideal is by no means easy to attain.

A pet delusion of the Gemini-born is that they are not interested in sex, so they seek a mate who is capable of catering to their varied mental interests and activities. A very real difficulty with them lies in the fact that their romantic notions are usually based upon high moral ideas. They should try to realize that love is not always logical.

As already indicated, if you were born under this Sign, you have definite ideas as to the type of person you are seeking for a partner. The following will serve to confirm you in your choice.

Gemini and Aries

These partners would find it hard to meet on common ground, due to the emphatic differences in their approach to sexual matters. Above all, Gemini respects the refined, intellectual approach to connubial bliss. The Arien is an impatient and emotional native of a fiery Sign, and may find the cool, calm Geminian, whose mind plays such an important part in love-making, frustrating.

Gemini and Taurus

These two are unsuited to each other because of their emotional outlook. The Mercurian Geminian's delight in all mental pursuits, and great love of variety is not compatible with the earthly outlook of the Venus-ruled Taurus. The fixed, slow, plodding, faithful Taurus would find it hard to adapt to the restless Gemini.

Gemini and Gemini

This should prove a compatible combination; at least both would understand each other's changeable natures. The sex demands and needs would be mutual. The one exception would be if one or the other has Scorpio rising at the time of birth. The demands of Scorpio would prove too much for the purely Mercurial Gemini nature, since Gemini's approach to sex is spiritual while that of Scorpio is more physical. A Gemini maiden would prove too puritanical for the Gemini-Scorpio rising male. This combination makes for excellent partnerships where the principals are engaged in corresponding vocations, such as singer-composer, author-publisher, etc.

Gemini and Cancer

The home-loving Cancer may find the club-loving Gemini too elusive for a good mate. While Gemini is constantly on the alert for change, Cancer is satisfied to become a truly domesticated mate. On the other hand, the Cancerian moodiness may become too much for Gemini to cope with. This combination does hold better possibilities for compatibility where the female is a Gemini and the male is a Cancer, especally if there are several children to occupy the Gemini mother's time.

Gemini and Leo

This combination will soon find out that they are emotionally unsuited. While Leo loves with the heart first, Gemini loves with the mind. There is great mutual attraction for both these Signs on the surface. Both Signs are naturally attracted to glamour, flattery, and the world of good fellowship. After these two return home from the party, the carefree, passionate Leo will surely clash with an unreasonable Gemini, who will complain that the Leo love nature is too material, possessive and demanding.

Gemini and Virgo

Not a good combination for connubial bliss. Mercury, the ruling planet of both these Signs, may prove too much over the long pull. In Gemini, Mercury is logical and calculating; in Virgo, it is demanding and critical. The realstic Virgo would be constantly at odds with Gemini's ever-present desire for change. One point of compatibility would be the desire for friends and associates who are engaged in intellectual and artistic pursuits. It is through these channels that many Gemini-Virgo combinations are formed.

Gemini and Libra

This is considered to be a good astrological influence for a long and happy life of marriage. Both Signs have much in common and enough contrast to make an ideal partnership. Venus (Libra) and Mercury (Gemini) is usually a good planetary configuration. Both favour similar changes of interests. In the case of this combination, Libra is the judge and Gemini the responsive jury in the nuptial courthouse. Their intellectual and artistic interests are compatible. Libra will readily understand both sides of the Gemini nature.

Gemini and Scorpio

Here Gemini finds a mate that can surpass the Gemini urge for action. From a mental standpoint, Gemini is more than a match for a Scorpio mate, but from a sexual and physical viewpoint, Gemini is too innately modest to meet Scorpio's demands. The jealous and possessive Scorpion nature will soon clash with Gemini's desire for freedom of action. While some Gemini-Scorpio combinations may work out fairly well, the pure Gemini-Scorpio alliance packs as much explosive as an atomic bomb.

Gemini and Sagittarius

Here are two Signs with one purpose—freedom of limb and action. Usually a compatible combination, both Signs are frank, outspoken, and cherish a certain amount of personal freedom. Inconstancy is mutually agreeable to these two astrological affinities. They meet on common ground, and can plan their lives with equanimity. Although there will be times when the love nest will become fairly ruffled and fur may fly, these lovebirds will battle more for the sake of diversion than blood.

Gemini and Capricorn

Here we find the Saturnian nature of Capricorn at odds with the fleet winged messenger of the Gods—Mercury. Patience is a virtue with Capricorn, but not so with Gemini. Unless there is a willingness on Gemini's part to slow down and heed the good advice of the Capricorn mate, much dissension and unhappiness is in the stars. Capricorn's great drive to excel, regardless of opposition, will prove too much for Geminians. Unless they both are willing to trim their sails, the Goat of Capricorn will go on butting until he gains the upper hand.

Gemini and Aquarius

The humanitarian instincts of Aquarius will find a ready haven with Gemini. Uranus, the ruling planet of Aquarius, is full of sudden surprises and changes which will suit Gemini perfectly. There will be sufficient variety to afford the stimulation that Gemini needs for its dual personality. The Gemini-born are always looking for surprises; the Aquarian will readily supply them. A note of warning to the Geminian—when the Aquarian mate wants to be alone, Gemini should not be offended. This is only a passing condition and will soon disappear—but at times the Aquarian must have these intervals of solitude.

Gemini and Pisces

The freedom of those of Gemini is at stake if they marry a Piscean. They must be prepared to give up all outside interests and devote all of their time and thoughts to the Pisces mate. The sensitive and distrustful Piscean nature will, no doubt, prove too much for the liberty-loving Gemini to cope with. Geminians must be prepared to change their personalities almost completely if they would seek happiness with a loving, possessive, and clinging Piscean mate.

Some Famous Persons Born in the Sign of Gemini

Jefferson Davis—Confederate President
Sir Arthur Conan Doyle—Author
Sir Anthony Eden—Statesman
James Montgomery Flagg—Artist
Errol Flynn—Actor
Judy Garland—Actress
Dashiell Hammett—Novelist
Bob Hope—Comedian
Jean Paul Sartre—Philosopher and Writer
Alfred P. Sloan, Jr—Business Executive
Igor Stravinsky—Composer
Josip Broz (Tito)—Yugoslav Statesman
Al Jolson—Actor
Thomas Mann—Novelist
Marilyn Monroe—Actress
Robert Montgomery—Actor
Sir Laurence Olivier—Actor
Dr Norman V. Peale—Clergyman and Author
Cole Porter—Song Writer
Queen Victoria—British Monarch
Richard Wagner—German Composer
Frank Lloyd Wright—Architect

4

CANCER

June 22nd–July 22nd

The Sign of Cancer symbolizes tenacity. The Crab is its symbol. The Crab, in order to move forward, is compelled to walk backwards. This illustrates the Sun's apparent motion when in this Sign when it commences to move backwards towards the equator again. Cancer also represents the fruitful, sustaining essence of the life force, hence we see the symbol of the Crab occupying a prominent position upon the breast of the Statue of Isis, the universal mother and sustainer of all. The Sign Cancer signifies the vital organs of the Grand Man of the Starry Heavens, and therefore represents the breathing and digestive functions of the human family. It also indicates the magnetic control of this constellation over the spiritual, ethereal, and vital essences.

Cancer governs the powers of inspiration and respiration of the Grand Man. The Sign Cancer upon the planisphere astrologically intimates the home of the Crab, the shore. It also expresses the varied powers of cohesion, and the paradoxical truths found in all contradictories. Cancer is the highest emanation of the watery Trigon, and is the constellation of the Moon.

Cancer signifies the equilibrium of spiritual and material life forces.

It is in the fourth House of the Zodiac and governs the breast and the stomach and represents tenacity.

Those dominated by its influx express the highest form of the reflective powers; they are timid and retiring. They are truly passive and constitute natural mediums. Cancer possesses but little of the intuitional qualities. That which appears to be intuition is direct inspiration. To the external eye, the natives of this watery trigon are incessant workers on the higher, or mental plane. This Sign expresses to us the conservation of forces. Its chief attributes are sensitivity and reflection.

The mystical gems of the Sign are the pearl and the moonstone. These gems are powerful talismans for all natives of Cancer.

The fortunate day is Friday. Fortunate numbers are eight and three.

The colours for this Sign are silver and white.

Best locations for these natives will be found near or on water.

Addressing a Cancer, I would say: You have an interesting, but somewhat enigmatic personality. You are a being of considerable reserve, but are, nevertheless, capable of joy and friendship. Though you have a great amount of personal pride, you are not egotistical or vain. You are often misunderstood and accused of being self-centred. Since you are an individualist, you have a good sense of your own worth. You will find it to your advantage to cultivate the art of self-expression in the presence of other people, because you can do so much to make others happy. You are straightforward, generous, upright, and loyal to your friends and to any cause in which you take an interest. You represent the type of personality that can be trusted with any important secret, commission, duty, or work. In fact, many of your close associates and friends rely on you at various times.

The true key to your disposition and temperament lies in your reflective memory. You have great depth of feeling and these feelings can be easily hurt, even though you keep this to yourself to a great extent. In fact, most of the time you would rather hide your feelings than express them. While you seldom hold a grudge, you never forget an unkind deed or action. You are apt to be extremely sensitive in emotional matters. You dislike anything that may be construed as a small or petty act. Your natural disposition is like the Sign under which you were born. Many people are seen by you as though they were children and in your noble, yet silent way, you guide them to the best of your ability with your logical philosophy of life. You are sympathetic and show much understanding.

You have good perception and very keep powers of observation. You are a natural student. You are meditative and have unusual powers of concentration. Except in periods of stress and emergency, you have good co-ordination between mind and body. There is very little that escapes your attention.

You endeavour to analyse your own thoughts and impulses. The faculty of imagination is very active in you. Musing about things and events that have taken place in the past is enjoyable to you. The ability to construct and reconstruct things in your imagination is another of your powers. This enables you to make improvements in various ways and to advance your own ideas and methods of doing things. It also helps you to be creative. There are times, however, when you are inclined to muse or daydream too much about the past. It is advisable to curb this tendency to a reasonable extent.

You can learn most anything you make up your mind to study. You are not always inclined to express your knowledge, but you can be a very good conversationalist when you so desire.

The average individual of your Sign has a natural tendency to study and analyse most of the impulses that arise from within. Those of your Sign that do not follow this process usually learn from bitter experience that it is not advisable to act upon impulse. Your excellent intuition thus gives you good insight into human nature and serves to give you foreknowledge of impending events as well as the ability to discriminate between fact and surmise.

You will find it to your advantage to study and learn more about the interesting faculties of your mind and the art of making them work for you. Very few, if any, ever understand the depth of your mind. It is seldom that you let anyone know what you actually think. You do not care to become aggressive unless circumstances and conditions make this a necessity. Your natural will and determination enables you to face obstacles. Patience and fortitude help you accomplish things long after others have given up. It may be advisable for you to share some of your interesting ideas and philosophy. It will help bring you the love, respect, and admiration you deserve.

Your birthsign presides over the stomach and the breast. Thus it is essential that you should use judgment in matters of diet in order to avoid stomach disorders. A sensible diet will do much to help you to avoid obesity and rheumatism. The problem of diet should be taken up with your family physician. Although you have a fairly good constitution, it is advisable not to overwork your body or mind and tax your sensitive nervous system. Avoid worry, moodiness, depression, and, above all, fears and complexes pertaining to ill health. Get plenty of fresh air and sunlight when you can. After the middle years of life, take up light exercises that will help to keep your body in good physical condition. Indications show that you are fond of the great out-of-doors and that you enjoy the beauties of nature. You find peace of mind and consolation around water. You derive a great amount of pleasure in reading or studying such works as interest you.

Indications show that you have a very sensitive, affectionate, and yet reserved, love nature. You do not always show your emotions but sometimes hold yourself in subjugation. This often proves to your disadvantage and is very apt to cause misunderstanding. In affairs of the heart you are tender, considerate, and affectionate. Love to you is something to be treated seriously. You are devoted to the object of your affection and have a tendency to be jealous. It is advisable to do all you can to avoid unreasonable jealousy. Owing to your sensitivity in matters of the heart, you are easily hurt, and once your feelings are deeply wounded it is very difficult for you to get over it. Many times such hurts cause you to change from one type of affection to another. Indications point to the fact that you can be among the happiest of all married people because of your love of home and the comforts of a wholesome domestic life. You are far happier in the married state than when single. Intellectual companionship plays an important part in your married life. Your personal love has a soothing and uplifting quality and you are devoted to the object of your affection. Be more demonstrative in the expression of your affection.

You have a great love for children. Your Sign is the parental sign and gives promise of some children. Your parental love is very deep rooted, but you must guard against becoming too critical of your children. If your home life is not harmonious, you will be quite unhappy. Owing to your natural sensitivity, unpleasantness in the home is apt to upset you deeply and more than the average individual.

There are times when it would prove to be to your personal advantage to take a trip or a short vacation away from your home surroundings. Avoid becoming a recluse. You are quite fond of travel, especially in the early years of your life. During the latter half of life you do not care to travel very far from your home. Your interesting mind and its remarkable powers of deduction and analysis indicate that your road to success lies mainly along professional lines. Your individuality must have its expression. Law, medicine, surgery, dentistry, navigation, instruction, salesmanship, mechanics and engineering are the vocations that are most likely to appeal to many Cancer people. Catering, running rooming houses, hotels, and restaurants also appeal to some. Cancer people also have latent and active artistic ability. Thus, you will find them designing clothes, composing music, painting, and active on stage and screen.

You have the type of personality and mind that creates its own destiny. Although others may help you at times, your actual progress depends upon yourself. Success to people of your Sign usually comes during the middle years of life, and usually continues until death. It is in the stars that you must exercise care in partnership ventures. You are industrious and conscientious and this often causes others to try to place too much responsibility and work upon your shoulders. It is true that you are capable and will not stand for much abuse. Under reasonably harmonious circumstances, you will do well in partnership ventures.

A fair degree of success comes to the people of your Sign who enter into business for themselves. When entering into such endeavour, it is advisable that you be well prepared to carry yourself over the periods of uncertainty until you get the proper start. Under such circumstances it is best to guard against becoming discouraged easily and giving up. Bear in mind that it takes courage and fortitude to achieve success.

Indications point to a varying cycle of financial success during the course of life. Your earning capacity is usually fairly good. However, you are generous and believe in purchasing the best that your money will afford. It appears that you would do well if you were to invest in real estate, government bonds, and the stocks and bonds of large corporations. You have, at times, an urge to gamble and speculate, but success in such matters is problematical. It is advisable never to speculate or gamble in big issues or to invest in get-rich-quick schemes. It is true that some Cancer people are quite successful in speculative ventures, and that their intuition helps them determine the value of a specific proposition. You are apt to experience financial difficulties during your early twenties, the thirtieth and sixtieth years of life. However, if you apply the conservative principles of your character to a reasonable extent, you will be able to attend to the problem of your own financial security in later years.

A person of your character and temperament needs but a few loyal friends. You will attract many people to you, but this is primarily because of what you may be able to do for them. You represent the type of individual who can be trusted by others and you will, no doubt, be in the confidence of many. The quality of your affection for them is usually of a parental nature. Although you are not particularly fond of an active social life, you will be able to enjoy a good social standing in your community. You take a keen delight in entertaining your close friends and associates at home.

You are meditative, and quite often like to enjoy the sacred seclusion of your own mind and thoughts; but you should also do all you can to avoid periodical spells of moodiness and brooding. Do all within your power to cast out useless fears and apprehensions that have a tendency to tax your mind and body and you will add greatly to your own progress. Indications show that your rise in life may be slow rather than spontaneous. Many of the people of your Sign work quietly for years and do not appear to get anywhere at all, but when opportunity comes they are usually ready and well prepared.

Use your higher psychic faculties to develop foresight. Realize that success must be born in your mind before you can ever hope to be successful in reality. Think it over. Investigate your own attitude and see what changes you need to make in order to create the success you are striving for.

The Cancer Child

Cancer children should never be forced to have personal contact with persons whom they do not like, as it will have an ill effect on their health. These children are usually very timid and retiring, yet they want and need friendship and sympathy, though they are very sensitive about seeking it. They sometimes have a tendency to take their friends for granted. At the same time, they are very conscientious in all things entrusted to them, and use considerable discretion in whatever they do. They are generally fond of home and parents and are easily influenced by those they love and admire. Ill health is very likely to come from the stomach. It is, therefore, essential to exercise great care with their diet. They also may suffer from bronchitis, coughs, inflammatory conditions, kidney trouble, and nervous exhaustion.

As the Cancer child is extremely receptive and imaginative, there is a possibility that at times he will become somewhat melancholy and moody. It is well to remember such possibilities when rearing the Cancer child. Also to be noted is a tendency to be lethargic. It is essential that the parent stimulate the child to action in a kindly manner. These children are versatile, and it is desirable for parents to encourage these children's ambitions in the formative years.

The Cancer Wife

The Cancer wife mothers everyone. She, typically, is the most motherly of all the Zodiacal wives. When at her best, she is a sympathetic, affectionate, protective woman. She is patient, devoted, adaptable, and satisfied with anything her husband provides for her. Her home is wherever her husband decides that it should be, and she gives the humblest place a permanent look. Her presence is sanctifying, and she understands how to serve. She is loved and respected in return for her devotion, and is the personification of all literature that idealizes "Mother." All of this, of course, depends upon the planetary combinations in the nativity.

Negative Cancer wives have some of these qualities, but too often they are moody, changeable, and unwilling to improve. It is very easy for a Cancer girl to marry; her natural inclinations are so sympathetic that marriageable men are drawn to her. She seeks protection, and it always comes to her. But if she is a girl without a great deal of character and background, she will need the help and guidance of her husband for strength to meet life's problems. Her husband is on a pedestal in her imagination, and if he fails her, the spiritual shock is crushing.

The wives of Cancer are passionately possessive and absorbed in the life of the family. Taken generally, their whole character is proverbially feminine, and the man who marries a Cancerian wife gets a complete feminine woman.

The Cancer Husband

The Cancer husband is not an easy person to live with, despite the Sign's reputation for easygoing good nature. The type is divided into at least two groups, one of which is dominant. The husband of this group loves his home, but he is exacting, fussy, and inclined to be critical and fault-finding.

The negative Cancer man as a husband is so passive, lazy, and self-indulgent, he often goes so far as to marry for money and position. Since this kind of man is persistent and agreeable when he chooses to be, it is often possible for him to attain his ambition.

Any Cancer husband spends more time at home than another man. He has a deep love for the traditional values of home and family, and has many of the same qualities in his nature that are significant to the Cancer woman. Moodiness, changeability, sentimentality, and effusiveness can be understood in a woman's nature, but transferred to a man, these qualities are not inspiring, especially in large domestically administered doses. The Cancer husband means to be devoted, and his whole mind is preoccupied by his wife and family, but this disposition is such that these feelings are translated into exacting demands for service. Nothing satisfies him and the most affectionate family feels the burden of this intensely possessive spirit.

Husbands born in Cancer are usually faithful enough if their desires are satisfied at home. The effort entailed in conducting outside liaisons is too much for the Cancer man. He is rather timid and abhors danger. Therefore, while his senses might lead him astray, he is unwilling to be involved in complications that require effort to sustain.

The Cusps of Cancer

(If your birthday is not within the cusp of your sign, the following does not apply to you.)

If the birthday is from June 22nd through June 25th

You were born in Cancer with Gemini tendencies. Your ruling orbs are the Moon and Mercury. This indicates that you are brilliant, decisive, and are usually in control of any situation that arises. You like to deal with the general public and are most content when you hold a position that brings you in touch with different types of people.

You are unduly sensitive and take things too seriously. In general, you have an analytical mind, but in some matters you are likely to overlook important details. You are somewhat moody but possess a good memory.

Frequently you tire of your regular routine in life and try to hunt up new experiences and associates. When you develop new friends, you have a tendency to neglect your old ones. You are fond of the good things in life. You are also interested in society, and the artistic things of life have a definite appeal to you.

If the birthday is from July 19th through July 22nd

You were born in Cancer with Leo tendencies. Your ruling orbs are the Moon and the Sun. This shows that you are original, clever, idealistic, and a good mixer. You possess a quick temper that is derived from Leo, but your Cancer qualities will usually keep it under good control. You seem to have difficulty in making ends meet. When things go wrong you sink into a depressed state of mind. If you have once made up your mind you can be stubborn and headstrong. Regardless of what others think, you will go on being just yourself. You usually possess a wide circle of acquaintances, yet few can be considered real friends.

You do not especially care for display or show. You prefer

to live a simple, comfortable life where you will be left alone whenever you are not in the mood for companionship. You do not impose upon others, but quite often they take advantage of your kindness.

The Decanates of Cancer

If the birthday is between June 22nd and June 30th

The personal orb for this decan is also the Moon, known as the ruler of the night, the great symbol of life's forces, and the natural reflector of the Sun. This planet governs the domestic, idealistic and maternal tendencies.

These natives possess a humane, kind disposition, and a dislike of dissension. By nature they are doubtful, apprehensive, and mediumistic. They may have a high temper and a tendency to pamper ill-advised impulses. Due to their critical and sensitive disposition, special care should be taken to overcome the negative tendencies which may develop in the character.

If the birthday is between July 1st and July 11th

The personal planet is Mars, known as the symbol of War and Centre of Divine Energy. It influences the energetic, courageous, active, and constructive tendencies. Mars will aid the native materially in overcoming some of the weaker and more negative aspects of the maternal orb, the Moon. It will give the necessary impetus to bring about the successful conclusion to many endeavours. Without this force it would be difficult to realize many cherished ambitions. The combination of the Moon and Mars is, indeed, a fortunate one, since Mars, being aggressive and powerful, forces its natives to attain their objectives.

If the birthday is between July 12th and July 22nd

The personal orbs are the conflicting planets Jupiter and Neptune. Jupiter is known to be the planet of Good Fortune and Blessing, with harmonious vibrations, while Neptune is known as the Spiritual Awakener, and governs the scientific, inventive, and artistic faculties. It sometimes acts to produce an involved, chaotic and nebulous state of affairs. This would indicate that the native possesses a very changeable and unpredictable nature. The greatest battle in life for those of this sector will be with themselves. The negative and positive qualities will be marked at an early age, which should give an opportunity to help eliminate the faults.

The Degrees of Cancer

Each Zodiacal Sign contains thirty degrees. The Sun transists one degree per day, each representing a birthday, and gives further influence on the native's character and destiny. The following will give the analyses of all birthdays (degrees) of Cancer.

June 22nd

A splendid character and a sympathetic nature coupled with deep emotions is indicated for this degree. The native is instinctively intellectual and matures early in life. It is essential that there be a happy environment; associates should be those whom the native can look up to and respect. There is a liking for outdoor activity and athletic pursuits. The emotional temperament yields to patient understanding rather than harsh treatment and dictatorial methods.

June 23rd

A serious, aspiring nature coupled with strong mental capabilities are imparted by this degree. The native is profound and practical. A strong sense of independence and a desire to help those in less fortunate circumstances is indicated. There is, too, a marked respect for superiors. Those born on this day can create their own destiny. Success in life is indicated through dealing with new enterprises and large institutions catering to the public welfare.

June 24th

A retiring and chaste nature is shown here. An envious streak should be curbed. There is fondness of literature, music, and art. There should be an effort to use any intellectual and commercial training to the maximum. Learn self-confidence and the ability to see the other fellow's point of view.

June 25th

Those of this degree possess an original, enterprising mind, and a harmonious, contented disposition. One aspect of this Horoscope indicates that the native will be easily satisfied. The practical methods by which success is achieved should be learned. Associates should be persons who are successful. High hopes and ambitions should be tempered with an awareness of reality.

June 26th

This degree imbues the native with a pleasing personality and splendid intuitive powers. A highly emotional nature can develop into an uncontrollable temper unless there is a real effort made to overcome this aspect. There is a tendency to brood and daydream too much if left alone for any great length of time. Above all, a "martyr fixation" should be avoided. The native may receive a great deal of help from someone befriended in the past.

June 27th

A flexible, happy nature and a clever, imaginative mind is bestowed upon the natives of this degree. Those of this birthday may be too generous and agreeable for their own good, and should learn that caution is the better part of valour. They are fond of mimicry and possess great liking for the stage and theatre. Losses due to extravagance and misplaced confidence may be avoided by controlling a tendency to be overly solicitous.

June 28th

A keen, intellectual mind coupled with excellent powers of concentration is indicated for these Cancer-born. A tendency to assume a too serious outlook upon life should be avoided. A bright, cheerful atmosphere and congenial company will help to eliminate this aspect. This highly magnetic personality and independent nature will make for great success in the business world. There is fondness of music and travel, and many profitable experiences in connection with both are indicated.

June 29th

An energetic nature and great skill in the execution of duties is shown here. Persistence and determination, even in the face of difficulties, will bring success and financial independence. Friends and associates are chosen with discrimination, and there is a display of considerable reserve at all times. Tolerance and consideration of other people's feelings should be practised. A tendency to impulsiveness is shown by one aspect here. This may lead to financial loss as a result of poor judgment.

June 30th

This degree imparts a gentle, kind, sympathetic disposition, and a good mind coupled with a charitable nature, which should endear this native to all. The magnetic personality and ability to attract staunch and loyal friendships may result in a dependent attitude. It is necessary to learn that independence and personal accomplishments are essential to success and happiness.

July 1st

These Cancerians possess a sensitive, idealistic nature and a friendly, kind-hearted disposition. Certain planetary aspects denote a tendency to be too generous for personal welfare. Recognition of the true from the false must be learned. There is fondness of travel by water, and indications of a long sea voyage which may result in a profitable business connection. A successful marriage is also indicated.

July 2nd

These Cancerians possess a sensitive, idealist nature and a pleasant disposition. Their keen sense of independence and diplomacy should be developed in order to check an adventurous spirit. An inquisitive and perceptive mind will lead to success in the professional world. Some may be naturally attracted to the study of medicine and medical research.

July 3rd

Shown here is an adaptable, versatile, and intuitive mind.

Concentration, if learned and practised, should be of great aid in overcoming many obstacles. One aspect shown indicates a tendency to tire easily and drift aimlessly from one thing to another. This charming personality coupled with a good sense of humour will attract many friendships.

July 4th

The natives of this degree are romantics, idealists, and dreamers. A rather "hard-to-please" attitude is shown at times, as a consequence of a self-centred, fixed point of view. There is a decided preference for the company of superiors and successful people. Tolerance and affectionate understanding is necessary when dealing with all co-workers, employers, or associates.

July 5th

This degree endows its natives with a pleasing, courteous disposition, and an alert, thoughtful, and intuitive mind. A tendency to dominate others and assume leadership regardless of consequences should be carefully curbed. Also indicated is great animal magnetism.

July 6th

Those of this birthday possess a courteous, pleasing, and sociable disposition. Their magnetic personality will attract many friendships and lead to popularity. One aspect in this Horoscope indicates a tendency to look on the serious side of life. This is an attribute of a sensitive and emotional nature. Successful friends will instill confidence and aid in overcoming pessimism. Too much excitement and dissension will cause an adverse reaction by the nervous system.

July 7th

This degree imparts an original, daring, and masterful mind. A strong will power coupled with the native's desire to have his own way should be curbed. A diversified education along commercial lines will be of great advantage. Much success is indicated in the business world. By exercising tolerance and patience, an overly energetic disposition can be subdued. There may be many ups and downs in domestic and personal affairs. Impulsive and radical changes should be avoided.

July 8th

These natives possess an unselfish and charitable disposition. The body is strong and healthy, and great interest and skill in sports is shown. It is important to overcome a tendency to attempt too many things at one time. The native can be a fluent conversationalist and prolific writer. Education and training towards some definite goal or profession will be a great asset. Once control of the emotions is achieved, success and public recognition will be assured.

July 9th

A resourceful mind and executive ability is indicated for those of this birthdate. Discrimination between right and wrong will help to overcome many difficulties. A diversified, liberal education will be an important factor in overcoming many of the negative qualities which may be inherent in this nature. Moderation should be practised at all times.

July 10th

These Cancer-born possess astute, practical, and intuitive minds. Artistic temperaments with marked humanitarian principles will bring many lasting and influential friendships. These people are generous, of good appearance, of kind manner, and charitably inclined. One aspect in this chart indicates a tendency to shirk responsibility and to get by with little personal effort.

July 11th

A benevolent, charitable, and sympathetic nature is shown for those of this nativity. A desire to help all those who ask assistance can result in extravagant expenditures beyond their means. This birthday brings susceptibility to flattery with attendant difficulties. One aspect in this Horoscope shows a tendency to become conceited due to excessive attention.

July 12th

This degree denotes an intellectual, scientific, and experimental mind. An independent, yet orderly spirit, coupled with a keen sense of diplomacy and tact will make it easy for those born on July 12th to get what they want in life.

July 13th

These Cancerians possess wholesome charm and great magnetism. They have inventive minds and show originality in ideas and undertakings. They will be susceptible to colds, and it is necessary that all precautions be taken to avoid drafts and sudden changes of temperature. A desire to speculate should be curbed, as many disappointments are shown if this characteristic is permitted to become a habit.

July 14th

Those of this degree possess a keen mind, and a calm, peaceful attitude towards life. A charming, openminded manner with humanitarian principles will endear these natives to all. Gain is indicated through sentimental associations and influential friendships. One aspect here shows a tendency to take good fortune and successful conclusions too lightly. Natural gifts must be appreciated and used constructively, rather than frivolously, all through life.

July 15th

Unusual mental qualities, and the ability to develop the mind along intellectual and scientific pursuits is indicated here. A steady and forceful disposition, and an ability to display independent thought is also shown. One aspect in this Horoscope indicates a desire to defy convention and become eccentric. This tendency must be overcome. Ambitions can be fostered, but high temper must be curbed.

July 16th

The natives of this birthday possess a keen, shrewd, and alert mind. They will be deeply moved by their higher sympathies and will become champions of human rights. There is a tendency to meddle in the affairs of others, and while the motives may be most charitable, many misunderstandings and disappointments are indicated until it is learned that life's greatest rewards come to those who mind their own business first.

July 17th

Those of this degree possess a bright, cheerful disposition and a kind, generous nature. They are just and righteous in both personal and social matters. They can pursue a professional career, where their fine minds will be demonstrated to good advantage. A strong attachment for home and family is shown. One aspect of this Horoscope shows a desire to be well dressed, in the height of fashion at all times. This urge can develop into the extravagant habit of purchasing many things of doubtful value and usefulness.

July 18th

An impulsive and somewhat radical disposition is indicated here. A brilliant mind and excellent intuitive powers are also shown. This combination of mental qualities is usually found in persons who attain outstanding success and recognition in public work. A tendency to be impulsive and erratic should be curbed, as the development of such characteristics can prove detrimental.

July 19th

These natives possess a bright, cheerful disposition and a splendid mind. Material success is indicated through the ability to make and hold influential and beneficial friendships. Marked originality and a good sense of humour will make for a position of prestige in the social world. A vivid imagination coupled with excess energy may cause impatience.

July 20th

Strong will power, a commanding, energetic personality, initiative, and good business acumen should enable the native to progress rapidly in the commercial world. A tendency towards extravagance should be curbed. The value of personal possessions ought to be appreciated.

July 21st

In this degree a versatile mind coupled with marked social capacity will be of great aid in gaining success and recognition in public service. One aspect here denotes a tendency to be too apprehensive concerning the welfare of loved ones and friends. Moderation of this golden virtue is necessary. Much affection for the parents is shown, and while this is a characteristic of most people, it is an especially marked one in this native. Cancerians of this day are liable to be deceived by their emotions.

July 22nd
A bright, cheerful, and affectionate nature is indicated for these natives. Great generosity, kindness of heart, and a desire to help others are also shown. One aspect of this Horoscope shows a tendency towards daydreaming and a desire to do too many things at once. Concentration must be developed. A magnetic sex appeal will bring much popularity with the opposite sex.

Compatible and Incompatible Signs of Cancer

Cancer is extremely imaginative and emotional, with a sex outlook that is romantic, sentimental, protective, and very largely maternal. In some ways it is a changeable Sign, still capable of great tenacity and faithfulness. There are two characteristics of great importance: one is the fear of ridicule, and the other is a hatred of criticism, both of which—especially the latter—may deeply affect the native's married life.

Cancer in the highest form imparts a domesticated nature, a love of home and possessions, strong maternal love, and a desire to cherish and protect others. It is self-sacrificing, and seeks little in return for the affection it pours out upon others. Unfortunately, the highest type of Cancer, as of any other Sign, is only too rarely encountered, and the under-developed specimen is much more common in everyday life, carrying a distortion of many Cancerian virtues.

The only way to get on with an afflicted Cancer type is to praise and flatter him or her on every possible occasion and to never utter a word which could be twisted into a semblance of blame or criticism. Astrology claims that Mercury is chiefly responsible for nagging, and it is true that both Gemini and Virgo can argue and scold incessantly if afflicted, but Cancer produces the real self-pitying nagger.

Even when an argument or discussion has come to an end, Cancer can usually be relied upon to revive it, and keep hammering at it. This tendency shows itself in many ways.

A chance word of criticism will entail hours of work on

the part of Cancer in cajoling the unfortunate critic into a recantation. Dislike of something that Cancer likes can produce an endless spate of reasons—or what passes with Cancer as reasons—for liking that particular thing; and he or she will not rest content until agreement is given. It is often for this reason that the husband of a Cancerian wife will be heard to lavish quite unwarranted praise upon her slightest action, for only in this way is it possible to keep her in good temper. In cases of an afflicted Cancer the temper is vicious and spiteful. Bad temper is one of Cancer's chief weapons; others include tears and nagging.

Cancerians are the sentimental, romantic type of lovers, and they need reciprocal sentiments from the opposite sex. Thus, it will not do for them to go in for the logical, practical types of humanity, for their feelings are bound to be hurt by such selections.

The trouble is that when Cancerians are in love, they are temporarily blind to realities, and often fail to perceive that the one they love is not the right one for them.

Their chief desire is to build a home and furnish a love nest, and they will never be satisfied until they have realized this dream. Cancerian women enjoy housework, and their homes are ever clean and tidy.

As lovers they are passionate, and personal feelings always play a big part in their lives. Marriage is the most important event in their lives, and it is especially necessary for them to select the right life-partner.

The general comparisons are as follows:

Cancer and Aries

This combination is not a wise one. Cancer, a Sign ruled by the Moon, will produce a temperament not compatible with the aggresive Martian (Aries) make-up. Cancerians have a tendency to live in the past, and any disagreement is not easily taken in their stride. The fiery, progressive Aries will not be likely to take time out for apologetic knee-bending after small breaches which are magnified in the Cancer-ruled mind and emotions. Cancer brings the impulse to back away from unpleasant or hurtful situations. In conditions which do not stir Cancerians emotionally they will show their native tenacity.

Cancer and Taurus

This would be an entirely compatible combination. Both Cancer and Taurus love a good home and much affection. Emotionally they are harmonious, but one thing the Taurus must take into consideration is that the Cancer mate is exceedingly sensitive, and will crawl into a shell in an emotionally trying situation.

Cancer and Gemini

The domesticated, home-loving Cancer will find it rather disturbing trying to keep up with the mobile Gemini. Gemini is ever seeking change, while Cancer is content in his own home. Gemini cannot be said to be as domesticated as the Cancer mate would wish. Also, Cancer's moodiness may be too much for Gemini's understanding. In those cases where the female is a Gemini and the male is a Cancer, there are fair possibilities of compatibility, especially if several children occupy the Gemini mother's time.

Cancer and Cancer

These two can make a beautiful love story of their married life, because each will have a sympathetic understanding for the other's moods, wishes, desires, and needs. Though there may be times when they are in complete disagreement, with each clinging to the experience and teaching of early childhood, each will understand the other. Both will have the tenacity of the crab who, once he sets his claws on to something, will hang on regardless of peril. Each will give sympathetic consideration to this trait in the other, and they should have no trouble in finding connubial bliss.

Cancer and Leo

This is usually a good combination, since the Moon (Cancer) reflects the light of the Sun (Leo). There is much to be said for this combination, especially if Cancer will be happy reflecting the admirable Leonian personality. Leo's big heart will soon forgive the moody outbursts that Cancer displays from time to time and which result from the strong influence of the Moon, Cancer's ruling planet. Cancer, more than any other Sign, responds to the Moon's aspects as it moves swiftly through the Zodiac.

Cancer and Virgo

Virgo's demands may prove too much for Cancer's desire for peace and quiet. The full, affectionate libido of Cancer will not be completely satisfied by Virgo's direct approach to the practical matters at hand. Cancer is sentimental, reticent, and even shy about sex matters, and this can be very frustrating to the Virgo temperament. Once Cancer crawls into his shell, all the tongue lashing and nagging of Virgo will not bring him out. This could drive the Virgo mate into a state of hysteria.

Cancer and Libra

Cancer is temperamentally unsuited to cope with the freedom-loving Libran. Once these two lovebirds get into a serious disagreement, they may go for days without so much as a nod of recognition. Libra's great desire for attention may bring on a period of sulking depression that could create a highly controversial situation. Though Libra loves justice and fair play, Cancer has a tendency to take advantage of all of these qualities for his own private use.

Cancer and Scorpio

Masterful Scorpio should make a good mate for reticent Cancer. While that "ole debil" Jealousy may plague both from time to time, their great mutual ability to love deeply will usually limit periods of dissension. Scorpio is well equipped to cope with Cancerian moods. Excess energy which Scorpio emanates will act as strong tonic for Cancer's reticence. Yes, Scorpio and Cancer could well prove the ideal marriage combination. More should try it.

Cancer and Sagittarius

TROUBLE may be spelled with capital letters should these two marry, unless each is willing to attempt a complete change of their star-predicted personalities. Cancer admires everything about the Sagittarian—therein lies the tender trap; but once Cancer has captured the busy-footed, roving-eyed Sagittarian, he or she will find it a "more-than-bargained-for" proposition. Cancer is not going to keep the Sagittarian partner close to the hearth. The Cancer's home is his castle, but for the Sagittarian, home is little more than a place to occasionally hang his hat. Watch out!

Cancer and Capricorn

Capricorn is 180 degrees from Cancer, and while this is an opposition in Astrology, it need not be so in life. The natives of both Signs have much in common. The Cancer's great sympathy and understanding is honey to the Capricorn's misunderstood complaints. Both these natives have a tendency to plod along until they get what they want. Capricorn has the ability to make Cancer's dreams come true, while Cancer is happy wishing for and wanting the success and security that the Capricorn mate strives for.

Cancer and Aquarius

The social whirl of the Aquarian may prove too much for the home-loving Cancer. Aquarians love to share their good fortune with the world while Cancer is satisfied to concentrate on personal obligations. Cancer's tastes are conservative; Aquarius' tastes are usually the opposite. The eccentricity of Uranus does not go well with the moods of Luna. The odds against a compatible marriage are really too great for this combination to overcome, unless, of course, one will become subservient to the other.

Cancer and Pisces

The marriage of these two sentimental Signs should prove to be astrologically ideal. Though both will have their moments of gloom and doom, they will soon come out into the sunshine and forgive and forget. Lovers' quarrels may be frequent, but the aftermath will be blissful. Home, possessions, and friends are cherished by both, and there will be mutual effort to fulfil all obligations.

Some Famous Persons Born in the Sign of Cancer

Louis Armstrong—Musician
Milton Berle—Comedian
Julius Caesar—Roman Emperor
James Cagney—Actor
George M. Cohan—Actor and Writer

Ernest Hemingway—Author
Charles Laughton—Actor
Kathleen Norris—Novelist
Ely Culbertson—Bridge Expert
Jack Dempsey—Boxer
Oscar Hammerstein II—Librettist
Nathaniel Hawthorne—Author
Cecil Rhodes—British Statesman
John D. Rockefeller—Philanthropist
Nelson A. Rockefeller—Governor of New York
Red Skelton—Comedian
Barbara Stanwyck—Actress
Isaac Watts—Inventor

5

LEO

July 23rd–August 22nd

THE SIGN Leo symbolizes strength, courage, and fire. The hottest portion of the year in the northern hemisphere occurs when the Sun is passing through this Sign. It is the solar Lion that ripens with his own internal heat the fruits brought forth from the earth by the moisture of Isis.

The Sign Leo signifies the heart of the Grand Man and represents the life centre of the fluidic circulatory system of humanity. It is also the fiery vortex of physical life. Those born under this influx are noted for the superior strength of their physical constitution and for their wonderful recuperative powers after being exhausted by sickness. The sign of Leo upon the esoteric planisphere is occupied by Judah, of whom his dying parent says, "Judah is a lion's whelp, from the prey, my son, thou art gone up. He stooped down, he crouched as a lion". This Sign reveals to us the mysteries of the ancient sacrifice and the laws of compensation.

Leo is the second emanation of the fiery Triplicity, and is the constellation of the Sun.

Leo signifies the sympathies of the heart. Those dominated by its influx are generous to excess with their friends. By nature they are deeply sympathetic, and possess that peculiar grade of magnetic force which enables them to arouse into action latent sympathies in others.

The mystical gem of Leo is the ruby, and it forms the most potent disease-resisting talisman for all governed by the Leonine influx.

The fortunate day is Sunday.

The fortunate numbers are five and nine.

The colours for this Sign are gold and orange.

Best locations for success are the wide open spaces.

Their star-ordained tendency is towards leadership and as orators, their earnest, impulsive, and impressive style makes them an irresistible success. An exceedingly fine specimen of Leonine oratory is given in Genesis, 44th chapter. This simple, eloquent appeal of Judah to Joseph probably stands unequalled for its sublime tenderness. The natives of Leo are impulsive and passionate, honest and faithful. Their minds are ever striving to attain unto some higher state, hence their ideas are always in excess of their means—large, majestic, and grand.

Addressing a Leo, I would say, you possess a good sense of humour and your jovial nature attracts many to you. Under ordinary circumstances, you are courteous and considerate of others. There is very little fear in you. You present a forceful, dynamic, and commanding attitude when necessary. You also have considerable ability to influence others and have them carry out your ideas. You are somewhat of an idealist and are rather generous; therefore, you are sensitive and easily hurt. Since you have a great amount of pride, it is essential that you guard against such excess and egotism, as would hinder you.

In character, you show sincerity of purpose and are courageous to the point of daring. You have a fairly quick temper. Under ordinary conditions you are not inclined to hold a grudge long. However, when angry, you can be forceful and unpleasant.

Anger upsets your nervous system, and it is advisable that you make every effort to curb or control yourself. In the main, you have what is known as a noble character. You show lofty ideals, generosity, and sympathy. In love you are inclined to be jealous. You are independent and do not lean.

Your powers of observation and perception are good. You enjoy doing your own thinking. You have a good sense of analysis, except in love and romantic affairs. Under such circumstances, your impulses rule your actions.

You are able to grasp facts and theories rapidly. Your quick perception is vital for your particular personality. A daring and adventurous nature brings you to face a great variety of situations and conditions. You have good co-ordination and can usually act as quickly as you think.

One of your temperament has an active imagination. Sometimes you get a great amount of pleasure in just musing and day-dreaming of romance. Your imagination can help you work out new ideas and express original thoughts. The naturally artistic nature of your Sign also gives you the power to visualize. This faculty enables many Leo people to be good artists, dancers, entertainers, musicians, actors, and actresses. You have a fairly good memory. You do not have much difficulty in retaining or recalling facts and ideas.

You take an interest in a great variety of subjects, which enables you to be an interesting conversationalist. You have good reasoning ability and judgment in business matters. As you are quite sensitive, it is advisable that you study all impulses that arise from within very carefully. Most of your impulsiveness is brought about by your sensitive reactions. You must also think over impulses relating to hazardous ventures or acts of daring. Think, analyse, and then act and you will be much more successful and happy.

You have an unusually deep insight into other people and their motives. Your intuition will provide you with the knowledge of the cause of your own failures and can give you the solution for progress.

Your birthsign endows you with a good constitution and good recuperative powers. Too many Leo people lead an active life before middle-age and then, suddenly, begin to take things easy and neglect light exercise. Your Sign rules the heart and the small of the back, and these parts are usually most easily affected. Your glands respond to your mental and emotional moods. Therefore, it is advisable that you avoid moodiness and mental strain. Learn the art of relaxing. Curb and control your emotional reactions. Endeavour to be reasonable in your diet. Enjoy good foods but avoid excess. If in doubt as to your diet, consult a doctor or an experienced dietician for the most reliable information.

Your birthsign represents the romantic and entertaining section of the Zodiac. It is evident that you possess a fondness for pleasure, recreation, adventure, entertainment, and travel. In youth, there is a temptation to engage in risky and hazardous ventures, and there is a great fondness for all kinds of excitement. You are by nature a romantic. In love, you are affectionate and passionate. Your feelings, when you let them rule you, are intense. You must bear in mind that ordinarily your judgment in romantic matters is not always reliable. Because of your emotional intensity, you permit your heart to rule your head. Remember that, unless we learn our lessons wisely, Fate will take a hand in teaching us, and Fate is not sparing in its methods of instruction.

You love children and are apt to be indulgent with them, but the general influence of your Sign does not show many children. You are fond of a good home and all the comforts thereof; you desire to have the best that your money will afford. Your nature is more or less fixed. You strive to have a specific place that you can call home. You are not, however, content to stay in one place too long. You are apt to become bored unless you have an opportunity for a change of scenery. Get away from home surroundings now and then, even for a short time. Your romantic nature has often caused you to be at odds with your parents. Better prospects for a settled home life usually come after the middle years.

You are more adapted to mental than to physical work. Under ordinary circumstances you have the patience and determination to work with a proposition until you have accomplished it. Most Leo people have the mentality, ability, and temperament that qualifies them for a business or professional life such as law or medicine; they also become proficient authors, bankers, merchants, brokers, real estate operators and salesmen. Many develop their natural, artistic qualities and become actors, musicians, and artists.

Your rise in life may not be rapid, but it is usually sure. You can hasten it only by judicious use of your wits. When Leos finally achieve success they remain quite successful for the rest of their lives. Sudden success is very apt to sway some Leo natives into a false sense of security, with the result that, in the end, they would have been better off without it. Too much pride and false self-confidence have proved the ruination of many.

You have good executive ability and are capable of assuming responsibilities. You will do well in a business for yourself. Indications point to reasonable success in any line of work or business dealing with the general public, as you have the sort of personality that is pleasing. You have good earning ability, but you are inclined to be a generous, and even lavish, spender. You believe in having a good time with your money.

During the first half of your life you are apt to be quite free with your money. You must bear in mind that in order to attain financial security, you must learn the art of making money work for you. You should begin to do this in a small way at first, and once you acquire the habit, you will be able to do it on a large scale. The easy come, easy go philosophy is not conducive to financial success and security. You should be reasonably cautious in all matters pertaining to gambling and speculation. You enjoy taking chances; it appears to be part of your nature. It is wiser to make good investments in the stocks and bonds of large industrial corporations than to engage in purely speculative ventures. Do not fall for get-rich-quick propositions that offer you wealth overnight. Cultivate the art of being reasonably conservative and you will gain financial security.

Your adventurous nature shows the urge for travel and change, and you will, no doubt, travel considerably during life. Many long and short journeys are indicated for the members of your Sign.

Your interesting and magnetic personality will attract many people to you during the course of life. You enjoy entertaining your friends in your home. True friendships will be among life's most pleasant experiences.

It is apparent that if you are not careful, your emotions may prove to be your own worst enemy. It is paradoxical that you have the courage to face and combat difficult obstacles without fear, and yet you succumb to the sensitivity of your emotions. Do all within your power to exercise rational control over your reactions or you will hinder your progress.

You have qualities that will enable you to rise above the circumstances of your birth. Your need is to understand yourself. Yours is the sort of personality that makes or breaks its own destiny. The art of looking ahead will increase your prospects for a successful and happy life.

The Leo Child

Leo children are born with a noble, ambitious, and aspiring nature; they develop into good leaders but poor followers. They usually scorn mean and sordid things and do not often stoop to do a mean act even under provocation. Their affections are strong and ardent. They have strong wills and can usually beat their way to the top despite all handicaps and obstacles. There is no halfway measure with the Child of Leo; it is all or nothing. If the lower nature happens to predominate, the above mentioned traits are reserved. When this occurs, parents with understanding should mould the child to encourage the better qualities to predominate. There will be a quick temper as well as a desire to rule over other children, and if you watch a Leo child playing with others, you will see Leo is usually the boss and the leader. Leo children usually forgive and forget readily and are generally sympathetic, affectionate, and charitable.

The vitality of the Leo child is generally strong, and the pathology of this group shows that the members' strength may be quickly overtaxed by impulsiveness and a strong desire to accomplish results at any cost. The Leo Sign has rulership over the heart. There is a tendency to fever and a possibility of poor circulation. However, as the fundamental vitality is strong, the general health should be good; but it is the parent's duty to know the ailments to which the Leo child is subject. Frequently an illness can be avoided when the parents have accurate knowledge. They should guard the child against cuts, burns, and accidents of the side, back and knees. The Leo child will enjoy the great outdoors, and particularly woods, mountains, rivers, and all wide open spaces.

The emotional character of the Leo child leaves a susceptibility to excessive rivalry and, sometimes, to cruelty. The mental characteristics favour the development of ambition, and a tyrannical desire for dominance if the Leo child is not trained properly. Very often a temperament develops with the urge towards the acquisition of power.

The favourable quality of the Leo child tends towards dignity; the unfavourable quality tends to dictatorship.

You may train the Leo child for any of the following

occupations—executive, government official, judge, lawyer, broker, jeweller, also any position connected with public utilities. Statesmen, presidents, producers, and physicists have been children of Leo. Leo children are very magnetic, intuitive, and often inventive.

The Leo Wife

The Leo wife is a splendid woman for a worldly and ambitious man. She has an aristocratic point of view and all of the social graces. She is a great manager. She can run an elaborate home, take first place in local social groups, and advance her husband's business chances by enjoyable entertainment. She attracts people to her home and commands great respect. She is the sort of wife a husband wants his boss to meet because the impression that she creates is helpful.

The love of a Leo wife is passionate, enduring, and self-sacrificing. These are the most loyal women. They give and feel and bestow and bless. Their families can never show sufficient gratitude for the wealth of attention lavished upon them and sometimes they appear to lack appreciation for such loving service. The truth is that no human being could repay the Leo wife's devotion to her home and husband. Her attitude is lush and generous in the extreme, unless the husband is a very dominant man—this type of wife will rule him and the result will be a henpecked husband.

Beauty often goes with this birth position and Leonine women are usually good to look at. They demand an active life; there is nothing of the languid about them. There is a certain amount of jealousy in their make-up though they seek a wide circle of friends of both sexes. They sometimes embarrass their husbands with open suspicions. If the Leo woman is lucky enough to marry a virile, commanding man, all of her good qualities will be elevated. She will have the opportunity to exercise her latent talents and put all of her heart and passion into her relationship with her husband. A supremely masculine man can supply her with the satisfaction that her passionate nature cries for, without requiring her to sacrifice her femininity.

The Leo Husband

The Leo man fits into the scheme of domestic life quite smoothly. Usually he is a good and generous provider. He desires his wife and family to shine in the community. He is tremendously proud of them and wants them to have the best of everything. For himself he demands the centre of the stage. He expects home life to revolve around him as the planets around the sun. He is affectionate, loving, and devoted in manner, but will not tolerate disrespect or insubordination.

The Leo husband is fixed in his opinions. His love is deeply romantic and very absorbing but he considers that he is the law unto himself. His attitude towards life is so conventional that he would never tolerate a wife who was disloyal. She must be above suspicion. As Leo men are acute judges of character, they usually select wives who meet with their high standards.

The average Leo man makes a fine husband. His generosity, kindness, loving disposition, and passionate loyalty in the big issues of life combined with great generosity, make him a safe and satisfying kind of husband for a clinging woman. The positive Leo man will be unhappy with a bossy, nagging wife. While he loves to show off his spouse and will usually buy her expensive gifts, he does so with the knowledge that it makes him look good in the community and among his associates.

The Cusps of Leo

(If your birthday is not within the cusp of your Sign, the following does not apply to you.)

If the birthday is from July 23rd through July 25th

You were born in Leo with Cancer tendencies. Your ruling orbs are the Sun and the Moon. This shows that you are methodical and practical. You aspire to higher things and should rise above the average station in life. You possess individuality, intelligence, and balance. You are not stubborn, and always dig into the cause for everything. You are fond of unusual entertainment and frequently get pleasure out of things other people consider tedious. You should watch your health, especially your blood circulation, stomach, and bowels. You are fond of your friends, and feel that you are fortunate in having so many. You have the ability to master any work or occupation. A professional life appeals to you. Being somewhat impatient, you seldom train yourself diligently enough in any one line. You are a leader among your associates and are always rated as a good fellow.

If the birthday is from August 19th through August 22nd

You were born in Leo with some Virgo tendencies. Your ruling orbs are the Sun and Mercury. This gives you self-respect and an awareness of detail in your work. You have artistic ability, and an appreciation of music and the refined things in life. You are attractive in appearance, possess excellent judgment, and are level-headed. An odd thing about you is that you can give good counsel to others, but are usually at a loss to solve your own problems. You need the companionship of a congenial person to help you over the rough spots. You often go to unhappy extremes in feelings and emotions. You have a strong physique, and possess an out-of-the-ordinary determination to succeed in spite of all hazards, even when you are discouraged. You are fond of outdoor life, and a vacation is exhilarating to you when it is not a luxury trip. You are energetic and possess much endurance; you are more capable than the average person.

The Decanates of Leo

If the birthday is between July 23rd and July 31st

Your personal and ruling orb is the Sun. This greatly stimulates your mental and physical activities. The double aspect of the Sun in your Horoscope is one of the most beneficent vibrations in the entire Zodiac. The Sun in this aspect creates a great love for change and the desire to reform. A noble and enthusiastic nature and the ability to lead others is also shown. The Sun will confer good fortune upon you, particularly if you will try to eliminate some of the negative tendencies which you may have developed.

If the birthday is between August 1st and August 10th

Your personal planet is Jupiter. It is known as the symbol of fortune and the royal planet of Divine Wisdom. It influences the intellectual, moral, and sympathetic tendencies. A noble nature, always acting honourably and gratefully, is one of the favourable aspects of this planet. Jupiter decrees harmonious surroundings imbued with devotion and happiness. It will confer good fortune and success upon you and assist greatly in offsetting some of the negative tendencies of your Sign.

If the birthday is between August 11th and August 22nd

Your personal planet is Mars, known as the symbol of war and the centre of divine energy. It influences the energetic, courageous, and constructive tendencies. Mars will materially aid you in overcoming some of the weaker and more negative aspects of Leo. It gives you the necessary impetus to bring about a successful conclusion to some of your endeavours. Without this force, it would be difficult for you to realize many of your cherished ambitions. The combination of the Sun and Mars is indeed a fortunate one, since Mars is powerful and aggressive, and forces its natives to attain their objectives.

The Degrees of Leo

July 23rd

You possess an ambitious, forceful, and somewhat brusque disposition. You are independent and have the ability to attain objectives in life without much assistance from outside influences. You must avoid hasty decisions in business and financial matters. You may meet with success and unexpected benefits from superiors. You have a good sense of authority.

July 24th

You possess a magnetic personality and affectionate disposition. You are fond of music and art, and enjoy the beautiful, refined, and aesthetic things in life. One aspect in this Horoscope indicates a tendency to self-indulgence, which should not be encouraged. You like to be pampered but this will only add to your difficulties when you come face to face with realities. You are best suited for an artistic or professional career.

July 25th

You possess an enterprising and trustworthy nature. You have excellent powers of expression. You are a born leader and possess the energy and ability to rule situations and command the respect of your friends and associates. One aspect of this Horoscope indicates danger through misplaced friendships. You may be more popular with men than with women. Beware the false female.

July 26th

You possess honesty and integrity. A powerful will helps offset a sensitive disposition. Marked introspection, with an inclination to become moody and despondent at the slightest provocation, indicates a retiring manner. You are capable of intelligent research of the highest order. Travel and seek favours but avoid extravagance. The opposite sex is desperately attracted to you.

July 27th

You are generous, courteous, obliging, and hospitable. Relatives, friends, and strangers will want to help you. Successful travel is also indicated. You will rise to the pinnacle of success. You have a prophetic inspiration and will show considerable skill in the financial world.

July 28th

You possess a bold imagination and a keen mind, ever seeking knowledge and sensation. You are affectionate with strong passions, and will gain through musical or literary activities. You will have fame as well as monetary reward in your chosen profession.

July 29th

You possess a magnanimous, open-handed, and free disposition. You have excellent mental faculties and many original ideas, but you are prone to hasty decisions. One aspect in this Horoscope indicates the ability to achieve fame in the fields of medicine or philosophy.

July 30th
You are firm, steadfast, and sure of yourself. You are intuitive and show unusual aptness in commercial matters. You are fond of mystery, and display a love for argument and debate. These will add to your store of knowledge and become a prime factor in developing your intellect and improving your security. While you are affectionate and magnanimous to your immediate family, you may show a tendency to be somewhat inconsiderate of other people and their feelings.

July 31st
You have broad views and wide sympathies. Although devoted to your friends, you may experience disappointment through them. You rely a good deal upon intuition rather than common sense. One aspect in this Horoscope indicates difficulty in getting along with your immediate family, because of a desire to impress outsiders. An outspoken and impressionable nature may mark you as an eccentric.

August 1st
You possess a warmhearted, shy, and sensitive disposition. You show a great deal of aptitude in making money for yourself and your associates. One aspect in this Horoscope indicates that many of your troubles will turn to blessings. It also indicates inheritance from wealthy relatives. Try to curb your extravagant tendencies.

August 2nd
You possess an optimistic and philosophical turn of mind. You have a fiery temper that may need restraint. One aspect in this Horoscope indicates disappointment due to misplaced confidence. You are restless and always on the move. You will be fortunate on the whole, and excel in some special field of endeavour.

August 3rd
You possess an energetic and courageous personality, but are

inclined to be stubborn and quick-tempered. You have a strong link with your family. You are fond of taking chances, and have an air of mystery about you. This is a degree that usually gains much public attention.

August 4th

You possess excellent powers of perception, but are inclined to be somewhat apprehensive. You will benefit much through older people and from an inheritance. You must avoid fraudulent schemes and speculative enterprises. Your sense of superiority may create some enemies from time to time. Avoid mental and physical overexertion.

August 5th

You are fond of learning and are artistic and studious. Care should be taken when travelling on water. You have good scientific visualization and can be successful in the field of philosophy. You are a natural teacher. You are, physically, attractive to the opposite sex.

August 6th

You are self-inspired and capable of great undertakings. You can become impetuous when your emotions are aroused. It is advisable to curb such tendencies. Your strong will power will enable you to overcome many obstacles in life. You have the natural ability to make friends readily because you have a good sense of values.

August 7th

You possess a good intellect with a great thirst for knowledge. You can gain success in the literary, artistic, or musical world. A magnanimous personality and the desire to help those who are in less fortunate circumstances may lead to many strange experiences during your life. You have humanitarian instincts which may lead to just rewards in the form of honour and fame.

August 8th

You possess a sympathetic, determined, and forceful nature. Watch your temper. One aspect in this Horoscope shows a judicial and perceptive mind coupled with a high-strung nervous system. It is therefore necessary to avoid excessive mental exertion which may result in nervous disorder. Indulge in outdoor physical exercise.

August 9th

You possess a gentle yet powerful nature, which coupled with sincerity of purpose may help to make you successful. Gains are indicated through elderly relatives, social contacts, and property. This is the degree of show business. You have latent talents as an entertainer. You are fond of ease and comfort.

August 10th

You possess an original, bold, and dashing personality. A strong, resolute nature, with the ability to express yourself impressively both in speech and writing are also indicated. You may show a tendency to become obstinate and reckless. A disregard for convention and a star-ordained desire to express your own radical views and impose your will upon friends and associates should be curbed to avoid animosity.

August 11th

You are a dogmatic, confident, and determined person. You have a passionate temper and at times may become obstinate and headstrong. You may have a delicate constitution and should take it easy if you can. Enlightenment through past experiences is indicated. There is some danger of losses and trouble through doubtful friendships and associations.

August 12th

You are proud, austere, reserved, and easily offended. A more tolerant outlook should be cultivated to avoid unnecessary animosity. One aspect in this Horoscope indicates a tendency to look upon the gloomy side of life. Seek well-lighted places. Patient self-training to instil confidence will help overcome gloom also. Undue excitement and too much dissension will have an adverse reaction on your nervous system.

August 13th

You have a generous and extravagant nature. You may have many trials and tribulations to contend with. Faith, tolerance and patience will be necessary in order to guard your health and finances. Consolation will come from the opposite sex in times of stress. You have good earning ability.

August 14th

You are industrious and commercially minded. You have good analytical ability, but may become somewhat self-centred and dogmatic. Such egotism could lead to difficulties with your co-workers or business associates. One aspect in this Horoscope indicates that you should curb a tendency to be too free with your money.

August 15

You possess a certain degree of prophetic foresight. You are an originator of plans and will have many interesting and romantic affairs. A happy and interesting life is foreseen, conducted with dash and verve. It is essential that you be on constant guard against accidents due to your carelessness.

August 16th

You possess an original and perceptive mind. You show a decided tendency to be contrary and mischievous. Artistic ability and musical talent will greatly aid you in the attainment of success in the entertainment world. Trouble with relatives is shown at various intervals in your life. Some trouble through property, documents, and journeys is foreseen. A kind, sympathetic nature with a desire to help relatives may bring disappointment because of unappreciative attachments.

August 17th

You possess a clever, critical mind and an intuitive nature. A strong will and a fiery temper may give you some cause for concern. Keen interest in literature and art, if pursued, will endow you with an intellectual personality. Curb a tendency to become sarcastic when your plans meet with outside interference.

August 18th

You possess an adventurous spirit and a star-prophesised desire to travel and visit strange places. You are also fond of company. You show a marked aptitude for organizing and controlling others. You are always ready to accept responsibility. You may receive considerable help from your relatives. At some time during your life you will develop a practical method for attaining success.

August 19th

You possess an enterprising and entertaining personality. You show a marked aptitude for finance and should be successful in the commercial world. Some difficulty with, or through, relatives is indicated. Unforeseen financial success from unexpected sources comes to many persons born in this degree. You have the qualities of a good executive. Beware of hasty marriage.

August 20th

You possess a good sense of humour and an analytical mind. You like to experiment with new and unusual ideas. Curb a tendency to become proud and overbearing in your dealings with those less fortunate than yourself. You can develop a martyr complex, which may eventually cause you to lead a retiring and lonely life.

August 21st

You possess an original, daring, and masterful nature. A strong will coupled with the overbearing desire to have your own way should be curbed. If you use your analytical mind in an intelligent manner, much success is indicated in the business world. By exercising tolerance and patience, you can subdue a restless and overly energetic disposition. Losses through law and imposition are threatened.

August 22nd

You possess an impulsive and somewhat radical disposition. A brilliant mind and illuminating intuitive powers are also indicated. This combination of mental qualities is usually found in persons who attain outstanding success in public service. Try to curb a tendency to be too impulsive and erratic, as such characteristics, if permitted to develop, can prove to be detrimental. This is a good degree for a politician.

Compatible and Incompatible Signs of Leo

The Sign of Leo is intensely loyal, generous, and magnanimous, but it is not as a rule fortunate in marriage. This may be due to misplaced affection, unwise and impetuous lovemaking, and a too implicit faith in human nature, but there is, generally, a deeper reason.

Some peculiarity of outlook will often spoil marital happiness, and in the majority of cases, the question of children will be involved.

Leo has a deep love for children, and is frequently denied them, or loses them by death. Leo often experiences sorrow through a child. Like all the fiery Signs, Leo is idealistic and tends to set loved ones upon a pedestal. This leads to disappointment and disillusion through broken engagements or unhappy marriages, in many cases. It has been noticed that the twenty-seventh degree (August 19th) appears to be particularly unfortunate in marriage. In love matters, Leo tends to adopt a protective role and likes to be looked up to and admired. Leo is often rather lordly and may be dominating on occasion, for Leo always likes to oversee the management of affairs. Leo women are good managers and excellent formal hostesses.

Extravagance due to lavish generosity and love of ostentation is a great failing.

In early life Leo men are sometimes lady-killers; Leo women seek admiration from whoever will bestow it; but the Sign is not really a fickle one and is capable of great faith and loyalty once the feelings are deeply aroused.

Leos are the romantic type of lover; they know how to provide the right blend of sentimentality and passion. Leo employs dramatic effort to achieve the right effect. There can be nothing commonplace about the Leonian way of doing things!

The basic urge to excel and to appear in a glorious guise is the manifestation of the Leo ego, which frequently develops into a superiority complex. Naturally, the degree to which this is pushed will depend upon the individual aspects in the natal chart which clearly define all tendencies.

Leo will profit, perhaps to a greater degree than many of the other Signs, by a close study of those life partners with whom there will be harmony and happiness.

The compatible and incompatible Signs for Leo follow:

Leo and Aries

As a rule, this union works out well for both. While Aries and Leo both are highly emotional in their make-up, Leo will lionize an Aries partner. If Leo can take over the stage and the audience on occasion and be the "whole show", everything will be fine. Aries, with the natal impetuosity in love-making, will find a welcome in the arms, heart, and home of Leo. Fiery Leo admires the aggressive tendencies of the equally fiery Aries.

Leo and Taurus

The Sun-ruled Leo and the Venus-ruled Taurus will be a happy combination if each studies and understands the shortcomings of the other. The sex appeal and splendid physical qualities of each are important to these natives, and, in this case, they seem to have found just what the doctor ordered in each other. Taurus, however, will have to soft-pedal a jealous streak. Taurus should let the beloved Leo have the opportunity to "show off" and all will be well with this combination.

Leo and Gemini

While both these Signs are attracted to the same things—glamour, flattery, and the world of good-fellowship, the combination is not a good one. Leo's love is heart-felt; Gemini's love is of the mind. After the rose-coloured cellophane wrapping is removed from this romance, Gemini will find Leo's passion too bossy, possessive and demanding. The zestful love nature of Leo will not find love life with the unresponsive Gemini. Not an advisable combination, so beware!

Leo and Cancer

Strange as it may seem at first glance, this can make a really good combination. The water (Cancer) would, on the surface appear to be an unwise mate for the Fire (Leo), but their real compatibility is provided by their rulers. The Moon (Cancer) reflects the light of the Sun (Leo) and if Leo loves anything, it is something which reflects his own shining glory. The big, generous heart of Leo will soon forgive the moody outbursts of Cancer. This is due to the strong influence of the Moon upon the Cancerian personality. Cancer, more than any other Sign, responds to the Moon's aspects as it swiftly moves through the Zodiac.

Leo and Leo

This should be a compatible combination, but, regrettably, it is not always so. Leo natives are positive people, who love to hold the centre of the stage. They want to be the head of their social groups. When the two marriage partners are constantly contending for leadership, unhappy results can readily be imagined. The only hope for a successful partnership here is if the female is content to rule the home and the male to shine in the business and social world.

Leo and Virgo

There is a good chance here for a happy union. Magnanimous Leo will overlook Virgo's tendency to be critical, while Virgo will take pride in Leo's accomplishments, good humour, and lovable nature. Leo will respect Virgo's clever and alert mentality. If Virgo will permit Leo to hog the limelight and refrain from being too critical of Leo's star-predicted desire to hold the central place in the family circle, there should be no real barriers to a happy and successful partnership. This is no easy task.

Leo and Libra

The hale and hearty Leo may prove too much for the sensitive Libra nature, although there are many exceptions that could make this a fairly good combination. The Sun (Leo) and Venus (Libra) usually form a strong and luxurious aspect. Both Signs love luxuries, are subject to flattery, and are artistically inclined. The chief difficulty may lie in the fact that Leo demands constant adulation; Libra may get the idea that what's good for the goose is good for the gander.

Leo and Scorpio

This combination brings together two shining personalities. They have much in common, especially where the Leo is the wife and Scorpio is the husband. The Scorpio wife may be too demanding for her Leo husband. Jealousy here plays an important role in causing many serious family quarrels. Basically, this should make for one of the most compatible combinations, but the long and happy partnership will be far better when a Leo female marries a Scorpio male.

Leo and Sagittarius

This usually makes an excellent combination. It is said that fire should be fought with fire, and this seems applicable to marriage between these two Signs, with very few exceptions. Both love change and excitement and possess a great zest for life. The one danger lies in the fact that both are domineering; this could lead to trouble if the Leo tried to relegate the Sagittarian to the sidelines. The independent nature of Sagittarius would rebel, and this could lead to a serious rift in the partnership.

Leo and Capricorn

The slow, plodding Capricorn may prove too much for the carefree nature of Leo. Leo forgives and forgets; Capricorn is slow to anger and seldom forgets. This combination would not form the ideal basis for mutual understanding. This is especially true in matters of sex. The Capricorn has the tendency to be suspicious of motives, while Leo will wholeheartedly enter the arena with no thought of consequences. The "hail-fellow-well-met" attitude of Leo's nature will prove too much for Capricorn to cope with over the long run.

Leo and Aquarius

This combination of the Sun and Uranus is usually a good one. Leo likes surprise and Aquarius will certainly supply it. Both Signs are at their best when doing things for others. Leo loves the world, and Aquarius loves humanity. This makes an excellent combination for partnership that deals with or caters to the public.

In intimate matters there is a mutual understanding of

each other's needs and desires. Aquarius may hold many surprises for Leo, so there should never be a dull moment in their lives.

Leo and Pisces

The strong and hearty temperament of Leo may prove too much for the subtle and sensitive Pisces. Pisces, with resilience, takes on the changing moods of any partnership. Impressionable Pisces is easily hurt by any trivial or imagined wrong, and becomes very difficult to cope with, and dangerous to boot. While Leo is flattered by the dependency of others, if he abuses Pisces, the just resentment of Pisces may be too much for Leo to take over a long period of time.

Some Famous Persons Born in the Sign of Leo

Gracie Allen—Comedienne
Lucille Ball—Actress
Ethel Barrymore—Actress
Ingrid Bergman—Actress
Napoleon Bonaparte—French Statesman
Bernard Baruch—Financier
Fidel Castro—Cuban Leader
Cecil B. DeMille—Movie Director
Marshall Field—Merchant
Henry Ford—Industrialist
Dag Hammarskjöld—Secretary-General of UN
Alfred Hitchcock—Movie Director
Herbert G. Hoover—US President
Aldous Huxley—Novelist
Carl G. Jung—Psychiatrist, Psychoanalyst
Benito Mussolini—Dictator
Madame Pandit—Indian Ambassador
Sir Walter Scott—British Writer
George Bernard Shaw—Playwright
Mae West—Actress
Orville Wright—Inventor

6

VIRGO

August 23rd–September 22nd

The Sign Virgo symbolizes chastity, and forms the central idea of a great number of myths. When the Sun passes through this Sign the harvest is ready for the reaper, hence Virgo is symbolized as the gleaning maid with two ears of corn in her hand.

The Sign Virgo signifies the solar plexus of the Grand Archetypal Man, and, therefore, represents the assimilating and distributing functions of the human organism. Consequently, we find that those born under this influence possess fine discriminating powers as to the choice of food best adapted to their particular organic requirements. This constellation, as governing the bowels of humanity, is highly important since the intestines comprise a very vital section of the digestive organism.

Upon the esoteric planisphere, Virgo is occupied by Asher. "Out of Asher his bread shall be fat," says Jacob, "and he shall yield royal dainties, thus typifying the riches of the harvest." Virgo is the second emanation of the earthly Trigon, and is the constellation of Mercury.

The mystical gem of Virgo is the sardonyx, a stone possessing very important virtues.

The fortunate day is Wednesday.

Fortunate numbers are eight and four.

The fortunate colour for this Sign is grey.

Best locations for success are in small cities.

The Sign Virgo signifies the realization of hopes. Those dominated by this influx are calm, confident, and contented; they are reflective, studious, and extremely fond of reading. Consequently they become the mental repositories of much wisdom and learning. These desirable qualities, combined with the penetration of Mercury, which this Sign contains, all conduce to make the native of Virgo pre-eminently fitted for the close application of scientific study. They possess large, well-balanced minds, and superior intellectual abilities, and make clever statesmen when thrown into the vortex of political life.

They are courteous, diplomatic, and present a neat and attractive appearance, as they are inclined to be critical in the matter of dress. They may appear to be rather cool and reserved, but this is because of their independence of thought and observation. Their natural bearing and demeanour will command the respect and admiration of others.

They have an intellectual and nervous temperament. They are kind and sympathetic, but generosity with them is a more practical proposition than it is with most people. Their excellent powers of observation make them critical of the most minute detail. They must learn to criticize constructively. Unwise use of this ability can lead to misunderstanding in personal and social contacts with others.

Virgoans are honest, trustworthy, sincere, and reliable, and will take their full share of responsibility in matters of importance.

Their emotional nature is to be somewhat sensitive and reserved. They derive much pleasure from ideas and observations. Most people do not realize that these natives are thinkers. They have excellent powers of analysis, with unusually quick and keen perception. They should do all within their power to develop persistence and fortitude, for if they do not develop these qualities, circumstances of life will force their development. Though Virgoans have good reasoning powers, there are times when they must guard against their conclusions being influenced by personal prejudices.

True logic is as impersonal as sunlight; false logic based on personal feelings is conducive to intolerance, selfishness, and prejudice. Virgoans are quick to recognize and absorb the facts surrounding a proposition, and are, therefore, able to learn much faster than those of many other Signs. They are good at analysing all angles of a given issue.

By nature those of Virgo are fact-finding individuals; imagination is used to practical ends. There may be times when they day-dream about personal or romantic affairs, but in other matters they are realistic and practical. They also try to visualize improvements in conditions and circumstances around them; they use their imagination in the same manner that a builder, inventor, or creative artist uses this same faculty. The memory is very good, because of the deep interest and attention given to all that they observe.

These natives also have the ability to express knowledge gathered. This faculty is valuable in business and social contact. They can help many people with their sound advice and constructive ideas. A good conversationalist is always appreciated. The one error they must be constantly aware of is becoming critical. These natives are naturally subject to impulsive action, but, fortunately, they are the type of individuals who will analyse their impulses before acting upon them. This is a good habit to acquire, as it can save much heartache and misunderstanding. Sound judgment, free from all prejudice, is essential to success and happiness.

The Sign Virgo imparts to its natives the power of inspiration. A study of the lives of many prominent Virgoans reveals that they have been inspired men and women. This inspiration is an attribute of the subconscious mind, as is the faculty of intuition. Active intuitive power gives those of this Sign a deep understanding of human nature and the motives of others. It also helps them recognize truths, and often warns of impending danger. Such intuition should not be confused with ordinary fear or apprehension. An intuitive impression is sudden and spontaneous, and has no association with any previous thought or experience.

Others may have some difficulty understanding Virgo people, but this is because they are apt to mistake the Virgoan reserve for indifference. In ordinary conversation, they keep to themselves and do not volunteer information. They are natural students and enjoy the independence of their own minds.

A good physical constitution capable of withstanding the rigours and vicissitudes of life is indicated. They, being of a mental and nervous temperament, should avoid excesses which have a tendency to weaken the resistance and irritate. Since Virgo is the Sign ruling the digestive organs and intestinal tract, judgment in the diet is advisable. A balanced diet of animal and vegetable food is the natural sustenance essential to human well-being, but many Virgoans are inclined to dietary fads and fancies. Consult your doctor before going overboard on a diet. Plenty of fresh air, sunlight, and rest will do much to maintain strength, and health and appetite.

The Virgo is fond of sports, entertainments, and travel. Much enjoyment is also derived from reading, and from lectures. Pleasure comes more from intellectual pursuits than physical pleasures, although the out-of-doors is greatly enjoyed.

Their innate reserve and sensitivity keeps these natives from showing their real feelings. They are more mental than emotional in the affections. It sometimes appears as if they are afraid of love. When subjected to love, they are apt to begin to lead an intellectual and mechanical sort of life which is devoid of emotion, sentiment, and affection.

This attitude is not normal and, in time, will react upon the body and mind in accordance to natural laws.

Hurt or disillusionment—especially in a love affair—is apt to deeply affect those born of this Sign, and they are not inclined to get over it easily. In friendships, they like individuals because of certain particular characteristics they possess, but when it comes to marriage, a mate cannot be accepted just for certain qualities. The mate must be acceptable for all qualities, and these must reasonably blend with the native's own mental, emotional, and physical make-up. If such blending does not exist, an inharmonious marriage results. This, in turn, would cause the native to become extremely critical and distorted by the disillusionment he feels. In the state of marriage, it must be borne in mind that things may happen from time to time which will cause irritation. In this event, understanding must be striven for, or else eventual separation and sorrow will result.

These natives possess a great degree of parental love and may be jealously fond of their children. Two things should be guarded against in regard to children—over-indulgence and over-criticism. Indications show an unsettled state of affairs in their home life during childhood and youth.

The Virgoan ideals regarding home life are high, but there is a restless element in the nature leading to a desire for mental and physical changes in matters connected with home life and surroundings. Close and confining places tend to irritate them. The native may not be aware of this consciously.

Those of this Sign are critical of the appearance of the home and its furnishings; disorderliness is utterly foreign to their nature. Disorder irritates their finer sensitivities more quickly than anything else.

Though they are methodical, monotony is apt to upset the sensitive nervous system. It is to their advantage to get away now and then, even though it may be only for a short time. They are often misunderstood by their own relatives, and, if married, by some of the mate's relatives. This is caused primarily by their independent natures. However, the Virgoans try their best to get along with others. They are willing to co-operate with kinsmen, but the latter rarely reciprocate unless it is to their advantage.

The Virgo-born will be much happier and accomplish more when they live apart from relatives. Those of this Sign are naturally industrious, conscientious, and sincere in their work. Their quick perception enables them to make improvements in their labours. They are adapted to intellectual rather than physical labour; they represent the type of personality well adapted to professional life. Many Virgo people are found in the law, the healing arts, literature, and bookkeeping. Their particular type of mind is suitable for any line of work which requires careful analysis and judgment. Many of the world's scientific minds belong under this practical Sign. Good mechanics and machinists as well as hotel and transportation people come under Virgo. They are practical in anything they do. When choosing a job or profession, they should select the kind which will give their abilities the greatest expression. It is advisable they take advantage of the high degree of persistence in their natures.

They will get along well in partnership ventures, but they require a free hand to carry out responsibilities. Indications are that financial standing will vary considerably through the course of life. Their pecuniary outlook ranges from conservatism to free spending. Because of their natural industry earning ability is good. They seldom reach the level of dire want. They will do well to consider real estate, transportation lines, and mercantile and chemical companies as fields for investment. Success in speculative ventures appear to be very limited. Small business enterprises and backing new inventions appear to bring fairly good results. However, in the main, Virgoans financial conditions are very much under their own direction, and they will, no doubt, have many opportunities in life to better their finances.

The choice of friends runs to the intellectual and idealistic types of both sexes; though the native is loyal and solicitous, there is a disposition, at times, to be critical of friends. Much pleasure is derived from social activity. Ability to be a good host or hostess creates a good impression on guests and friends..

The Virgo Child

The children of Virgo are governed by the intellect and are seldom sympathetic. They are quick mentally, but are inclined, at times, to get into a "rut" and become overly fond of taking things easy. Sometimes they cause enmities of a lasting nature, but more generally make very good friends, treating their friends well.

They are sensitive to any suggestion of ill health and can become chronic hypochondriacs. In dealing with the Virgo child, the parents should stimulate the child's interest in health and recreation. The mind of this child should be kept busy in order to avoid an uncertain mental state. Virgo children are, at times, hard to understand, and it will be to the interest of the growing child if the parents take an interest in all the activities of their offspring. A review of the health potential for the Virgo child shows that the vitality can be termed moderate. The system will have a tendency to an acid condition. Special note should be taken when this child begins to walk, as he or she may tend to poor circulation, indigestion, and bowel disease. It is well to avoid drugs as much as possible; the best tonic is care in diet, and mental and physical exercise. Fear in the mind of this child is likely to cause illness.

In considering the best occupation for the Virgo child, great care should be taken to ascertain his or her likes and dislikes. This is of the greatest importance as it can set the stage for a career. The occupations for which the Virgo child is eminently suited are connected with the earth and its products. They make fine bankers, inventors, librarians, nurses, physicians, promoters, psychiatrists, scientists, and statisticians.

The mental characteristics of this child will tend to make him critical, with a strong tendency to worry over trifles.

Music and art will always play a big part in the life of a Virgo child, and such attributes should be given every opportunity to develop. Many times opportunity is lost because the parents do not realize until too late that certain star-ordained gifts could have been developed to enhance the possibilities of success later in life.

The Virgo Wife

When the Virgo woman marries, she makes an excellent wife in most respects. Her concept of marriage is that it is a legal partnership, to be run as a business. She is usually capable and arranges her housekeeping routine perfectly. The home is spotless, and under her care everything seems to remain new. She is vigilant and efficient—she is everything that can make a home run like a well-oiled machine. There is no waste or neglect in her home.

Her disposition may not be perfect all the time. In some cases, the Virgo wife is apt to be fussy and nagging. She guards the family purse jealously and, in extreme cases, she is stingy. In all her responses to life she shows the same parsimonious attitude.

Emotionally, this woman is often way below par. She handles traditional duties well but the intimate companionship and emotional ecstasy so necessary in a wife are often entirely absent. She has in her make-up a selfish coldness that resents demands for personal warmth. The Virgo wife never recovers from her maiden beliefs that she is sinning when she accedes to her husband's purely physical attention. A very clever man who is deeply in love might alter this frame of mind, but since the Virgo woman seldom inspires great intensity of passion, her best hope is for a mate as restrained, practical, and material as herself. In such an environment she makes a successful wife. It must be remembered, of course, that other planetary influences can alter the emotional intensity of the Virgo woman.

The Virgo Husband

The Virgo husband in search for the best kind of wife would do well to choose a Virgo woman. These men are not usually interested in love in the passionate, personal, and possessive senses of the word. Virgo husbands are conventional, traditional-minded men who accept domesticity because it is part of the social scheme. They are willing to conduct their private life on a partnership basis, as if it were a commercial enterprise. In many cases they would prefer to be bachelors; this Sign produces many of them. They are abstemious and stingy, the latter which has kept many a man from matrimony.

The Virgoan is capable, and makes comfortable provisions for his wife and family, but he is fussy, critical, peevish, and complaining (especially about health or expenses). He safeguards his home and is careful to protect it from disaster.

Unless there are other stimulating factors in his Horoscope, the Virgo husband is not virile. He has little male dominance in his make-up, and is as loath to demand surrender as he is to give of himself. He does not have a passionate urge, and his deepest approach to love is flirtation. Eroticism and flights of passion would never be attempted by him, since his opinion of passionate sexual performance is not favourable. The one great exception to the rule can be a Virgo husband with Scorpio rising in his Horoscope. This contributes to a passionate attitude by giving a physical desire for ever-fresh, stinging pleasures.

The Cusps of Virgo

(If your birthday is not within the cusp of your Sign, the following does not apply to you.)

These natives are born in Virgo with Leo tendencies. The ruling orbs are Mercury and the Sun. This cusp shows kindness, optimism, and unusual success in whatever the natives set out to do. They have a good sense of humour and should capitalize on their varied talents. They are loyal to their friends and delight in doing things for others. They are fond of diversion, travel, and novel contacts. They possess an aptitude for science, invention, and original enterprises. They never betray a confidence or trust. Should they meet with financial reverses, they will make a comeback and start again with their former courage.

Through persistency they will make some of their plans come true. While at times there may be a tendency to follow the course offering the least resistance, they soon control this and get back on energetic planes. At times they worry too much over trifles. They are clear thinkers and early in life should train themselves to see both sides of any problem.

If the birthday is from September 19th through September 22nd

These natives are born in Virgo with Libra tendencies. The ruling planets are Mercury and Venus. This indicates that they are full of many ideas, but lack a plan to carry them out. These people are kind, thoughtful, and will go to extremes to make a good impression upon strangers, though those who are closest to them are often overlooked. They possess some literary and musical ability. In romantic matters they are sincere, and anyone fortunate enough to receive their interest may count on their loyalty.

These natives benefit from past experience and seldom make the same mistake twice. Because they always try to make sure that they are right before they go ahead, they are likely to be more successful than the average person. They have the ability to accomplish any reasonable desire. Throughout life they will be popular, and will have the good will and respect of their circle of friends.

The Decanates of Virgo

If the birthday is between August 23rd and August 31st

Your personal and ruling planet is Mercury. It is the symbol of knowledge and the Swift-Winged Messenger of the Truth. It rules the rational part of the soul and mind, and indicates an alert, ingenious, perceptive, intellectual, studious, and forceful personality when in favourable aspect. In unfavourable aspect, it inclines towards an inquisitive, meddlesome, careless, cunning, radical, imitative, shiftless, forgetful, and effusive nature. This planet is said to be the great mental ruler, for without Mercury's influence, we would be devoid of memory and the powers of speech and expression.

If the birthday is between September 1st and September 11th

The personal planet for this decanate is Saturn, known as the symbol of time. This planet is restrictive in its influence. It governs the thoughtful and meditative tendencies, and inclines to make its subjects careful, patient, and considerate. Saturn is chiefly concerned with lending fixity to all affairs that may be classed as concrete conditions. Its powers lie in stability, endurance, tenacity, and perseverance. Gain through thrifty methods and careful investments is indicated. These natives possess a magnanimous spirit and a kind, benevolent, and sympathetic nature.

If the birthday is between September 12th and September 22nd

The personal planet is Venus, which is known as the symbol of Love and Beauty and gives constancy to the affections.

It denotes a sensitive, generous, harmonious, perceptive, and artistically well-balanced mind—a mind capable of taking a dispassionate view of life.

These natives possess a good sense of proportion and are able to see both sides of a subject clearly. Praise and admiration will influence them to develop the more positive tendencies of their nature. They share their earthly possessions, especially with those who are near and dear. A generous spirit is indicated by the influence of Venus in this Horoscope.

The Degrees of Virgo

August 23rd

These natives possess a romantic nature, and may be idealists and dreamers. A rather "hard to please" attitude is shown at times, due to a fixed, self-centred viewpoint. You of this birthday may show a decided preference for the company of persons having a great deal more money than you have. When dealing with those who are less fortunate, it is necessary to use tolerance and consideration. Old friendships should not be neglected or discarded.

August 24th

This degree imparts a resourceful mind and natural executive ability. Marked determination to succeed in all undertakings may make you work alike for good or bad. Discrimination between right and wrong should ever remain the keynotes. A diversified, liberal education is an important factor in overcoming many of the negative qualities which may be in this nature. Moderation and conservative principles will pay the best dividends in success and happiness.

August 25th

Here is a sensitive, impressionable, and reserved nature. There is a tendency here to depend too much upon others for help and advice. Wealth by marriage often makes life easier for this degree. Obstacles in business may come from elderly persons who have put you under obligation. There is a marked interest in politics, law, and humanitarian activities. Any sacrifice made to obtain a college education will well repay you.

August 26th

Those of this degree possess a serious, aspiring nature coupled with a strong intellectual capability. You are profound and practical. A strong sense of independence and a desire to help those in less fortunate circumstances is also indicated. At times you may become too magnanimous for your own good. Learn the value of financial conservatism. Show a respect for your superiors. You will create your own destiny.

August 27th

These Virgo-born possess a retiring, studious, and analytic nature. An envy streak should be curbed. You are fond of literature, music, and art. Make the maximum use of your intellectual and commercial training. Learn self-confidence and the ability to see the other person's point of view. Due to lack of emotional stability, you may be hard to understand at times.

August 28th

The Virgoans of this birthday possess unusual mental qualities. You display independence of thought and possess a steady and forceful disposition. One aspect of this Horoscope shows a desire to defy convention. This tendency should be curbed. It should be borne in mind that best chances for success and happiness come through valuable friendships that are made and held.

August 29th

A keen mind and a calm, peaceful attitude towards life are bestowed upon the persons of this degree. Gain is indicated through sentimental associations and influential friendships. One aspect of this Horoscope shows a tendency to take good fortune for granted. Persons of this degree are possessed of great sexual potency.

August 30th

This chart shows an adaptable, versatile, and intuitive mind. The value of concentration should be recognized. One aspect in this Horoscope indicates a tendency to tire quickly. One thing should be completed before another is started. A charming personality coupled with a good sense of humour will attract many friendships.. Diligent application of the many capabilities shown for you will aid in the attainment of success once a constructive mental attitude is developed.

August 31st

You possess a sensitive and idealistic nature. Certain planetary aspects show a tendency to be too generous for your own personal welfare. Learn to recognize the true from the false. Fondness of travel by water and a long sea voyage are indicated.

September 1st

You are endowed with an original mind coupled with a rather sensitive and retiring nature. One aspect in this Horoscope shows that you may lack the incentive to overcome obstacles. Develop self-confidence. Be practical. Pursue success. Cheerful companions and friendly associates will do much to help attain social ambitions and make life bearable.

September 2nd

These Virgo-born possess a bright, cheerful disposition. You are just and righteous in both business and social matters. You will probably pursue a professional career where your mind will be exercised to the best advantage. A strong desire to be well-dressed at all times is shown. This can develop into the extravagant habit of purchasing many things of doubtful use. Pull in your horns and practice parsimony.

September 3rd

Those of this birthday possess an astute, practical, and intuitive mind. An artistic temperament with marked humanitarian principles will bring many lasting and influential friendships. You are generous, of good appearance, kind-hearted, and charitably inclined. One aspect of this chart indicates a tendency to shirk responsibility, a desire to get by with little personal effort.

September 4th

Strong will power and an energetic, commanding personality is shown by this degree. Initiative and good business acumen will enable you to progress rapidly in the commercial world. There is a tendency, however, towards extravagance. The value of personal possessions should be learned. An ardent, highly emotional nature, desirous of adventure and full of wild dreams, should be moderated.

September 5th

A flexible, happy nature and a clever, imaginative mind are indicated here. You may become too generous for your own good, and too agreeable to protect your own interests. There is a fondness for mimicry, the stage, and theatre. One aspect of this chart shows a tendency to scatter your forces, talents, and energies in too many directions at the same time. Concentration of purpose should be exercised.

September 6th

These natives are the possessors of sensitive, impressionable, and inquisitive natures. Love of travel to distant lands is indicated. At times, you show an erratic disposition and a cross temper. This should be checked as soon as possible. One aspect here shows a rather extravagant nature, which must be curbed so as to avoid loss of credit from time to time. A marked interest in political, legal, and humanitarian activities will aid materially in achieving success.

September 7th

The natives of this degree possess a keen, shrewd, and alert mind. They can be deeply moved by their higher sympathies. There may be a tendency to meddle in the affairs of others. While the intentions may be most charitable, there will be misunderstandings and disappointments until it is learned that life's greatest rewards come to those who mind their own business.

September 8th

This degree imparts to its natives an energetic nature and great skill in the execution of duties. Persistence and determination, even in the face of difficulties, will bring success and financial independence. Friends and associates should be chosen with discrimination. Other people's viewpoints should be treated with tolerance. There is a tendency here to become somewhat impulsive, especially in affairs of the heart.

September 9th

Those of this birthday possess a keen and intellectual mind coupled with excellent powers of concentration. A tendency to regard life with too serious an outlook should be avoided. A bright, cheerful atmosphere and the company of successful friends will greatly aid in eliminating this trait. A highly magnetic personality and an independent nature will make for great success in the business world.

September 10th

Wholesome charm and magnetism are the endowments of this degree. You have an inventive mind, and show a high degree of originality in all of your undertakings. You are susceptible to colds and it is necessary that all precautions be taken to avoid draughts and sudden changes of temperature. A rampant desire for speculation should be curbed.

September 11th

This degree bestows a splendid character and a sympathetic nature coupled with deep emotions. These natives can really succeed in life if they will curb a tendency to become too easily satisfied. It is essential that they have a happy environment and friends who are appreciative of their talents. The emotional problems will yield to patient and understanding treatment.

September 12th

An expansive and genial personality is shown here. You can attain much popularity in your social life. You have a charming personality and talk well. Love of travel is indicated. The emotional nature should be stabilized. An artistic temperament coupled with a magnetic personality will make for success in a professional rather than a business career. Public recognition through literary abilities can be insured by proper education. One aspect here warns of the tendency to become too much of a carefree dreamer.

September 13th

You possess a bright, cheerful disposition, a splendid mind, and a magnetic personality. Success in a material way is indicated through the ability to make and hold influential and beneficial friendships. Marked originality and a good sense of humour will help towards a position of prestige in the social world. A vivid imagination coupled with excess energy may cause restlessness and carelessness at times. Some danger when travelling is shown.

September 14th

This native possesses a pleasing personality and splendid intuitive powers. A highly emotional nature may develop into an uncontrollable temper unless you develop an ironlike self-discipline. There is a tendency to brood and daydream too much if left alone for any great length of time; this is, no doubt due to a most imaginative mind. Many persons born on this day will evince much artistic, musical, and literary skill. Avoid solitude.

September 15th

Those of this degree possess an intellectual, scientific, and experimental mind. Being excellent conversationalists they should enjoy great popularity. An independent, yet orderly, spirit coupled with a magnetic personality is also shown. These fine qualities should make it easy for these natives to get what they want from friends.

September 16th

You possess a kind, sympathetic nature, and a pleasing disposition. You should develop a sense of independence and a faculty for diplomacy in order to utilize a too-adventurous spirit. Due to an inquisitive, aspiring, and perceptive mind, success is indicated in the professional world. You may be naturally attracted to the study of medicine. An indicated ability to get along well with all types of people will aid materially in attaining success. Conservative financial principles should be followed.

September 17th

A benevolent, charitable, and sympathetic nature is imparted by this degree. A desire to help all those who appeal for assistance may result in extravagance beyond your means. You are subject to flattery and can easily become the prey of designing friends and associates. One aspect in this chart shows a tendency to become conceited due to excess attention. Beware of false friends.

September 18th

These natives possess a good mind coupled with a charitable nature, which will endear them to all. The magnetic personality and ability to attract staunch and loyal friendships may result in a dependent attitude. The early home environment may also tend to encourage the shirking of responsibility. It would be wise to concentrate on concrete personal accomplishments which are essential to your success and happiness.

September 19th

Great ambition and a keen perceptive mind are indicated for those of this birth date. A highly magnetic personality and an enterprising, forceful disposition will attract many respected and beneficial friendships. At times it will be necessary for these natives to overcome an exaggerated sense of self-importance. A wayward spirit and a star-influenced desire to make frequent changes is shown. This aspect should be moderated by intelligent training towards a more modest and stable viewpoint.

September 20th

You possess a pleasing, courteous disposition and alert, thoughtful, and intuitive mind. A tendency to dominate others and assume leadership, regardless of consequences, should be carefully noted, and proper education and training should be sought in order to overcome these tendencies. There is industry and self-reliance shown here, and a highly ambitious and determined nature. Help may be received from persons in superior positions. Cultivate humility.

September 21st

A polite, agreeable, and companionable disposition is shown here. The attractive personality will draw many friends and bring much popularity. One aspect here shows a tendency to look upon the dark and gloomy side of life. This is, no doubt, due to a highly sensitive and emotional nature. Patient training to instil confidence will help overcome this pessimistic attitude. Undue excitement will cause an adverse reaction of the nervous system. Pleasant surroundings and cheerful friends are essential to you.

September 22nd

You possess a bright, cheerful disposition and a generous nature. You are just and righteous in both financial and social matters. A professional career, where the fine mental faculties shown here may be demonstrated to the best advantage, is advisable. There is a strong attachment for the home and family. These natives are extremely clothes-conscious, and wish to appear in the height of fashion at all times. Sometimes this small vanity leads to unnecessary extravagance.

Compatible and Incompatible Signs of Virgo

The outstanding Virgo characteristic is self-sufficiency. The old maid of caricature, with her cat or parrot, her fussiness and faddiness, her curiosity, and her love of malicious gossip, is a typical product of Virgo.

The Sign is a discriminatory and critical one, and is not easily satisfied. Virgos are fastidious, dislike being criticized, and have a deep-rooted fear of infections and ailments. These factors all play an important part in the sex outlook of its natives.

In marriage, Virgo is dutiful, and may desire to be more affectionate than appears on the surface, for the extreme shyness of the Sign prevents outward exhibition of affection. Virgo makes a faithful partner but not necessarily a sexually exciting one. The matter-of-fact, critical, and fussy manner is not calculated to win another's heart easily.

Neatness and tidiness are usually strong Virgo characteristics, and are by no means confined to the women of the Sign. These tendencies are evinced in their style and dress, and also in the care lavished upon the home and possessions. Virgo rarely praises anything, and more often grumbles and criticizes. The general efficiency of the Sign leads its natives to assume that no one else can do anything as well, as neatly, and as methodically as they can.

Virgoans have quiet, cultured, demeanours, as a rule, and

they certainly know how to interest the opposite sex. Love to them is an adventure. They believe that they are interested in the opposite sex for psychological reasons only—just the simple student of life to whom the study of the behaviour of others is the supreme interest—but their interest is not by any means as detached or coldly analytical as they would have one believe. Despite their explanation, the fact remains that they provoke the amatory susceptibilities of the opposite sex. In other words they can be veritable teases!

Virgo is flirtatious and intensely curious. If their penchant for criticizing others results in a rebuff, they feel hurt, and sorry for themselves. This state will not last long before the barometer changes and they come up smiling—more provocative than ever! They are interested in so many members of the opposite sex, in each of whom they see "points" others haven't got, that they are sometimes baffled as to which one is best for them. It would be good for the Virgoan to study the following comparisons of the Signs and discover the compatible and incompatible Signs for the Virgonians.

Virgo and Aries

This combination is certainly not the "happily-ever-after" affair. Mercury-ruled Virgo will not take kindly to bossy, dictatorial Aries (Mars), and the impulsive, fiery Aries would soon become dissatisfied with the prissy, critical Virgo. Usually a difficult combination.

Virgo and Taurus

Taurus is apt to have a love-at-first-sight attack for Virgo, but Taurus does not like criticism, which is usually Virgo's strongest weapon. In addition, Taurus can be as stubborn and obstinate as the Bull which is the symbol of that Sign, and Virgo will be inclined to do a lot of nagging and push the Taurus mate into a fury.

Virgo and Gemini

Though both these Signs have the same ruler—Mercury—this combination may prove too much for both over the long run. Mercury in Gemini is logical and calculating; in Virgo it is demanding and critical. Virgo would soon be out of breath trying to keep up with Gemini's constant desire for change. There are some points of compatibility between these two—the love of good clothes, a predisposition to neatness, and mutual desire for friends and associates who are in artistic and intellectual pursuits. It is through these channels that many Gemini-Virgo combinations are formed.

Virgo and Cancer

The demanding Virgo may be very disturbing to the Cancer's desire for quiet contentment. Virgo is apt to be too realistic and direct in the approach to everyday events. Sentimental Cancer is reticent—even shy—in sex matters. This will probably frustrate the Virgo and cause him to harshly criticize and nag. Such treatment would put the Cancer native in a sulking, silent mood, and Virgo would probably become hysterical. Only those who are on the highest plane would find this a compatible union.

Virgo and Leo

This could be a very happy combination, since each seems to have what the other needs and wants. Warm-hearted, forgiving Leo will be likely to overlook Virgo's sharp tendencies and Virgo will regard the Leo mate's accomplishments with pride. Leo's good humour and lovable traits will do much to melt any Virgo coolness. Leo's respect for Virgo's mind and cleverness will nourish the Virgonian ego. If Virgo will permit Leo to hold the centre of the stage, and soft-pedal criticism, there should be few barriers to happiness in this partnership.

Virgo and Virgo

It would be difficult indeed for these two to find anything resembling compatibility. The traits of each here would make for a battle of wits with the opponents evenly matched. Each would exaggerate the faults of the other. At best it would be a commonplace marriage, with the possibility of husband and wife talking each other to distraction.

Virgo and Libra

This is another combination that would have trouble in finding mutual grounds for marital bliss. If there is one thing Libra cannot take it is criticism, and, of course, Virgo is a champion in that department. Virgo is very meticulous in all matters pertaining to detail, while Libra is easygoing and detests details. The conflict of interest here will surely cause storm signals to be run up soon after the sex novelty has worn off.

Virgo and Scorpio

This combination usually belongs to the mutual admiration society. The exploring Virgo mind is fascinated with the mysterious and intriguing Scorpio. If there is any Sign that can curb Virgo's tendency to sulk, it is Scorpio. Virgo respects Scorpio's ability to analyse all situations and thereby sidesteps countroversial issues before they become a basis for disagreement. If Virgo will avoid hurting Scorpio's pride, this combination will be happy and enduring.

Virgo and Sagittarius

The Sagittarian love of freedom and change may prove too much for the meticulous Virgo disposition. The Sagittarian male is easily attracted to the Virgo female. Her spic-and-span appearance intrigues him, but once he is married, he may soon find that he got more than he bargained for. He may find the things he liked most before marriage may put him into a strait jacket after marriage. One thing Sagittarius cannot take is bickering—and Virgo thrives on it.

Virgo and Capricorn

There are points of similarity and compatibility in these two Signs. They are both very exacting. This eliminates many areas of disagreement. They both have great pride in appearance and surroundings. They can cry on each other's shoulder when outside influences prove too much to cope with. This Mercury-Saturn combination should find mutual ground for an agreeable partnership.

Virgo and Aquarius

Aquarius may hold too many surprises for the conservative Virgo nervous system to cope with. This is an elaborate combination to analyse. Much depends on the cultural and educational levels of the partners. If there is a marked difference between the two, the chances for a happy and enduring marriage are almost nil. However, if both parties happen to be college sweethearts, or do the same sort of work, chances for a happy marriage are greatly enhanced. This combination is either very good or very bad—no happy medium here.

Virgo and Pisces

Pisces is the exact opposite of Virgo. In the Zodiac they are 180 degrees apart. While opposing Signs are considered astrologically unfavourable, opposites often find much compatibility. This may be because contrast makes for interest, and in Virgo and Pisces the contrast is very marked. It will take a great deal of patience and understanding on the part of Virgo to cope with the moody, sentimental nature of Pisces over a long period of time. A little sentimentality on the part of the Virgo mate will go a long way in making this combination happy; however, a little sentimentality is a dangerous thing.

Some Famous Persons born in the Sign of Virgo

Leonard Bernstein—Composer and Conductor
Pierre Curie—Physicist and Chemist
Theodore Dreiser—Author
Greta Garbo—Actress
Johann Goethe—German Dramatist and Poet
Arthur Godfrey—Entertainer
Alexander the Great—Conqueror
Oliver Wendell Holmes—Poet
Sophia Loren—Actress
Grandma Moses—Painter
Friedrich Nietzsche—German Philosopher
John J. Pershing—US General
J. B. Priestley—Author
William Saroyan—Author and Playwright
Upton Sinclair—Novelist
William Howard Taft—US President
Cornelius Vanderbilt—Industrialist
H. G. Wells—Author

7

LIBRA

September 23rd–October 22nd

THIS CONSTELLATION symbolizes Justice. Most of our readers, doubtless, have seen the Goddess of Justice represented by a blindfolded female holding in her hand a pair of scales. This conception is purely astrological. The Sign Libra signifies the reins and loins of the Grand Celestial Man, and therefore represents the central conservatory or store house of the reproductive fluids. It is also the magnetic vortex of procreative strength. This constellation represents, in its most interior aspect, the equinoctial point of the arc in the ascending and descending cycle of the life atom. This Sign contains the unification of the cosmic forces as the grand central point of equilibrium of the sphere.

Libra signifies external perception balanced by intuition. The union of these produces reason and foresight. Those dominated by this influence constitute the rationalist school of the world's thinkers.

Libra upon the esoteric planisphere is occupied by Dan, the patriarch, in his blessing—thus referring, to his celestial nature: "Dan shall judge his people as one of the tribes of Israel." Libra represents the interior equilibrium of nature's forces, and contains the mystery of the divine "at-one-ment" of the ancient initiations.

Upon the universal chart, this Sign becomes Enoch, the perfect man. Libra is the second emanation of the airy Triplicity, and is the constellation of Venus.

Its mystical gem is the chrysolite. As a magnetic talisman, this stone acts as a repulsive force, and combines with the magnetic sphere of those born under its influence to repel the emanations from foreign bodies.

The fortunate day is Friday.

The fortunate numbers are six and nine.

The fortunate colour for this Sign is pastel blue.

Best locations for success are places of social activity.

Theoretically, Librans are strong supporters of such conceptions as universal brotherhood, universal equality, and the rights of man, but actually they seldom (unless it pays) put their pet theories to actual practice. The natives of Libra, though possessing a finely balanced mental and magnetic organism, are seldom elevated into very prominent positions. This is because they are too even, both mentally and physically, to become the popular leaders of any radical or sensational party.

It is one of the attributes of Libra to infuse a tendency within all born under her influence to accept and adopt the golden mean, or as it has been termed, "the happy medium". Hence, they generally command respect from both sides on questions of debate, and their intuitions are light and golden.

The true Libra personality is charming, attractive, pleasing, and graceful. Libra usually indicates beauty, and many of the world's most handsome men and lovely women are born under this Sign. Ordinarily Librans show considerable poise. They usually possess a personality that is responsible for the creation of its own destiny throughout life. This orientation gives one a good start in life, but the actual carving of destiny depends upon the strength of the mind behind the personality.

In disposition, the native is kind, sympathetic, generous, and loyal, under ordinary circumstances. They have a touchy emotional nature. Their temperamental responses vary with the particular mood at the time Librans are aroused. Sometimes they are quick to anger, and at other times they are very patient and will stand for much nonsense. They dislike pettiness and injustice, yet there will be times in their lives when it will be advisable for them to take stock of themselves and see if they, themselves, are not guilty of injustice. Though they may not show it, they are selfish and self-willed, with independent natures. They resent any intrusion upon their independence of thought or action. In their business and social life they manifest the same sort of personality, often impetuous and impulsive.

Though Librans possess good sense, there are two things they must guard against. They should not get into the habit of considering things from the viewpoint of their personal feelings and prejudices, and they should avoid jumping to conclusions because of analogies or comparisons.

Such reasoning, based on either emotions of the moment, prejudices, or erroneous comparisons, is no safer than a leap in the dark.

The perception of these natives is aided by their intense desire to learn. In their eagerness to learn, however, they must guard against glossing over—or missing—some of the minor, but important, details of a subject or proposition. They are inclined to be intelligent in any matter other than their own feelings. They should be aware of this fact and do their best to view their emotions with more caution. It is hard to regard your own feelings impersonally, but with desire and the will to do so, a few lucky, determined Librans can accomplish it.

Imagination plays an important part in the life of Librans. They are natural daydreamers. They take keen delight in going over pet ideas in their minds. Romantic ideals become quite vivid in their imaginations. Excessive indulgence in such habits is apt to create the conditions for sad disillusionment in love, romance, and marriage. Bear in mind that good ideals are lovely things so long as they are possessable in reality as well. Imagination should be used to visualize the steps necessary for progress.

Libra gives its natives good powers of expression. Though they are somewhat self-willed and just thinkers, there are times when they lack continuity of purpose—they do not always stick with an idea or proposition to its logical conclusion. There are times when they appear to be evasive, even blind, and times when they show good ability to concentrate. Emotionally, they are impulsive. Think over and analyse impulses, just as any other idea or proposition. If Librans will do this, they may not always act in haste and repent in leisure. They may be content to dream about ideas and never carry them out. A minor setback could lead them to abandon an entire project.

Libras also have the faculty of intuition, which enables them to understand human nature. There are times when they can see through and understand the motives of others. They often take an intuitive dislike to certain people they meet, but they do not know why. Time usually proves their "hunch" was right. However, when it comes to their personal feelings and emotions, they are apt to ignore their intuition and act contrary to it. They must learn to understand this voice for it will materially aid their progress.

Libra birth brings a good physical constitution; but it is imperative that Librans exercise reasonable care in diet. They should avoid excesses. Their Sign rules the kidneys, back, and loins. They should also guard all periodical spells of moodiness and depression by seeking gaiety and diversion. They must avoid overdoing and attendant fatigue, nervousness, and irritability.

Native Librans enjoy travel, sports, recreation, dancing, and the theatre. Their artistic tastes must be satisfied and the fancies of their imagination catered to. They enjoy motion, rhythm, and the beautiful things in life and nature.

Indications show that the Libra-born are affectionate, tender, sympathetic, and warm in love. Their moods, however, vary according to their mental activity. They may appear poised and calm while hiding the intense warmth of an affectionate nature, but when conditions are ideal, they are expressive and demonstrative. Their feelings are easily hurt in love affairs, but they will endure much, and willingly sacrifice much, for those they love. They are often misunderstood by their lovers and may even be accused of being flirtatious, because they take an interest in many people. This frivolity is based on intellectual rather than physical interest. They enjoy meeting and talking with anybody whenever they get a chance. In all love and romantic ventures, it is advisable that they do not permit some of their ideals to prevent good, practical judgment. Librans must remember that, regardless of whom they love, they should accept the whole person, and not make a conquest just for certain characteristics that arouse temporary romantic interest. Until they learn this, they are apt to experience disillusionment in love affairs.

There should be reasonable, harmonious balance between natives of Libra and the objects of their affections from mental, emotional, physical, and idealistic viewpoints. If such balance does not exist, the Libra-born are inclined to lose interest. They must learn to heed the voice of their intuition, making sure to guard against all impulsiveness in romantic matters. The Libra nature, even though it is self-willed and independent, revolves around others. The ideal mate must be understanding, intellectual, sympathetic, patient, demonstrative, affectionate, and idealistic.

Indications show much love for children. This birthsign is not a barren one, but it does not give promise of many children during the course of life. Certain indications denote that the domestic life of these natives may not always be as harmonious and peaceful as they desire—or expect—it to be. This will not always be due to any particular fault of the native.

Their independent natures may cause them to be at variance with their parents. They are intensely devoted to their parents and relatives, but are not always understood by them. In the home, these natives want all comfort and beauty possible. The domestic life may, at times, be unsettled because of a desire for changes of scenery. Monotony bores them, so they should take a short trip now and then. When conditions permit, Libra-influenced people enjoy entertaining in their homes. During the last half of their lives, they are inclined to be more settled.

This chart indicates adaptability and talent. In fact, Libras may possess more active talents than they know what to do with. They may experience difficulty in discovering just what they are best equipped to do in this world. Regardless of their education, their experiences may lead them restlessly into many varying lines of diverse endeavours before they find themselves. They will lean towards the intellectual and artistic pursuits.

Libra people exceed in any capacity which may take them before the general public. Libra attorneys make good judges. The Libra-marked are also to be found in all sorts of entertainment work, for Libra is the natural Sign of beauty and imitation. Librans make good instructors, writers, doctors, architects, and aviators. Under ordinary circumstances, they are highly efficient in their work, and very ambitious, energetic, and successful.

Many Libra people are apt to get discouraged too quickly at times. They should make every effort to develop "stick-to-it-iveness".

Good earning power is indicated, but there is a tendency towards being a big spender. In partnerships, success will depend upon the type of partner. It is necessary for Libra people to exercise restraint over their feelings. They are capable of accomplishing much if given a free rein; they achieve a good degree of success by entering into business ventures for themselves. They are by nature thrifty. There are times when money is spent in response to a desire or impulse; then they must start saving all over again. It will pay well to develop a certain consistence in conservatism.

The Libra-charted are inclined to be somewhat speculative and it is advisable for them to be reasonably cautious in this matter so their natural impulsiveness will not lead them. Great risks should never be taken except for great stakes. Librans are often conservative in their ideas pertaining to investments, but their adventurous nature often urges them to have a small fling at some longer chance. They will achieve far more satisfactory results if they stick to such investments as government bonds, or transportation, aviation, and chemical stocks.

An attractive personality will bring many friends and acquaintances to the Libran in the course of his life. Many will be drawn because of the natural charm. Great loyalty to friends is shown here, but there is a deplorable tendency to be too critical at times. However the Libran's unusual understanding of human nature will bring many friends with their confidences.

These natives have every prospect of rising to the social position they desire. They should make the most of their natural charm. Their worst faults are a fondness for day-dreaming and a lack of tenacity. They must resist depression and be ever watchful to their health. Proper training will enable them to attain the full measure of their aims and ambitions. Librans have far more in their favour than against them, and it is up to the individual to apply his star-granted energy constructively for progress, success, and happiness in life.

The Libra Child

Libra children are generally very good-looking. The complexion is usually smooth and clear, and the hands and feet well shaped. Parents will find their Libra child very ardent in almost everything he or she does. One of the principal faults is that children of Libra find it hard to settle down into steady effort. The parent must urge this child to overcome vacillation. Don't be surprised if the Libra child is cheerful and then, suddenly, without apparent reason, depressed.

These children are exceedingly fond of music and art. They must have their minds constantly engaged; otherwise pent up energy may lead them into trouble.

The vitality is moderate, and the pathology shows that the nervous system may be depleted by jealousy and moodiness. Physical ailments from which they may suffer are indigestion, headache, backaches, and diseases of the stomach, liver, or kidneys. Libra children are easily thrown off balance in health, but yield readily to treatment.

Generally speaking, the Libra child will achieve greatest success if trained for work of an artistic nature. Parents should be careful about the selection of a career for their Libra-born because of Libra's tendency to drop one subject and start another. The best plan is to observe the child closely in the formative years. These children will be rather imitative and somewhat fickle because of their changeability. They are extreme in feelings and somewhat subject to negative moods, so proper early training is of great importance.

The Libra Wife

The Libra wife possesses one of the most interesting love natures in the Zodiac. The Sign has a decided feminine leaning, with the highest Venus influence prevailing. These women have delicate, spiritual appeal. A Libran is an ideal wife for a wealthy, successful man who is stimulated by union with a woman who is like an orchid. The Libra wife is exotic in appearance. Actually, these women are not as fragile as they appear. The Libra wife is a fine intellectual companion, wise in the ways of partnership. One of her special gifts is a talent for harmony. She attracts an interesting social circle. At the same time, she never neglects her own family, but gives them all the loving attention of which her gracious nature is capable.

The Libra wife is a luxury. She is usually quite attractive, and always has a group of admirers seeking her favours. While she requires a varied social life, she is too well-balanced to encourage indiscriminate flirtation, but if she were to find herself emotionally involved, her response would never be underhanded. This type of woman does not encourage scandal. Because she is so attractive, her life is sometimes more complicated than the existence of plainer women. Her passions are voluptuous, and demand a "quality setting." She is responsive, intuitive, and intellectual.

Her passionate response to married life is extremely satisfying, and in many respects she is the best suited of all the Zodiacal types to be a wife in the strictly personal sense of the word.

The Libra Husband

The Libra husband is not an easy man to please. The monotony of domesticity is not to his liking, but he is a passionate man and a respecter of tradition. The Libra husband is reasonable. He is a born judge, and no other Zodiacal type can order his life with so much wisdom. His superior ability to guide the destiny of the home is one of his greatest virtues. Negative Libra characters do not have this power. They have surface smoothness, but not the high intellectual development of which the best Libra men are capable. Libras provide well for their families and they seem to feel with the same intensity as a woman the necessity of elegance and luxury in the home surroundings.

The Libra husband is a passionate man, to whom love is a high art. His passions are overwhelming, and he rises to great heights in the expression of them.

This kind of husband would be deeply disappointed if he did not meet with satisfactory response to his passions. Even when the domestic partner is very agreeable, he might be tempted to seek variety. The Libra husband does not seek divorce unless the conditions of his life are not adjustable.

He has an instinctive distrust of the untried, and will strain with his judicial talents to guide domestic routine to satisfy his fastidious taste.

The Cusps of Libra

(If your birthday is not within the cusp of your Sign, the following does not apply to you.)

These persons were born in Libra with Virgo tendencies. The ruling planets are Venus and Mercury. This indicates that these people are intuitive, impulsive, and considerate. They are, at times, jovial and at other times depressed. Moments of depression come suddenly and for no apparent cause. They are ardent and sincere, but will have many heartaches and troubles in romantic affairs. Marriages brought about through emotion rather than love are seldom happy. These Librans should not marry early in life, and when they contemplate marriage, they should take considerable care in choosing a mate. More unhappy marriages are contracted by Librans than any other Sign.

They are neat in dress and take pride in their surroundings. They are endowed with so many talents that they are apt to follow the wrong one and engage in a line of business for which they are not suited. They have the faculty of seeing both sides of any problem and their judgments can be relied upon. It is desirable for them to follow their hunches and impressions. They are well-liked by many and will make many friends throughout life. If they do not scatter their energy they will become successful and prosperous individuals.

If the birthday occurs from October 19th through October 22nd

These persons are natives of Libra with Scorpio tendencies. The ruling planets are Venus and Mars. With their magnetic powers they could become outstanding sources of inspiration to others. They are skilful, conscientious, and original. They are of cheerful disposition and use good judgment. They are rather impatient to succeed, and are constantly devising means to improve themselves and their environment. They possess originality of thought and should be successful organizers, managers, inventors, or directors. They are rather unconventional, and the mysteries of life and nature appeal to them. They are not as punctual as they should be, are quick to anger, but easily pacified. They like to be praised and complimented openly. They enjoy popularity with their friends, who assist them. These of this cusp have ideals and ambitions which, with a little encouragement, may frequently be attained.

The Decanates of Libra

If the birthday is between September 23rd and September 30th

Your ruling and personal planet is Venus. It is the symbol of love and beauty, giving constancy to the affections and denotes a sensitive, generous, perceptive, and artistically well-balanced mind, capable of taking a dispassionate view of life. You possess a good sense of comparison, being able to see both sides of a subject clearly. Praise and admiration will help you develop the more positive tendencies of your own nature. A magnanimous spirit is indicated by the double influence of Venus in this Horoscope.

If your birthday is between October 1st and October 11th

Your personal planet is Saturn, which is the symbol of time. This planet is restricting in its influence, and governs the meditative tendencies. It inclines to make its subjects careful, patient, and considerate. Saturn is chiefly concerned with fixity of all affairs that may be classed as concrete conditions. Its powers lie in stability, endurance, tenacity and perseverance. Gain through thrifty methods and careful investments is indicated. You have a capacity for kindness and sympathy.

If the birthday is between October 12th and October 22nd

Your personal planets are Uranus and Mercury. Uranus, symbol of Air signifies originality and gives its natives the ability to become advanced thinkers. It inclines them towards the profound, mystical, and more serious problems of life. Mercury is known as the symbol of knowledge and truth, and rules the rational part of the mind. It indicates an alert, perceptive, and commanding personality.

The Degrees of Libra

September 23rd

You possess a forceful and progressive spirit. You are kind-hearted and hospitable, and would excel in the medical profession or charity work. You can also be successful in dealing with property and insurance. An elderly relative may be particularly helpful. One aspect in this Horoscope indicates possible disappointment in a love affair.

September 24th

You are kindhearted and artistic, but lacking in self-confidence. You have a humane and sympathetic disposition that will make you a champion of civil liberties. You will always take the side of those in less fortunate circumstances. Your intuition and inspiration are well blended.

September 25th

You possess an active and inquiring mind. You are just, sympathetic, affable, and socially inclined. You are easy-going, fond of luxury, your home, and your relations. You have marked literary talents. You have the natural ability to make friends readily because of your pleasing personality, but you must use more than ordinary precautions when signing legal documents.

September 26th

You possess a loving disposition and you are steadfast in your friendships and affections. You can be depended upon to fulfil your obligations. One aspect in this Horoscope indicates the ability to achieve fame in the fields of medicine, philosophy, psychology, and humanitarian pursuits.

September 27th

You possess a critical mind. On the other hand you must beware of deception when negotiating or contracting for the purchase of anything of value. Your keen interest in the welfare of others may cause you to become careless of your own. Do not permit your highly sensitive nature to make you too faultfinding of your close associates.

September 28th

You are idealistic and romantic, with a tendency to be self-sacrificing. You are very devoted to your loved ones. You could make a great success in the social world. You are best suited for an artistic or professional career, rather than for business or commercial pursuits.

September 29th

You possess a quick mind and a fertile imagination. You may become too impulsive for your own good and should exercise caution. Curb a tendency to indulge yourself in food and drink. One aspect in this Horoscope shows a tendency to scatter your talents and energies in too many directions at the same time.

September 30th

You possess a resourceful, capable, and practical mind. You are endowed with great courage, but have a somewhat fatalistic outlook on life. You are a born leader and possess the energy and ability to rule situations and command the respect of your friends and associates. One aspect in this Horoscope indicates danger through misplaced confidence. Success is assured from dealings with elderly relatives in business ventures.

October 1st

You possess a tactful, sympathetic, and proud nature. You show a great love for fine clothing and a desire to be well-dressed at all times. You possess natural aristocratic bearing and may have a tendency to attach too much significance to outward appearances. One aspect in this Horoscope indicates the possibility of loss through treachery in love and business.

October 2nd

You have a capable and sympathetic nature. You show a great deal of adaptability and unusual aptitude at reproducing and imitating. One aspect in this Horoscope shows that you have great love for children. You have a desire to gain wide recognition for your artistic talents.

October 3rd

You possess a gentle and retiring nature, full of sympathy and understanding. You are an excellent judge of human nature and a loyal friend. Special care should be taken with your health. You may benefit from an inheritance. You should be on guard against financial loss through deceit.

October 4th

You have a progressive mind. You must guard against misdirecting your energies. Difficulties in romance and marriage are indicated. A penchant for speculation must be moderated. Your fine intellect and keen understanding of life's problems would make you an excellent judge.

October 5th

You possess a receptive nature with psychic tendencies. You are resourceful and self-reliant. You will derive many benefits from strangers. You are fond of mysteries and display a love of argument and debate. This will add greatly to your store of knowledge and become a prime factor in developing your mental faculties and social background. You are very affectionate and magnanimous to your immediate family.

October 6th

You possess an adventurous spirit and a star-influenced desire to travel and visit strange places. You are also fond of social activity. You are very impressionable and likely to suffer through deception. You are versatile and have a quick mind; you ought to exercise concentration of purpose in order to achieve happiness.

October 7th

You are ambitious and enterprising, with a well-balanced personality. Business associates should be chosen with care. Some danger exists which arises from attempted exploitation of others. The influence of the mother is strong in this degree. You are an excellent speaker and would do well in politics. An urge to speculate should be curbed.

October 8th

You possess an energetic personality, with latent ability to be successful in the promotion of large industrial combinations. This powerful degree also denotes much talent for scientific endeavour. Curb a tendency to take needless risk in business and personal affairs.

October 9th

You are capable and courageous, but may be overly critical of your friends and associates. You usually get what you go after, regardless of opposition. You may experience some trouble through servants or co-workers. Tone down a tendency to make erratic changes without good cause or reason.

October 10th

You are somewhat self-centred, obstinate, and extravagant where your own pleasures are concerned. You should restrain a strong tendency to lavish luxuries on those you wish to impress. Be careful when signing important documents or contracts. Financial loss through carelessness is shown.

October 11th

You are a clear thinker with an open mind and are willing to work hard to attain your goals. Through tact, perseverance, and courage you will overcome most of your obstacles. An inheritance usually comes to those born in this degree. You are attractive to the opposite sex in a rather basic manner.

October 12th

You possess a strong character and a fine intellect. You are a progressive person with some unusually fine ideas. You will be fortunate in many different ways. Care should be taken where important documents are concerned. Possible loss through carelessness is shown.

October 13th

You possess a well-balanced mind, great determination of

character, and a kind, affectionate nature. You have a magnetic personality and, at times, may be somewhat temperamental and headstrong. You may have a delicate constitution; you should not overexercise or go to extremes in mental exertion. You have excellent artistic and musical talents. Many profitable and lasting friendships will prove useful in attaining success and happiness.

October 14th

You possess an impulsive, alert, and generous disposition. You will take advantage of many opportunities, but self-indulgence and too many romantic alliances may adversely affect your health. Many persons born in this degree will travel far and wide. Good fortune will come from a keen intuition.

October 15th

You are industrious, ambitious, and of keen perception, but somewhat self-seeking. You will be liable to deception in some of your business transactions. The development of musical or scientific talents will bring monetary and personal rewards. Some danger of ill health from romantic and emotional troubles is shown.

October 16th

You possess a refined and artistic temperament. You have an active and progressive mind. Your health will need continual care. Domestic and business troubles will threaten from time to time. Many trials and tribulations are shown for persons of this degree. This is particularly true where the children of the natives are concerned.

October 17th

You possess remarkable artistic and musical talents and will be successful in these fields providing excesses in love of pleasure are controlled. You show great enterprise in acquiring the good things in life, and success will be attained mostly through your own efforts. Avoid both mental and physical overexertion, as one aspect indicates the possibility of nervous ailments.

October 18th

You are exceedingly clever, and possess a fine character. A versatile mind coupled with marked social instincts will enable you to gain success and recognition in public service. One aspect in this Horoscope indicates a tendency to be too apprehensive concerning the welfare of your loved one and friends. Learn moderation of this golden virtue, as it is apt to cause misunderstanding. Much affection for your parents is indicated.

October 19th

You are sympathetic and good-natured, thus, are likely to be imposed upon. You are financially fortunate, but sometimes too pleasure loving, which ascertains varying degrees of success and happiness. A great love of animals is shown by this degree. This may include horses, with the speculative tendency towards betting on them. Remember, lady luck is elusive.

October 20th

You possess an adventurous, mystic nature, and a scientific trend of thought. A great love of travel and the sea is also indicated. A magnanimous personality and a desire to help those who are in less fortunate straits may lead you into many strange experiences during your life. Studies of a scientific nature which can be used for the good of humanity and the alleviation of sorrow and suffering will bring success and happiness.

October 21st

You are frank, outspoken, and fond of travel and sports. You have a charming personality which is much admired by the opposite sex. Do not permit your fortunate qualities to make you conceited and arrogant. Your love of ease should be kept under control.

October 22nd

You are courageous, determined, ambitious, and desirous of public acclaim. Your intellectual faculties are well-developed, but care should be exercised when dealing with legal matters. Possible trouble through writing or signing documents is also shown. Being very impressionable, you will readily react to your environment. It is, therefore, necessary to select the right type of friends and companions.

Compatible and Incompatible Signs of Libra

The compatible and incompatible Signs for the Libra-born will yield a wealth of information as to just who should fit into the love-life and marriage plans of those born September 23rd to October 22nd. Although Libra is the marriage Sign by virtue of its relation to the Seventh House of the Zodiac, the fact that Libra is rising or strongly occupied in a Horoscope by no means implies that marriage will take place. Libra has an intense desire for sympathy, love, and understanding, and is hard to satisfy. Libra has a real interest in recreation, and this characteristic is shared by both men and women of the Sign. The women are romantic and tend to be "in love with love" rather than any particular person. They crave admiration and flattery even when they know it is merely flattery. There is no Sign quite as capable of believing what it knows to be untrue as Libra.

It is incorrect to say that Libra is an affectionate Sign. Actually Libra has an affectionate manner, tempered with selfishness. People's troubles are never quite real to Libra. It is a Sign which prefers to ignore ugliness and build a world of its own.

There is no doubt about the personal charm of Libra, which is never entirely lacking even in its negative representatives. Sometimes this charm is an unconscious one, but more often it is deliberately exerted in order to obtain help, favours, and protection. Libra women make ideal hostesses, but to be at their best they must have plenty of servants to do the actual work. Libra, though capable enough, dislikes manual labour, especially if it entails soiling the hands. Libra much prefers to snuggle back into a pile of cushions and press the bell.

The sexual side of marriage is not of primary importance to Libra women, though it sometimes appears to be so. The girls and young women of the Sign are usually surrounded by many admirers and obtain a reputation for flirting. In reality, they are seeking admiration. They are flattered at the attentions they receive but are in no hurry to give in, for that would spoil the good time. As a result, they play one admirer off against another, until finally they may lose them all. In this event, they remain unmarried or rush into marriage with the first available person. This little tragedy is played by a great many Libra women, and explains why Libra marriages are not, as a rule, really happy. In many cases the "first available person" is a man who may have been rejected by someone else or is wealthy and seeks someone to grace his home; and entertain and impress his important business acquaintances. In either event, the marriage is one of convenience for Libra, and the affection is on one side only. Usually, however, such a marriage is successful enough from a material viewpoint, for Libra women can be content with a dream world all their own. Libra men, on the other hand, are not so disposed to make the best of marriage. They find it extremely difficult to resist feminine wiles and flattery.

Librans are equable, generous, and sociable people, with quite a good deal of sentimentality. When an appeal is made to their generosity, they rarely have the heart to say "No!" They are exceptionally good mixers, and are at their best in social life. They are lovers of music and the arts, and there is nothing that pleases them so much as to be considered a connoisseur of these things.

Their intellectual qualities are often above average. They are also good conversationalists, and really delight in repartée.

As lovers they are sentimental—and susceptible! Thus, their emotions are capable of being worked upon, especially as they have somewhat passionate natures. They react badly to slights, and are often sensitive in this respect, and when they do form a bad impression of someone, it usually sticks. They are at their best when among artistic, sociable types, and they admire clever people. Thus is unconsciously shaped for them the kind of partner they should seek.

There are some types, however, with whom a happy marriage would be problematical.

The general comparisons are as follows:

Libra and Aries

This is a combination that is tops for perfection. The warmth and passion of Libra blends perfectly with the fiery, aggressive, impetuous qualities of Aries. Their rulers, Mars and Venus, are in good accord, and each seems to have what the other needs and wants. This will be even more evident if both persons are on the same cultural and intellectual level. Libra's refined and artistic temperament will be appreciated and reciprocated by Aries.

Libra and Taurus

These two are basically compatible so far as their positive qualities go. Both have the same or similar interests. Unfortunately, negative qualities are present in most people, too. In such instances, one marriage partner should have a good quality to offset the negative one in the other. In such case, all should go well unless both of these "Bull" partners get angry at the same time—then the tempest and the mad fury may cause an irreparable damage to the relationship, for when the Taurean gets really angry, he sees red!

Libra and Gemini

This looks like a good partnership all the way around. Mentally and artistically these two could "make the scene," and Libra can understand Gemini. There is just enough contrast to make things interesting—with little combat expected. Mercury (Gemini) and Venus (Libra) can make a very happy home together.

Libra and Cancer

Libra is too fond of freedom to endure the absorbing, confining tendencies of Cancer; and Cancer's interests are too concerned with home and family to understand the Libran love for social flitting. Libra would never be happy with a partner who is likely to sulk and sink into deep depression if things do not go the Cancer way. They would both pout—perhaps for days—over a routine family spat, so, perhaps, both should look for another partner more compatible with their own qualities and expectations.

Libra and Leo

These two have qualities that blend well. The Sun (Leo) and Venus (Libra) form an impressive aspect together. This is a luxurious aspect as both love luxuries. Both are artistically inclined, and both love attention and flattery. Leo demands these things to make him happy—Libra expects them as just due. Constant adulation and the centre of the stage at all times must be given to Leo; eventually Libra may get the idea that it's a bum piece of rubber that doesn't stretch both ways! If Libra is willing to always "play up" to Leo, these two could really "have a ball" in marriage.

Libra and Virgo

This is most likely a "no go" affair in many ways. All may appear well at first, while the sex novelty still possesses its shine and curiosity still stimulates, but when both land back on earth to take up life and its cold routine, there is little chance that either of these two will change his basic qualities willingly. If there is one thing that Libra resents, it is criticism; and with a Virgo mate (who takes top prize for knowing how to dish that out) poor Libra may bear soul-marks from the tongue lashing and carping of Virgo. Virgo insists on perfection while easy-going Libra hates detail. The conflict of interests here make this alliance no more than a dalliance.

Libra and Libra

Here is a truly "made-in-Heaven" combination, unless one had an incompatible Sign rising at birth. Both have the same basic interests and qualities, so there would be great mutual understanding between these two partners. While both like to be admired, and may cast a roving eye away from home territory, each is understanding of the other's motives. There is so much in favour of this combination and so little against it (a possible incompatible Sign rising in either birth chart) that there can really be no hesitation in advising it.

Libra and Scorpio

There is much sympathetic magnetism between these two Signs. While Scorpio is the more dominant Sign of the two, the Libran's beauty and sense of fair play appeal to Scorpio's good judgment. In Scorpio, Libra sees all the virtues she admires, for Scorpio's sex drive is all that Libra's hopes to be. There is much to recommend this union, for they have many sympathies in common. As lovers, Librans are sentimental and susceptible. This "accepting quality" appeals to Scorpio's dominant and possessive urges. As long as the pride of Scorpio is not wounded, Librans will find what they are looking for when they marry a Scorpio.

Libra and Sagittarius

Libra may not find it easy to cope with the free and easy-going Sagittarian philosophy of life. However, this is a good marital combination. Libras will get all the excitement they want if they marry Sagittarians. The only question is, will Libra's endurance be able to last with this partner? The Libran love of beauty, luxury, and social whirl appeals to the Sagittarian, but he will not be tied to the Libran apron-string. Sagittarius hates confinement, and will not tolerate bondage, whether it be legal or not, and will use all the means at his command to break through bonds.

Libra and Capricorn

These two personalities seem to be opposites on the surface, but the taciturn Capricorn is very much intrigued by Libra. If Libra does not find the steady Capricorn nature too boring, there is good chance here for a successful marriage. The Capricorn mate is far more liberal in his views on sex before marriage than he will be afterwards. Libra had better screen the social environment to suit Capricorn's views or there may be some embarrassing moments later on.

Libra and Aquarius

This could be a most suitable combination for marriage. Aquarians have perfect affinities for Librans. Their mutual love of beauty, society, and people help to make this an ideal union. One of the few possible causes for a misunderstanding is that the Aquarian mate is unpredictable at times, and, for no reason at all, may seek seclusion and refuse to communicate. In that event, the best thing to do would be to let him enjoy his solitude. He will soon revert to his lovable self, and all will be well if Libra doesn't insist on explanations.

Libra and Pisces

There is mutual attraction here, but it seldom lasts long. This is especially true under intimate circumstances. Pisces will be content with Libra's exclusive company, but Libra's love of social affairs may generate jealousy and disharmony in the intimate life. Libra can get along well with most people, but the Piscean is more discriminating, and therein lies the source of many Libra-Pisces disagreements. Nothing can make a Libran more miserable than a sulky, complaining Piscean.

Some Famous Persons Born in the Sign of Libra

Brigitte Bardot—French Actress
David Ben-Gurion—Israeli Statesman
Sarah Bernhardt—French Actress
Charles Boyer—Actor
Edward W. Bok—Philanthropist and Editor
Dwight D. Eisenhower—Commander and President
William Faulkner—Novelist
Henry L. Mencken—Editor and Writer
William Penn—Statesman
Eleanor Roosevelt—US Stateswoman
Mohandas Gandhi—Indian Statesman
Lillian Gish—Actress
Helen Hayes—Actress
Vladimir Horowitz—Pianist
Thomas W. Lamont—Banker
Walter Lippmann—Social Writer
Groucho Marx—Comedian
Ed Sullivan—Columnist
Gen. Paul Von Hindenburg—German Statesman

8

SCORPIO

October 23rd–November 21st

The Sign Scorpio, in its symbolical aspect, symbolizes death and deceit. It is the allegorical Serpent of matter, mentioned in Genesis as tempting Eve. Hence the so-called fall of man from Libra, the point of equilibrium, to degradation and death by the deceit of Scorpio. No wonder the primitive mind, when elaborating this symbol, tried to express a spirit of retaliation.

The Sign Scorpio typifies the generative organs of the Grand Man, and consequently represents the sexual or procreative system of humanity. It is the emblem of generation and life; therefore, the natives of Scorpio excel in the fruitfulness of the seminal fluids, and this creates a corresponding increase of desire.

A distinct reference to the fruitfulness of this Sign will be found in Gen. xxx: 10-11, wherein Leah, when she beheld the birth of Zilpah's son, exclaimed, "A troop cometh."

Scorpio upon the esoteric planisphere is occupied by Gad, of whom the dying Jacob says, "Gad, a troop shall overcome him: but he shall overcome at the last" (Gen. XL: 19); intimating the fall of man from a state of innocence and purity through the multitude of sensual delights, and his final victory over the realms of matter as a spiritual entity. This Sign represents the physical plane of the attributes of procreation.

It contains the mystery of sex, and the secrets of the ancient phallic rites.

Scorpio is the second emanation of the watery Trigon, and is the constellation of Mars.

The mystical gem of Scorpio is the topaz, the natural talisman of those born under this influence.

The fortunate day is Tuesday.

The fortunate numbers are three and five.

Their best colour is dark red.

Best locations for success are near water.

Upon the intellectual plane, the Sign Scorpio signifies the generation of ideas; hence those dominated by this influx possess an inexhaustible resource of ideas and suggestions.

Their active, evolutionary minds are ever busy with some new concept, and their brains are full of inventions. They possess keen perception, fine intuitional powers, and a positive will. Hence they excel as medical practitioners, chemists, and surgeons. In the various departments of the surgical art, natives of this Sign have no equal. In addition to this mechanical ability, they are endowed with a powerful, fruitful, magnetic life force, which they sympathetically transmit to their patients. This is why they become such successful physicians. Sexual desire is naturally strong, hence they have the potential for excess in this direction.

Scorpio natives have an attractive, magnetic, and dynamic personality, but they are quite difficult to understand because of a tendency to be secretive. Under ordinary circumstances, they are likeable, and capable of influencing and soothing others. The personality, if properly developed, will prove a strong factor in their efforts and endeavours to attain success. It may prove to their advantage to become more expressive.

Ordinarily, they are courteous, generous, loyal, sympathetic, and patient. However, if they are aroused, there is no fury like the fury of a Scorpio. They not only get angry, but become obstinate and headstrong as well. They can speak bitterly and cuttingly, losing all appreciation of the sensibilities of themselves or others. When this happens they become cynical, self-willed, and selfish. They should do all within their power to avoid this type of expression, as it may be the cause of much heartache and sorrow.

The Scorpio-born have the class of mind which will enable them, with effort, to attain the degree of self-control essential to their progress. They are, then, sincere and may be depended upon. Their friends will be inclined to rely on them, and will often appeal to the Scorpio native for help when faced with disturbing situations and personal problems.

Their powers of observation are keen. They possess the ability to meditate. They are independent thinkers, and not inclined to take the other fellow's opinion as final without investigation. They rarely advance an opinion unless it is asked for by others, except in case of emergency. Where emergency exists, Scorpio people think and act simultaneously.

The more sensitive types may lose all sense of self-composure and become incapable of constructive action. Those who react this way should make every possible effort to change their ways. It is true that they are individuals with intense feeling and emotion. Nature has a method of compensation for all things, and in their case, they are furnished with all the essential qualities of mind, which, if properly applied, will enable them to apply rational control to their emotion.

With their keenness, things seldom escape their notice. They have the ability to learn things easily. When their feelings are not aroused, they can perceive the realistic value of their own ideas and impulses. Their reflective minds cause them to daydream sometimes, but, as a rule, they use their imagination to visualize facts. Their good memory springs primarily from the fact that they consciously and unconsciously pay close attention to the details of any proposition. They have fairly good powers of self-expression and make interesting conversationalists when they so desire, but as a rule, they are apt to be quite reserved in their opinions and judgment, unless it is asked for by others. They possess the type of mind that absorbs facts quickly. They have the qualities of persistency and determination of purpose which enables them to overcome many obstacles in life.

They are not mentally impulsive, but their feelings play an important part in their life. Their personal reaction to their emotions makes it most difficult for them to judge matters impersonally once the emotional thermometer rises. Once they are aroused, they are apt to be very outspoken. Calling their attention to this fact is not fault-finding, but only an effort to help them understand themselves. The corrective measures can only be applied after they understand their faults.

They have an active faculty of inspiration. There are times when inspired ideas flash into their consciousness. Some of the world's most progressive men and women have been born under the Sign of Scorpio. They were inspired beings and they worked out their inspired ideas. The same can be learned by all Scorpios—to act upon inspirational ideas and bring them to fulfilment.

They also have a good insight into human nature. It gives them an awareness of truth, and makes them difficult individuals to deceive. Their intuition often gives them foreknowledge of impending events.

The greatest asset of these natives is their power of will and determination. It enables them to overcome many obstacles which would compel others to give up. They should endeavour to keep their reason in the face of intense emotional crises. They have the type of mind which will enable them to go far in life, if they will but learn to direct and apply mental energies wisely.

This birthsign presides over the organs of reproduction, and the various glands of the body. By reaction, the head and throat are susceptible to minor ailments, thus it is advisable to avoid exposure to common colds. These natives are fond of the good things of life. Reasonable care should be taken to avoid a fondness for too much rich food, sweets, and alcohol.

Many of the major ailments of Scorpio people could be avoided by the use of judgment in diet. Physically these natives possess a fairly rugged constitution, but it is not advisable to overtax it. If the law of moderation is applied, there will be no worry about health. Indications in this chart show a great fondness for recreational activities. There is also a deep appreciation of art and the beautiful things of life.

Travel, too, is enjoyed, though most Scorpio people get tired of too much of it.

The emotional nature is deep and intense, and the love nature is affectionate, somewhat aggressive at times, sympathetic, deep, and passionate. The Scorpio's feelings in love matters can be their best friend or their worst enemy.

These people are extremely serious and intensely devoted to those they love.

They are not always sure of themselves in romantic affairs. Once their love is constructively aroused, acknowledged, and returned, they become happy, affectionate, magnetic, and they radiate a most pleasant personality. It is advisable that these natives do their utmost to avoid unreasonable and unwarranted jealousy, because they are apt to become selfish. They evince poor judgment when their feelings get the upper hand. This will, no doubt, lead to many misunderstandings and disappointments in romantic matters.

The Scorpio's affectionate, aggressive, and passionate nature requires a normal expression and outlet. Love acts as an inspiration for the progress of these natives. It helps them to take an interest in their work, and stimulates their desires and ambition for accomplishment.

When the planetary aspects blend to a reasonable degree, their friendships are lasting, and free of the misunderstandings that usually plague relationships.

It is impossible for love to live with excessive selfishness and jealousy. It is evident that the Scorpio native is far happier in the marriage state than when single. These people must guard against traits which tend to destroy the very foundation of all they care for.

This birthsign is known as a fruitful one and gives promise of children. People of this Sign usually have an intense love for them but are strongly advised not to be too indulgent with them.

It is necessary that the emotional and domestic life be as ideal and harmonious as possible for Scorpios, as domestic matters play an important part in their lives. They desire a permanent state of affairs. They get much enjoyment from the comforts of their home, and want the best they can possibly afford in its furnishings. They feel pride in their home surroundings, and endeavour to keep them attractive and artistic. They have the natural qualifications of a good host or hostess. The Scorpio person is usually active, industrious, and quite capable. They are naturally ambitious, efficient, conscientious, and sincere in their efforts. Whenever they do anything, they desire to do it well. Though they have independent natures, they are capable of efficiently executing orders. They do not, however, like to feel that they are being forced to do anything.

Scorpio is a loyal, dependable, and trustworthy employee. If in business for themselves they are capable of managing affairs with a good degree of success.

Their particular intellectual talents enable them to stick to a proposition until it proves successful. In a general analysis of this Sign, it is impossible to say just what kind of work they are particularly suited for. This information must be determined by the individual's aspects in their natal chart, and since no two people in all the world are exactly alike in every respect, the personal Horoscope, cast and analysed for a Scorpio native, will give the truest advice.

Men and women of this Sign are found in all types of work, and nearly all of them have good business ability. In partnership matters they usually get along fairly well, especially when there is no occasion for serious domination. They will often shoulder more than their share of responsibility when handled tactfully.

This birthsign has a natural affinity for financial matters. This does not mean that all Scorpio people are financial successes, but they have good earning ability. Naturally, the more conservative type will amass the greater wealth. The weaker type of Scorpio can save to a certain extent, but is inclined to be an impulsive spender. They may save for a definite purpose and be doing all right; but when they see something they like, and want—they buy it.

It follows that this type will not be able to amass much money in the course of their life. The true art in back of all financial success and security lies in one's ability to put money to work. There are many Scorpio people who are clever in money matters and make good investments.

It must be admitted that in most Scorpio natives there is a speculative streak. Generally speaking, Scorpios have their share of financial reverses, but most of them seldom get in dire financial trouble. Investments in government bonds and the stocks and bonds of large industrial corporations usually prove quite profitable. Some of these natives make good in real estate and mining ventures.

Scorpios are capable of leading an active social life with a good degree of success. Their greatest obstacle is their own emotional nature. They must learn to understand and to control their emotions, and avoid becoming too headstrong and temperamental. Envy, jealousy, and selfishness need continual efforts to be overcome. These natives have the power of will and determination to overcome all obstacles. They can reach their desired pinnacles of success financially if they will but apply the conservative principles of their nature and avoid impulsive extravagance. It is up to them to apply themselves wisely and attain their full measure of success.

The Scorpio Child

Scorpio children will develop according to the way they are trained. They are always ready to take up an argument, either in their own behalf or for someone else. They are never content with half measures and will always go to extremes, good or bad. They are not underhanded and operate in the open and above-board. They have an uncertain temper; this should be taken in hand by the parent at an early age. Efforts should be made to instil within them a tolerant attitude. Much care should be taken to teach the Scorpio child sex hygiene, because this group is under the planetary influence that rules the generative organs. It is essential the parents see to it that their Scorpio child is physically and morally clean.

The fundamental vitality is strong, but wasting or scattering of life forces will be most detrimental to the health. This child should not partake of highly seasoned foods, and should have rest and fresh air in abundance. They are subject to ruptures, toxic diseases, haemorrhoids, and sometimes prostatic stricture. They develop diseases of the blood, fevers, and inflammation. They must be protected from the possibility of burns, scalds, and mishaps due to carelessness. Since these children are usually endowed with strong vitality, the above-mentioned ailments need not develop. Scorpio children are very temperamental, and can be quite vindictive. They are subject to emotional extremes. The parent should be watchful for, and guard against, the development of a nasty temper and suspicion. They are boldly courageous, with an inclination to be overventuresome. These children usually develop a firm, yet delicate, touch, making them very skilful with their hands. This is a necessary requirement for surgeons and dentists; they could succeed in either of these professions. These children are inclined to have an "all-or-nothing" attitude, and it will be very beneficial to train and develop the child along the lines of moderation.

The Scorpio Wife

The Scorpio wife is one whose deepest feminine instincts are aroused by the functions of being a wife. She takes marriage seriously, and has an old-fashioned reverence towards domestic responsibilities as long as she is in love with her husband. Should this condition change, she follows, without thought of consequences, the dictates of her heart. Happy Scorpio wives are loyal and courageous, and need no hothouse atmosphere to keep their love in bloom.

They enjoy responsibility, and a large family is a delight to them. These women are very capable. Once they are settled into domestic life, they put all of the energy of their passionate nature into the home. They have the gift of homemaking, and frequently organize a much better home than the Cancer or Taurus women who are famous for their homemaking instincts.

The Scorpio woman loves luxury, and has considerable taste in decorating. She is blunt and fearless in character, doing everything passionately from the depths of her being. Her devotion to her husband is wholehearted, and she idolizes those she loves. Her reactions to life are intensely realistic, and she sees her man exactly as he is. Since she is neither shy nor tactful, she expresses herself with the greatest force. Her sexual appetite is large, and she requires vigorous satisfaction. The Scorpio person is inclined to excess. While the moral sense rebels against the animal appetites, satisfaction usually comes first and repentance afterwards. It takes a very virile man, with a deep sympathy for sexual indulgence, to satisfy the Scorpio wife.

The Scorpio Husband

The Scorpio husband is one of the most difficult to live with in peace and harmony. The only way this can be accomplished is for the wife of a Scorpio man to be receptive to his every wish, and follow his instructions with complete obedience. He is a typical old-fashioned "Lord-of-the-Manor" and can be just as tyrannical and overbearing in his home as he is in everyday life.

Many astrological warnings have been given about marriage to a Scorpio man with bad aspects in the seventh house of marriage. He is too extreme in his love life.

The Scorpio man, himself, is often successful and able to support a wife and a large family, but his personal passion and the possessive attitude of his devotion can prove to be a strain on the most devoted family. No matter how much love and attention he receives, he will remain suspicious.

The depths of his affection for his wife and children are genuine, but he cannot seem to curb his inherent jealousy. Such selfish love is bound to cheat itself as the unhappy Scorpio man makes his stubborn way through life.

Sexual excesses are often a part of the negative aspects of this Sign. As in the case of the Scorpio woman, the Scorpio man has a strong moral side to his nature. He suffers deeply for his indulgences and always makes inward promises of temperance after the appetites have been satisfied.

The Cusps of Scorpio

(If your birthday is not within the cusp of your Sign, the following does not apply to you.)

If the birthday is from October 23rd through October 25th
The native was born in Scorpio with Libra tendencies. The ruling planets are Mars and Venus. This denotes that great importance is placed upon wealth; there is much admiration for those who hold positions of authority and power. They like to be among people of culture and refinement. They are aggressive, determined, and somewhat critical. Self-assurance and a positive attitude may lead others to believe that the native is unsympathetic, but he really is not as difficult as his attitude appears. These natives are not easily convinced against their will, and frequently ignore advice. They are reasonably cautious and possess good judgment. They generally accomplish what they set out to do. Each effort

spurs them on to greater achievement. Some of their best qualities are developed in competition, as they like opposition. They are usually excellent conversationalists, but also good listeners. They are capable and can accomplish more by themselves than in a group. They are distinguished in appearance. A quick temper and a restless nature should be restrained to retain poise and good-naturedness.

If the birthday is from November 19th through November 21st

The native was born in Scorpio with Sagittarius tendencies. The ruling planets are Mars and Jupiter. They are positive and determined. They show a fondness for travel and will have many adventures. Their word is law, and they will adhere to it, unless they discover they were wrong. They will make sacrifices for those they love, and are usually more generous to others than to themselves. They possess occult, mediumistic tendencies and can become successful clairvoyants.

They are quick-tempered, high-strung, sensitive, and are easily hurt. Those who are fortunate to win them as friends may be assured that these natives will always be loyal companions who will stick to their friends through thick and thin.

The Decanates of Scorpio

If the birthday is between October 23rd and October 31st

The personal and ruling planet is Mars, which is doubly forceful in this aspect and tends to bring out the more dominant, dictatorial, and positive side of the nature. It is important that these natives practice patience and understanding. An active body and a highly impetuous and spirited nature is shown by the double aspect of the planet Mars in this Horoscope. There is the determination to have their way in all matters, so it is highly advisable to practise restraint for best results.

If the birthday is between November 1st and November 11th

The personal planets for this decanate are Jupiter and Neptune, considered somewhat conflicting. Jupiter is known to be the symbol of Good Fortune and Blessing, while Neptune is known as The Spiritual Awakener. This would indicate that these natives have dualistic tendencies and a very changeable and unpredictable nature. Their greatest battles will be with themselves. Their natural negative and positive qualities were definitely marked at an early age. This should help them to overcome and eliminate their adverse tendencies, and constructively and beneficially develop the more positive ones.

If the birthday is between November 12th and November 21st

The personal orb for this decanate is the Moon, which is the great moulder of character. She is the Queen Mother of Heaven, and has chief rule over the earth. This orb indicates a highly emotional, imaginative, changeable, and proud nature.

Marked ability in artistic and dramatic fields of endeavour is indicated. This native's personality contains a sense of romance, imagination, and mystery. Popularity and recognition will be gained through the magnetic personality and sympathetic nature. The combination of the Moon and Mars is indeed a fortunate one, since Mars, being aggressive and powerful, strives to force its natives to attain their objectives.

The Degrees of Scorpio

October 23rd

These natives possess a determined, yet flexible nature. Capability in dealing with the masses, and success through association with influential and prosperous friends is indicated. Proper education will equip them for a life of public service. They are not receptive to any dealings that do not coincide with their own inherent sense of justice and fair play. It is necessary that they learn to rely upon their own judgment.

October 24th

Strong will power and a commanding, energetic personality is shown here. Initiative and good business acumen will enable this native to progress rapidly in the commercial world. A tendency towards extravagance should be curbed at all times. These natives should realize and understand the value of personal possessions. An ardent, highly emotional nature, full of adventure and wild dreams, should be moderated.

October 25th

These Scorpio-born possess a clever and perceptive mind, which coupled with great intensity and sincerity of purpose may tend to make them over-critical and intolerant when their plans and ambitions are interfered with. They can avoid the development of this aspect by carefully analysing the inevitable reactions and consequences. Physical activities should be encouraged as much as possible in order to offset the possibility of over-taxing the mind by too much study.

October 26th

Those of this degree possess a retiring, studious, and chaste nature. An envy streak, which may become apparent from time to time, should be curbed. These natives are fond of literature, music, and art. They should make the most of their intellectual and commercial training. Self-confidence and the ability to see the viewpoints of others must be nourished and developed. Due to lack of emotional stability, these people may be hard to understand at times.

October 27th

You are endowed with an intellectual, scientific, and experimental mind. An excellent conversationalist, you should enjoy great popularity. An independent, orderly spirit coupled with a keen sense of diplomacy is also shown. These fine qualities will make it easy for you to get what you want from your friends and associates in life. One aspect in this Horoscope indicates the possibility of becoming self-centred and easily spoiled.

October 28th

Those of this birthday possess a splendid character, a sympathetic nature, and deep emotions. Being instinctively intellectual, they may show a tendency to become too reserved and serious. It is essential that they have a happy environment and associate with persons they can look up to. Outdoor activities and athletics are advisable. Their emotional temperament needs patient and understanding treatment.

October 29th

A clever, critical mind and a sympathetic nature is shown for these natives. A strong will power and fiery temper may give them some cause for concern during their life. Keen interest in literature, art, and writing will endow them with the qualities of an intellectual personality. They should develop the practical side of their nature in order to attain the greatest measure of success and happiness in life.

October 30th

These natives possess an unselfish and charitable disposition. They have strong, healthy bodies, and show great interest and skill in sports. They should learn the value of concentration in order to overcome a tendency to attempt to do too many things at one time. They are fluent conversationalists, and could become prolific writers. A passionate sex nature is also shown.

October 31st

These Scorpio-born possess pleasing dispositions, and alert, thoughtful, intuitive minds. A tendency to assume leadership regardless of consequences should be curbed. They are industrious and self-reliant and possess a highly ambitious and determined nature. There are some difficulties through the opposite sex indicated.

November 1st

You possess unusual mental qualities and the ability to develop the mind along intellectual and scientific pursuits. You display independence of thought, and have a steady, forceful disposition. One aspect in this chart indicates a desire to defy convention and become a bold innovator. An inherent desire to become self-willed should be guarded against.

November 2nd

These natives are endowed with a shrewd and alert mind. They are deeply moved by their higher sympathies, and can become champions of human rights. There may be a tendency to meddle into the affairs of other people. While this may be prompted by the most charitable intentions, many disappointments are indicated until the native learns that life's greatest rewards come to those who mind their own business first. Success is shown in the fields of art, letters, and science.

November 3rd

You of this birthday possess an impulsive and rather radical disposition. A brilliant mind and excellent intuitive powers are also indicated. This combination of mental qualities is usually found in persons who attain outstanding success and recognition in public work. An inherent tendency to be impulsive and erratic should be controlled. These characteristics, if permitted to develop, can prove detrimental.

November 4th

This chart shows you to be sensitive, impressionable, and inquisitive. You love travel, and long journeys to distant lands are indicated. At times, you may become hard to manage and show signs of developing a cross temper. This should be checked constantly. One aspect in this Horoscope shows an extravagant nature, which should be curbed.

November 5th

These natives possess a keen intellectual mind coupled with excellent powers of concentration. A tendency to assume a too serious outlook upon life should be avoided. A bright, cheerful atmosphere and the company of superiors will greatly aid in eliminating this aspect. A highly magnetic personality and an independent nature will make for great success in the business world, especially if the native will strive to overcome some of the more negative tendencies shown in his Horoscope.

November 6th

You Scorpio-born possess a keen mind, and a calm, peaceful

attitude towards life. A charming, open-minded manner coupled with humanitarian principles will endear these fortunate people to all. Gain is indicated through influential friendships. One aspect in this chart shows a tendency to take good fortune too lightly. Learn to appreciate your many natural gifts, and use them constructively.

November 7th

Those of this degree possess an astute, practical, and intuitive mind. An artistic temperament with marked humanitarian principles will bring many lasting and influential friendships in life. These natives are generous, of good appearance, kindly mannered, and charitably inclined. One aspect here indicates a tendency to shirk responsibility and get by with little personal effort. It must be remembered that diligent application of the natural talents is necessary to success.

November 8th

A benevolent, charitable, and sympathetic nature is indicated for these natives. A desire to help all those who ask assistance can result in extravagant expenditure far beyond personal means. These natives are subject to flattery, and can easily become the prey of designing friends and associates. One aspect in this Horoscope indicates a tendency to become conceited.

November 9th

The natives of this birthday possess an original, daring, and masterful nature. Strong will power coupled with a desire to have their own way should be curbed at all times. A diversified education along commercial lines will be of great advantage. Much success in the business world is indicated. By exercising tolerance and patience, a restless disposition can be subdued.

November 10th

These natives possess a pleasing personality and splendid intuitive powers. A highly emotional nature can develop into an uncontrollable temper unless constant and patient efforts are made to overcome this aspect. There is a tendency to daydream and brood too much if left alone for any great length of time. They should associate with persons of their own class. Above all they should see that they do not become the victims of a martyr fixation.

November 11th

These Scorpio-born possess an energetic nature and great skill in the execution of duties. Persistence and determination, even in the face of difficulties, will bring success and financial independence for many persons born on this day. They usually choose their friends and associates discriminately, and display considerable reserve at all times. One aspect in this chart indicates impulsiveness, which should be toned down.

November 12th

Those of this degree possess a sensitive, idealistic nature and a friendly, kindhearted disposition. Certain planetary aspects indicate a tendency to be too generous for their own welfare. They should learn to recognize the true from the false, and remember that while charity is a great virtue, it should be given only to those truly deserving of it. Fondness of travel by water is shown, and there are indications of a long sea voyage which may result in a profitable business association.

November 13th

Great ambition and a quick, perceptive mind are indicated. A magnetic personality will bring many respected and influential friendships in life. You should curb an exaggerated sense of self-importance. A desire to make changes frequently is indicated. Success will come through the possession of property.

November 14th

The natives of this birthday possess a serious, aspiring nature coupled with great intellectual capability. They are profound and practical. A strong sense of independence and a desire to help those in less fortunate circumstances is also indicated. At times they may become too magnanimous for their own good, and must learn the value of financial conservatism. They show marked respect for their superiors. These natives will create their own destiny.

November 15th

You are endowed with an expansive and genial personality. You can attain much popularity in your social life through your charm and excellent powers of conversation. The emotional nature is stable. An artistic temperament coupled with a magnetic personality will make for success in a professional rather than a business career.

November 16th

You possess a romantic nature, and can become an idealist and dreamer. A rather "hard-to-please" complex is shown at times. This is due to a self-centred point of view. You show a decided preference to associate with persons much more prosperous than yourself. This tendency should be modified as there is grave danger of suffering severe financial loss at some time in your life due to misplaced confidence.

November 17th

Those of this birthchart possess an adaptable, versatile, and intuitive mind. The value of concentration of purpose should be realized. One aspect here indicates a tendency to tire easily, and drift aimlessly from one thing to another. You should complete one thing at a time. Your charming personality coupled with a good sense of humour will attract many friendships.

November 18th

A resourceful, energetic, prudent, sincere, and intuitive nature is bestowed upon these natives. Much success is foreseen for many persons born on this day, especially in law, journalism, and business. However, discrimination between right and wrong will be necessary in order to avoid serious loss. Marked determination to succeed, regardless of risk, may cause the native to work alike for good or evil.

November 19th

Those of this degree possess an original, enterprising mind, and a harmonious, contented disposition. One aspect in this Horoscope indicates that you may be easily satisfied, and because of this trait may lack the incentive to overcome obstacles. You should learn self-confidence and practical methods of achieving success. Cheerful companions and successful friends should be acquired.

November 20th

These natives are endowed with wholesome charm and great magnetism. They have inventive minds, and show originality in their ideas and undertakings. They may be susceptible to colds and it is necessary that all precautions be taken to avoid draughts and sudden changes of temperature. An inherent desire for speculation should be curbed. Success in the field of science is shown.

November 21st

These Scorpio-born possess a bright, cheerful, and affectionate nature. Generosity, kindness of heart, and a desire to help others is indicated. One aspect in this Horoscope shows a marked tendency to daydream, and a desire to do too many things at one time. By scattering their forces, these natives are likely to become "Jacks-of-all-trades and masters of none". They must learn concentration of purpose, and the importance of completing one task before starting another. A magnetic love nature will bring much popularity with the opposite sex.

Compatible and Incompatible Signs of Scorpio

The Sign Scorpio is by far the strongest and most extreme of all. The natives of no other Sign can rise to such great heights or sink to such abysmal depths as those of Scorpio. It is a strongly sexed Sign, and the Scorpio native can stand long continued excesses which would quickly break down the constitution of most other Signs. As might be expected, the outlook is usually a markedly sexual one, though it is not invariably so, for the ability for continence and self-control is quite as great as the desire for self-indulgence.

The Scorpio native has an eye to material things, and frequently contracts a marriage that offers considerable worldly advantages. The Scorpio nature is not an intensely proud one, and marriage is often entered into in order to obtain money and position. In many cases, the Scorpio native tends to seek affection or adventure away from home, but he never allows such entanglements to disturb his domestic life.

Perhaps the chief faults of Scorpio are intense jealousy and a domineering disposition. There is nothing of the "wishy-washy" about Scorpio women. They have character, a keen—if sometimes peculiar—sense of justice, and the capacity for deep and lasting loves and hates.

As might be expected from the extreme nature of the Sign, marriage can be either very happy or entirely the reverse. A seriously afflicted Scorpio tends to evolve fits of gloom or depression, and a persecution mania is quite common, according to the degree of affliction.

Its rulership over the sex organs make it an important factor in cases of sexual excess.

Scorpians have great strength of character, and a large supply of energy with which to put over their personality. It is this great amount of vital energy which is the real crux of their problems. Something really has to be done about it, for this energy has to be expended. If they employ it to useful, creative ends, all will be well. If they do not—well, that is another story.

Their love nature is, as a rule, far more intense than that of the average person. It can be a transcendental love, with a devotional fervour that seems to know no limits. But they have a special requirement connected with this. They need a lover who knows how to reciprocate, for they have need of constant demonstrations of affection.

Once they are convinced they have found their true love, they are in deadly earnest in their love-making. Light flirtation is not their bent and they have no time for it. When they love, they love.

Undoubtedly natives of this sign know how to choose, for they appear unerring in their character determinations, and know the merits and demerits of those whom they contact. Their moods are complex, and not readily analysed. It takes a clever person to assess them accurately, and frequently those who attempt to do so make grave mistakes in their judgments; for the powers and talents of the Scorpio reside below the surface. They are proud of spirit, not with the same kind of pride as the Leonian, but with the pride of self-mastery. It is this pride which makes them the great fighters that they are. Woe betide those who wound them!

They are remarkably thorough in whatever they do, and if they take up a subject they certainly can master it. They are tireless in their efforts and nothing is too much trouble if an end is in view. That is why people remark upon their diligence and patience. It is not at all a question of patience, but that inner force which makes them persevere, levelling by sheer will any obstacle in their path.

They know their assets and their limitations very well, indeed, and they take care to work within these limits.

They are critical, but their criticism lacks the carping quality of that of the Virgoan. It is those who do not know them who dub them cool and calculating. Those who do know them know the warmth of feeling and great generosity of nature that is just beneath the surface.

Being natural psychologists themselves, it is doubtful if they really need too much guidance, for they know people.

The following will be a comparison between Scorpio and the natives of those Signs which may be compatible or incompatible:

Scorpio and Aries

One throne with two kings upon it would be quite out of order, and one house with two aggressive Mars-ruled "heads-of-the-house" would be more so. These two are only compatible from the sexual viewpoint, unless one is able to become a meek and pliable little lamb who willingly steps down and lets the other rule. This is highly improbable, as a Mars-ruled person doesn't stay meek and mild very long, even in the throes of wild young love. This combination is not advisable unless both enjoy hurricanes of turmoil in the home.

Scorpio and Taurus

This is a compatible combination for both, as the natives of these two Signs have much in common. Mentally, physically, and emotionally these two could really make a go of it—IF they are both able to eliminate the strong streak of possessiveness and jealousy that exists in each. If either is afflicted with a "roving eye", an "H" bomb rehearsal would be the result. However, these two are well suited, so let them look before they leap—then leap!

Scorpio and Gemini

Gemini will love Scorpio's urge for action, and Scorpio will adore Gemini's mentality; but Scorpio would be a bit strenuous for Gemini physically, and the jealous and possessive Scorpio would certainly put a damper on Gemini's love of freedom. Some types of Scorpians may combine with Gemini, but it is still too much of a chance considering the star-predicted characteristics of both.

Scorpio and Cancer

Here are two who love deeply, and each has much to give the other. What dissension may arise from jealousy in both natures would probably be of short duration. There would also be sympathetic understanding by Scorpio of the "gloom and doom" of the Cancerian moods, and the vigorous Scorpio energy will act as a strong, stimulating tonic for the gentler, home-loving Cancer. A GOOD combination!

Scorpio and Leo

Here are two of the "Royalty" who are most compatible IF the Leo is female and the Scorpio male. Were this reversed, a Scorpio wife may stir Leo's anger by her demands, for they would be many. Leo MUST be the centre of attention at all times, but a Scorpio woman would not permit this. Jealousy is still lurking in the corners here, and could cause many really big blows—so the best bet here is if the wife is the Leo who can, with wifely submission, make it a happy marriage.

Scorpio and Virgo

These two admire each other in every respect. Virgo, whose mind is always searching, meets a worthy match in Scorpio. Virgo's often destructive critical tongue can be quickly silenced by the sarcastic lashing of which Scorpio is capable. Too, Scorpio's penetrating mind can see right through the motives of Virgo. In this event, Virgo will conveniently change the subject to avoid making the home a battlefield.

If Virgo can be considerate of Scorpio's pride, this can be a good marriage.

Scorpio and Libra

Libra's need for affection and to "belong" will be just what Scorpio desires. The Scorpio half of this team will be the more dominant one, but the possessiveness of this Sign will please Libra, rather than irk. Libra sees in Scorpio all the virtues ever dreamed of, and all the vices desired; for the intense Scorpian love-nature is what Libra would like to have as a personal trait. Here again it will be necessary to handle the Scorpian pride with care; but the effort will surely pay off for Libra in a happy union.

Scorpio and Scorpio

Here is one that is baffling in its outcome. If both of these individuals have a thorough understanding of their inherent traits, they can have deep sympathy for each other. The dominant, possessive, and jealous temperaments of each are things which BOTH will have to handle with extreme consideration. They are both intense in their love nature, and can get just what they are looking for in each other. If one should forget to consider the other's tender spots, or does anything to rouse the other's jealousy, then the storm will rage. This can be a wonderful—or terrible combination.

Scorpio and Sagittarius.

The dominant Scorpio will have trouble keeping her Sagittarian partner in tow. This freedom loving Sign will surely bring out the worst in Scorpio's nature. Mutual distrust is easily developed here, and the Scorpian possessiveness will make life unbearable for Sagittarius. It is true that from the sexual viewpoint, Scorpio is intriguing to the Sagittarian appetite, but there the compatibility ends. Not an advisable combination.

Scorpio and Capricorn

A rather difficult combination to analyse. The strength and power of the Scorpio personality may clash with the Capricorn desire for the last word when it comes to important decisions pertaining to the family welfare. Capricorn can be mighty disagreeable when frustrated, and Scorpio will have to use the sting of the Scorpian barb to move the Capricorn goat from a set course. The result usually spells emotional incompatibility that becomes unbearable for both parties.

Scorpio and Aquarius

This combination usually winds up in a battle of nerves. Aquarius is too unpredictable for the solid Scorpio temperament. Aquarius has too many outside interests to suit a Scorpio mate. Aquarians are too reserved to meet the passionate demands of Scorpio. Scorpio admires the Aquarian's humanitarian instincts, but does not want to share them with the world.

Scorpio and Pisces

This is a love-at-first-sight combination that seldom endures the test of time. All is well until Pisces begins to pout about the many little outside interests that are always intriguing Scorpio. The possessive qualities of Pisces are not appreciated by Scorpio, who feels that possessiveness is his own sacred domain. The clinging-vine type of Piscean has Scorpio's sympathies, but respect is soon lost for the weaker member, and the partnership falls apart.

Some Famous Persons Born in the Sign of Scorpio

J. Ogden Armour—Industrialist
Adm. Richard E. Byrd—Explorer
W. Averell Harriman—Statesman
June Havoc—Actress
Katherine Hepburn—Actress
Vivien Leigh—Actress
Jawaharlal Nehru—Indian Statesman
Ignace Paderewski—Pianist and Statesman
Pablo Picasso—Painter
Auguste Rodin—French Sculptor
Will Rogers—Humourist
Theodore Roosevelt—Soldier and US President
Gen. Chiang Kai-shek—Statesman
Robert Louis Stevenson—Author
Ella Wheeler Wilcox—Writer
Dr Jonas Salk—Polio Vaccine Researcher

9

SAGITTARIUS

November 22nd–December 21st

This constellation, in its symbolical aspect, represents both retribution and the hunting sports. We find it depicted as a Centaur, with the bow and arrow drawn to its head ready for shooting. It is frequently used to designate the autumnal sports and the chase. The Centaur is a symbol for authority and worldly wisdom.

The Sign of Sagittarius signifies the thighs of the Grand Universal Man. It represents the muscular foundation, or the seat of locomotion in humanity. It is the emblem for stability, foundation, and physical power. This Sign also represents authority and command.

Sagittarius, upon the esoteric planisphere, is occupied by Joseph. "His bow abode in strength," says the patriarch, "and the arms of his hands were made strong." We see in Joseph, the Egyptian ruler and law-giver, a true type of real authority.

Sagittarius is the lowest emanation of the fiery Trigon, and is the constellation of the planet Jupiter.

It represents the powers of "Church and State", and symbolizes the might of civil, military, and religious codes.

It indicates to us the organizational powers of humanity.

The mystical gem of this Sign is the turquoise, a talisman of great virtue to its proper natives.

The fortunate day is Thursday.

Fortunate number is nine.

The fortunate colour for this Sign is purple.

Best location for success is the great outdoors.

Describing those born under Sagittarius, I would say persons of this Sign are loyal, patriotic, and law abiding. Such natives are generous and free, energetic, and combative.

They are hasty in temperament, ambitious of position and power, besides being charitable to the afflicted and oppressed. They possess strong conservative ideals, and their chief mental characteristics are self-control, and the ability to command others.

Sagittarians have attractive, interesting, magnetic, and dynamic personalities. They are fond of being looked up to, and they enjoy meeting a great variety of people. Under ordinary circumstances they are likeable and command respect and admiration.

In character they are honest, sincere, frank, and trustworthy.

In disposition they are kind and generous to their friends, diplomatic and tactful in most matters, but have a hair-trigger temper. Although they are quick to anger, they are usually over it soon and are not likely to hold a grudge.

They are changeable, impulsive, and subject to varying moods. Their impulsiveness may either be intellectual, emotional, or both. They have considerable personal pride, but not many of this Sign are unusually egotistical. Personal pride is useful when it implies enlightened self-interest. In most matters Sagittarians display an independent nature; they usually rebel at any form of restraint.

However, they have a good sense of humour and express much joviality with sharp wit when they so desire. They have a fair degree of determination and will power, but if they are crossed they can be most obstinate and headstrong.

If you are of Sagittarius, you have good powers of observation, good perception, good reasoning ability, and show good judgement in most matters, except those which relate directly to your emotional nature. In matters pertaining to work, you show accurate judgment; yet when it comes to your own personal life, you are apt to make errors in judgment. It is advisable that you make an effort to correct this tendency.

The mental grasp of Sagittarians is very quick, and they can learn most things quite readily. Sagittarians are inclined, especially during the first half of their life, to place themselves in all sorts of conditions and circumstances where quick thinking is necessary in order to avoid unpleasant consequences.

These natives have vivid imaginations, yet are not dreamers. It is true that they have flights of fancy about love, but, in the main, Sagittarians use their imagination for practical things. That happy faculty is the progressive purpose of their imaginations. Such a faculty enables man to visualize and construct the ideas essential to progress.

Sagittarians seldom forget important details. This is because they consciously or subconsciously take an interest and pay attention to all that is going on about them. They have the ability to concentrate on either what interests them, or what they need to meditate upon. Good expressive powers make them excellent conversationalists.

Their intuition serves as a warning of impending events. It helps them to become aware of the truth in important matters and gives them an unusual insight into human motives. You of Sagittarius should study and learn more about this interesting faculty and apply it in everyday affairs.

Indications point to a good physical condition that is able to withstand much abuse; but Sagittarians have a somewhat nervous temperament, and it is essential that they take reasonably good care of their health. They require balance in their mental and physical activity; they should use judgment when eating and drinking. Health is too precious to be tampered with! This birth-sign presides over the hips and thighs, and, by reaction, over the chest and lungs. It is advisable to guard against colds, as they are apt to seriously affect the respiratory system.

Indications for this birthsign show a love of sports, games, travel, motoring, the solitude of the forest, streams, mountains, and the desert. These natives have the spirit of adventure.

They enjoy social affairs, and they have a deep appreciation of art, music, and dancing. Their restless and active nature will find its expression in change; a Sagittarian will move as often as possible. Travel stimulates their minds and affords them great relaxation. Indications show that although they are highly emotional, they are capable of showing reserve. Their love nature is affectionate and passionate, but its intensity varies with the personal mood of the moment. In other words, they are ardent one moment, and indifferent the next. This may cause them to be misunderstood by their loved one. Sagittarians should learn to overcome this shortcoming and adjust their mental and emotional life so that it will not bring misunderstanding and disillusionment. If they have occasion to look back upon some of their previous disappointments in romantic matters, they will no doubt find that their own fluctuating emotions may have been the actual cause for the complicated series of events that followed. Their restless and highly-charged natures require expression. They are not sure of themselves, so they usually have more than one romantic attachment.

Nevertheless, they are of the type that finds a happier state of affairs when married than single, and are very considerate of their mates. The ideal type of mate must be intellectual, adventurous, affectionate, and have a good degree of patience and understanding. In the selection of a mate those born under this Sign must guard against emotional impulsiveness which may lead them to accept an incompatible person.

Love is the power that inspires progress and constructive living. Sagittarius is not a barren Sign, but gives promise of but few children.

Indications show that Sagittarians are not always happy and securely settled in their home lives. Their active and adventurous natures sometimes make them restless and desirous of change, and if it is at all possible, they will arrange it. Sometimes even a few days away from home will help them get over a restless period. People possessing a more fixed nature may not understand these natives.

Persons of this birthsign are industrious, studious, and progressive. They forge ahead in life, primarily due to their determination and clever intellect. The proper development of their personality will enhance the prospects of success in any business or profession they choose to follow. They require work which gives both mental and physical activity. They are the kind of individuals who are well fitted for duties which bring them into contact with the public. A great number of these natives become lawyers, teachers, doctors, and authors—both literary and journalistic. They also enter businesses, such as publishing and transportation, usually in a managerial capacity. They become mechanics, scientists, research workers, and aviators.

Many Sagittarius natives are inclined to follow more than one line of work. If prepared for a professional career they may have a hobby which proves practical and remunerative.

It is apparent from the indications that one of this temperament is so constituted that he or she could enter into partnership ventures with a good expectation of success. These natives are co-operative, efficient, and reliable. Their financial prospects in the course of life may be considered fairly good. They will succeed best when working for large corporations and industries rather than small ones. They have good earning abilities, but they are inclined to be careless spenders. They are not conservative in money matters. There are times when they impulsively buy a thing regardless of its actual worth to them.

When it comes to the planning for financial security, they should consider their spending habits. Their adventuresome natures incline them to speculate with varying degrees of success, but conservative investment usually proves more advantageous in the long run.

Indications show that you of Sagittarius will attract many friendships. Sportsmanship and frankness and a sense of humour will go far in creating many friendships.

The Sagittarius Child

The Sagittarius child is likely to be rather changeable, with an inclination to become confused and uncertain. This changeability often makes them difficult to understand. They are of fiery temperament, and are very unpredictable. The moulding of such a child will tax the ingenuity of the parents.

These children are born with ambition, and the formative years can be the training ground for the realization of such dreams. Their vitality is fundamentally strong and they generally enjoy good health. These children should be taught deep-breathing exercises and should be encouraged to spend as much time as possible in the wide open spaces.

The pathology of this Sign is interesting, and the parent of every Sagittarian child should bear in mind that nervous depletion can be caused by restlessness, which can result in injuries and accidents.

The children of this Sign are more subject to accidents than those of any other Sign. Indulgence of the appetite should be guarded against. Care in diet is absolutely essential.

Intellectually, Sagittarian children are ambitious, curious, and frank. Emotionally, they are daring, energetic, idealistic, impatient, and often not very domestic. They should be taught to guard against extravagance which is an adverse Sagittarian aspect.

It will be noted that they have a fondness for animals.

The Sagittarius Wife

Here is a type of woman who takes an intelligent interest in her husband's business. She is not an intruder and has enough reserve to wait until her advice is asked for. She is not only a sympathetic listener, but a useful helpmate as well.

In the field of hobbies and sports she is a real companion. All outdoor life attracts her, and she enjoys fishing, hunting, riding, and even the competitive sports.

A man does not have to search for a companion with whom to enjoy his hobby if he is married to a Sagittarian woman. She is enthusiastic about all kinds of activity, from civic affairs and social life to sports and an occasional fling at gambling. It is easy to see that a husband would have a very full life with such a companion.

In the home, she is competent, tidy in her housekeeping, and sympathetic in the care of her children. In all of her reactions to life she is clever and well balanced—a woman to be trusted entirely, if that is possible. These wives are not, however, very tactful; they are outspoken in the extreme. Both the husband and children may expect to hear any errors frankly discussed.

Born under Sagittarius, her passions are healthy, joyous, and swift. She does not make a fetish of physical indulgence, but she is rather highly sexed and demands stimulating, adventurous excitement. Her responses are enthusiastic, and her approach to physical love is highly refined and inspiring of great efforts. She brings out the best in a man.

The Sagittarius Husband

The Sagittarius husband requires a wise, tactful wife. This may be true of all husbands, but this man has much to give; and frequently his family sees the worst side of his nature rather than the best.

A Sagittarian man is not ideally fitted by the stars for domestic life. His interest in world affairs is great, and his business or profession is usually chosen from a purely monetary standpoint. He is very much of a businessman. His basic mental strength goes into his business obligations, and his personal affairs become unimportant by comparison. If his personal tastes change, he sees no reason why he must continue to express a devotion that no longer exists.

The wife of a Sagittarian must be exceedingly broad-minded and free from jealousy. She will have to be a good deal of a psychologist to hold his interest, in any case.

All Sagittarians do not stay married, but many make good husbands. They are very gifted men, with whom it is a privilege to live. It is necessary for the wife to widen her own horizons so that she may see eye to eye with him.

The passions of the Sagittarian are lusty, sportive, and adventurous. They are joyous fellows who treat love like a happy adventure. All of the emotions accompanying this birthsign are high-strung and demand satisfaction.

The Cusps of Sagittarius

(If your birthday is not within the cusp of your Sign, the following does not apply to you.)

If the birthday is from November 22nd through November 25th

The native is born in Sagittarius with Scorpio tendencies. The ruling planets are Jupiter and Mars. This denotes that these people are courageous and progressive, and have unusual physical endurance. Frequently they take upon themselves too much responsibility and this tends to hold them back. They have strong inclinations which are often misunderstood, and they may be criticized because of them. They will encounter many obstacles and barriers, but they usually overcome them. They possess a good supply of reserve energy and recuperate quickly from illness. They overcome discouragement readily. They have a vivid imagination, and are painstaking in their work. While they are very sensitive, they seldom show it to others. They are not too considerate of other people's feelings, but do not intentionally offend.

If the birthday is from December 19th through December 21st

The natives are born in Sagittarius with Capricorn tendencies; their ruling planets are Jupiter and Saturn. These Capricornian Sagittarians are very entertaining to have around as they are genial, vivacious, witty and well-informed. While they possess many talents, they are somewhat critical of the viewpoints of others and, therefore, may incur the enmity of those who disagree with them. They have a strong sense of duty and accept responsibility as a matter of course. They are dignified, honourable, and capable. They have a good imagination, and they always do their work quickly and thoroughly. They keep a promise and are quick to make decisions, and do not procrastinate. If given the opportunity to develop their inclinations along their own lines, they will succeed and prosper.

They can be depended upon to do more than their share in any collective undertaking. They have a strong, magnetic, personality which attracts many to them. They seldom violate a confidence, or interfere in matters which do not directly concern them.

The Decanates of Sagittarius

If the birthday is between November 22nd and November 30th

The ruling and personal planet for this decanate is Jupiter, which influences moral and sympathetic tendencies. These natives are endowed with intellectual qualities of a high order. They have a lofty sense of justice and wisdom in all commercial and personal interests.

Because they are unusually sensitive and wise, they are

attracted by tenderness, love, and trust. A truly magnanimous spirit is indicated by the double aspect of Jupiter in this Horoscope.

If the birthday is between December 1st and December 11th

The personal planet for this decanate is Mars, the symbol of War, and the centre of Divine Energy. It governs the constructive, adventurous, fearless, and aggressive tendencies, and inclines its subjects to become ambitious, forceful, and courageous. This planet endows these natives with a burning ambition to attain success in all undertakings. Men who possess marked executive ability are influenced by the planets Jupiter and Mars. This interpretation indicates great success in the business and social world.

If the birthday is between December 12th and December 21st

The personal orb for this decanate is the Sun, known as Ruler of the Day. It is the centre of the Solar System, and the giver of life and individuality. It stands for dignity, loyalty, honour, and ambition. The Sun in this aspect creates a great love for change and the desire to reform. A noble and enthusiastic nature and the ability to lead and govern others is also indicated. These natives are full of enterprise and novel ideas. The Sun governs pride and personal ambition. It confers good fortune, particularly if the native will try to overcome some of the negative tendencies of Sagittarius.

The Degrees of Sagittarius

November 22nd

You possess an intuitive and prophetic nature, and are gifted with keen insight. Your constant search for knowledge will add materially to your success. You will be fortunate in a commercial or scientific career, but difficulties in romantic affairs are indicated. You also have exceptional talent for philosophy and research.

November 23rd

You are a practical visionary and can carry your ideas to

successful conclusions. You will be more successful working with others than you will be in business for yourself. You may meet with obstacles at various times, but you will eventually overcome them.

November 24th

You are broadminded and good-natured. You are a champion of the underdog. Many persons of this degree marry a distant relative. It will be necessary to tone down a rather high-strung and erratic temperament. You may display marked artistic, musical, and psychic abilities. Success in one or more of these fields is indicated.

November 25th

You are affectionate and demonstrative. You are very fond of your home and relatives. Success in the field of electronics is indicated. Care should be exercised when on water. Your health will need careful attention at all times. Friends may not be as reliable as they appear on the surface.

November 26th

You possess much creative ability, artistic inspiration, and prophetic insight. You have the ability and determination to overcome all obstacles. You will not have an easy life, but you will triumph in the end. Hindrances through deception is also indicated. Deal tactfully with elders, using the utmost discretion.

November 27th

You possess a persuasive manner and have the ability to influence others. You will be subject to varying degrees of good and bad fortune from time to time. Happiness and sorrow will curiously intertwine. Sports and travel will be your favoured activities. You have a powerful sex drive.

November 28th

You possess the ability to make friends of your opponents, due to your agreeable and harmonious nature. You are dignified and well fitted for an executive position. Although your progress may be slow, it will be sure. One aspect in this Horoscope shows that elderly relatives will contribute to your good fortune.

November 29th
Your keen insight and great fortitude will enable you to overcome difficult business and financial obstacles. Some trouble through relatives is also shown. A strong love of pleasure and a reckless attitude must be curbed.

November 30th
You possess a rather difficult personality. While you have good powers of concentration, you are somewhat headstrong and foolhardy in your personal activities. Many trials and tribulations are shown, but you seem to get help from some secret source. Happiness and success will largely depend upon your education and early upbringing.

December 1st
You possess a keen ambition and good executive ability. You have great love for truth and justice. Nothing will come easy to you, but on the whole you will be fortunate and successful. This degree usually receives an inheritance at some point during life. Occasional reverses will act as a tonic to stimulate your determination.

December 2nd
You are a profound thinker, and are aggressively assertive, generous, and good-hearted. Be on the lookout for possible errors in speculative judgment. Sudden losses through unwise investments are indicated. Care should be taken against accidents. You will lead an eventful life.

December 3rd
You possess a sensitive and somewhat restless nature. You are frank, prudent, and dependable. Success will not be easily achieved, despite help from friends and superiors. You are endowed with tremendous energy, both mental and physical, and you will lead a full life. One aspect in this Horoscope indicates sorrow through bereavement or extreme sensitivity.

December 4th

You will lead an active life and may experience varying degrees of success and failure due to a penchant for engaging in daring enterprises and risky ventures. This, a good-luck degree, will bring help from unexpected sources. A lucky hunch may result in considerable good fortune.

December 5th

You are sagacious, capable, efficient, and hard working. Some secret matter during your lifetime may develop into a powerful influence. Love of sensationalism may cause you to suffer depressive moods. A tendency to rebel against authority should be curbed. A successful marriage or partnership is indicated.

December 6th

You have a well-balanced mind with an intellectual outlook upon life. Friends will play an important part in your success. One aspect in the Horoscope suggests danger of heartbreak through an unfortunate romance. Being hospitable and good-natured you must be constantly on guard against unscrupulous associates.

December 7th

You possess an independent spirit and a great desire for freedom of action. You are able to acquire a great amount of knowledge with consummate ease. You are determined and restless and become quite despondent if required to remain in the same environment too long. One aspect in this Horoscope indicates occasional reverses due to elders and in-laws.

December 8th

You possess a philosophical, critical, adaptable, and ingenious mind. You would make an able journalist. You are venturesome yet capable of much discretion. You are well-fitted for a life in politics. Safeguard your health by avoiding chills and colds as much as possible. This is considered a fortunate degree.

December 9th

You possess an ingenious and approbatory nature with refined artistic tastes. Many friends among the opposite sex are indicated. Your literary and philosophical turn of mind qualifies you for a place of fame in the literary world. Both gains and lossess will come through secret dealings.

December 10th

You are aggressive, ambitious, and full of mental and physical energy. While you are normally conservative and economical, there is a tendency to make exceptions where the opposite sex is concerned. Legal troubles and excesses in diet are to be closely watched. Try to curb your extravagant and speculative urge.

December 11th

You are exceptionally fortunate, popular, good-natured, and sincere. You have excellent foresight in business matters and will be favoured by your superiors and people in high places. Do not permit success to warp your good sense of judgment, particularly where the opposite sex is concerned. Secret alliances here have a way of coming to the surface.

December 12th

You possess many fine traits and outstanding abilities. You will be a good debater and will excel as a lawyer or politician. You must always conduct yourself so as not to arouse jealousy in others. You should also curb an erratic temperament where the opposite sex is concerned.

December 13th

You are endowed with much strength of character and an affectionate disposition. You will experience many vicissitudes of fortune. Sudden events may completely change your life. Disappointment in love or friendships is threatened. You will have marked socialistic tendencies and are very liberal in your political outlook.

December 14th

You possess a sympathetic disposition with a psychic temperament. You are ingenious, volatile, and versatile. You must not throw caution to the winds as there will be grave risks at some time during your life of either accident or some other misfortune. This degree warns not to take needless chances, not only when travelling, but in all financial endeavours.

December 15th

You possess boundless vitality, are good-natured, hospitable, and reliable. You are very romantically inclined; none the less you have high standards of loyalty. The stage, music, literature, or art would provide a lucrative and suitable career. There may be many so-called platonic friendships among friends of the opposite sex.

December 16th

You possess much refinement, sympathy, and goodness of heart. You are bright, gay, and full of zest for life. You have a somewhat poetic and sensuous temperament, craving physical delights. Heavy responsibility brought on by your adventurous nature may give you cause for concern. Curb your desire for constant change.

December 17th

You possess a strong character with a great desire for fame and recognition. You will be very talented in a literary field. There are strong aspects for becoming an author, due to your keen imagination. Because you are talented you will be subject to treachery and jealousy. Close family ties are essential in order to offset disillusion caused by misplaced friendship.

December 18th

You possess an emotional and sensitive disposition. While you are fond of home and family, much travel is indicated. You are impressionable and therefore readily imposed upon. Choose your friends and associates wisely. Do not give of yourself until you are sure of the beneficiaries' motives.

December 19th

You will have a somewhat checkered career. Courage and faith will help offset sudden unexpected upheavals. Because you are charitable, kind, and affectionate, you are liable to imposition. You possess executive ability and some business or professional success is indicated.

December 20th

You are good-natured and have a positive outlook upon life. Care should be taken at all times near fire, machinery, and explosives. You show great enterprise in commerce and are also well qualified for a government or political career. Guard against deception in business and love. Be circumspect when meeting or dealing with strangers.

December 21st

You have a tendency to worry and fuss about matters over which you have no control. You possess good mental ability but will be in danger of reversals of fortune caused by emotional entanglements. Health will easily be affected through digestive weakness. Depend on your keen intuition in times of stress and strain. Do not hesitate to seek advice from true and trusted friends.

Compatible and Incompatible Signs of Sagittarius

Sagittarius is an easygoing Sign with a friendly and attractive manner. The natives are usually fond of outdoor games and exercises, and are intense lovers of freedom. It is not a Sign which favours marriage to any great extent, for both the men and the women value their freedom highly. The Sagittarian is not orthodox or conventional enough to be concerned with what people will say if he deviates from the established custom of love, marriage, and sex.

The desire for admiration makes Sagittarians apt to carry on numerous flirtations, but, as a rule, they do not mean very much, and do not seriously interfere with married life. Natives of this Sign are usually bad liars, but good detectors, and intuitively guess the truth behind any attempt to deceive them.

As marriage partners they are kind rather than over-affectionate. They are extremely inquisitive and full of well-meaning. There is much idealism and enthusiasm in the Sign, and an eccentric mentality which sometimes leads to the choice of a marriage partner for reasons which may not prove too sound.

Perhaps the worst partner for a Sagittarian is a person of narrow and restricted views. A marriage of this sort degenerates into sarcasm, bickering, and general unhappiness, which sometimes, though by no means always, leads to separation. If Sagittarius is not too restricted, marriage is generally reasonably satisfactory, and is not characterized by extremes of any kind.

Sagittarians have a generous, extrovert nature, distinguished by their frankness and straightforwardness. Naturally these traits are immediately observable in their mode of making love, for they rarely beat about the bush and cannot be said to be bashful.

Temperamentally they are flirtatious, frank, and carefree, and make friends readily.

They have the keenest regard for personal freedom and liberty, and this is the factor which makes them loathe to compromise and let themselves be tied down.

Since wrong types do not have labels to designate them as such, perhaps it will be useful to indicate those types in which Sagittarians may best seek or avoid:

Sagittarius and Aries

This combination should be a fairly happy one, though both the natives are of the fire Signs. Mars (Aries) and Jupiter (Sagittarius) blend very well. There will be sympathetic understanding of each other's impulsiveness, and neither will take too seriously the outside interests of the other. The Sagittarian's banner of "Liberty and the Pursuit of Happiness"—or even "the happiness of pursuit"—will be subscribed to by the Arien in most cases.

Sagittarius and Taurus

This combination does not, as a rule, prove that love can overcome everything. Taurus loves deeply and is very selfish and possessive of the loved one. Sagittarius will refuse to be contained, and no amount of argument will change him. Taurus is too jealous, and Sagittarius too freedom loving for this combination to work out well.

Sagittarius and Gemini

This is really a fine basic combination, since both have those qualities that do not have to blend, for they are both the same. Both love absolute freedom of limb and action; both can shrug off the inconsistency that is a common trait with them. Neither will dissolve in tears and recrimination if the other strays now and then. Truly compatible. If they battle at all it will be more for diversion than any serious difference.

Sagittarius and Cancer

Cancer would have to go to a Temperament Tailor and be entirely made over for this combination. Though they admire everything about the Sagittarians, Cancerians will never take lightly the Sagittarian tendency to drift. Cancers "gather unto themselves" all of the body, soul, and activities of their family. This combination can mean little more than trouble. Cancer will cry, Sagittarius will flee—usually not a good combination for marriage.

Sagittarius and Leo

These two, both fire Signs, are very compatible in most things. Both love change, excitement, and have a great zest for life. There may be occasional explosions since both are extremely domineering, but basically these two have qualities which are in sympathy. A good combination!

Sagittarius and Virgo

With the critical and meticulous Virgo, Sagittarians are letting themselves in for a bed *not* of roses. Certainly Sagittarius admires the perfection of Virgo—the orderly, spic-and-span appearance, the "just-right"ness of Virgo; but these qualities may prove to be ropes of steel in marriage, for they certainly will not permit the freedom of action that Sagittarius must have. Too, Sagittarius does not take to the criticism and bickering which Virgo gives out so freely. Not a good chance to take.

Sagittarius and Libra

The Libran sense of justice and fair play may make this combination work out—but it is going to be tough on the Librans, for they will have a hard time accepting the free and easy Sagittarian philosophy of life. Librans will get everything they're looking for—and admire—in Sagittarius, but over a long period of time the sense of justice and fair play may wear thin. Both love the same things—luxury, beauty, and social-whirling, but Libra may have a tendency to attempt the old apron-string technique on Sagittarius, which, of course, will not work. The Sagittarian hates confinement of any kind. Chances for life-long happiness are just fair here.

Sagittarius and Scorpio

Scorpio, with the strong will to dominate, will not find Sagittarius a willing subject. The fierce Scorpio possessiveness will simply make Sagittarius look for the nearest exit, and the mutual distrust between these two will not make for sweetness and love in a marriage. They are very compatible so far as physical love goes, but there is little else that could be considered in a union here. Only a good psychologist will be able to hold this marriage together.

Sagittarius and Sagittarius

Strangely enough, unless these two are on the same intellectual and social plane, this combination is not too promising for happiness. They will have to do everything together—or not at all. They must have the same interests in social and business matters. Both are freedom loving—but they will find that even freedom must be enjoyed TOGETHER, as neither the male or female will be willing to sit at home while the other goes out on the town. A good look before the leap is made is strongly advisable.

Sagittarius and Capricorn

Unless Sagittarius can clip their wings a little, this combination does not get the go-ahead signal. These two are entirely different in their temperaments—one is optimistic, the other is pessimistic. Sagittarius has a devil-may-care attitude, while Capricorn has a sombre and restrictive temperament. This would be a very unhappy combination for the Sagittarian, as he—or she—would have to have the type of love that "passeth all understanding" to find any joy in this combination.

Sagittarius and Aquarius

This is generally an easy combination for success. Both temperaments have much in common. This is a purely social combination that will revel in a large group of friends and public-spirited associates. Sagittarius will readily understand the Aquarius moods and peculiarities and make the necessary allowances, as he expects and appreciates reciprocal treatment. They both love travel, change, and excitement, so this should work out well.

Sagittarius and Pisces

Free and easygoing Sagittarius may find Pisces too heavy a load to carry. While there is much here that makes for an interesting and sincere friendship, Sagittarius may find a marriage with Pisces too confining. Love would soon be replaced by pity, and then it would be a struggle between conscience and duty. Centaur, think twice before marrying a Pisces.

Some Famous Persons Born in the Sign of Sagittarius

Thomas Carlyle—Author
Sir Winston Churchill—British Statesman
Noel Coward—Playwright, Actor, Director
Gen. George A. Custer—Soldier
Charles De Gaulle—French Statesman
Joe DiMaggio—Baseball Player
Walt Disney—Animated Cartoonist, Producer
Douglas Fairbanks, Jr—Actor
Ira Gershwin—Lyricist
Mary Martin—Actress
John Milton—Poet
Robert G. Menzies—Australian Statesman
Diego Rivera—Painter
Pope John XXIII—Religious Leader
Lillian Russell—Actress
Mark Twain—Humourist

10

CAPRICORN

December 22nd–January 19th

This Sign, in its symbolical aspect, represents sin. The universal offering of a kid or young goat as an atoning sacrifice for sin is significant.

The different qualities of the sheep and the goat, from a symbolical standpoint, are used by St John in his mystical Apocalypse.

The Redeemer of mankind, or Sun God, is always born at midnight directly when Sol enters this Sign, which is the winter solstice.

"The young child" is born in the stable and laid in the manger of the goat, in order that he may conquer the remaining signs of winter and death, and thus save mankind from destruction.

The Sign Capricorn signifies the knees of the Macrocosm and represents the first principle in the Trinity of locomotion. It represents the pliable and moveable parts of the body, the joints. It is the emblem of material servitude.

Capricorn, upon the esoteric planisphere, is occupied by Naphtali, whom Jacob says, "is a hind let loose, he giveth goodly words". Here we have two distinct references; the first, to the symbol a hind, or young deer, i.e., a goat with horns (goat and deer are equally significant of the earthy, mountainous nature, and are fond of high hills); the second, is the Christmas proclamation, he giveth goodly words, "Peace on the earth, good will to man".

This Sign represents regeneration, and reveals the necessity of "new dispensations".

Capricorn is the lowest emanation of the earthly Trigon, and is the constellation of the planet Saturn.

The mystical gem of this constellation is the onyx.

The fortunate day is Saturday.

The fortunate numbers are seven and three.

The fortunate colour for this Sign is dark green.

Best locations for success are secluded places away from noise and excitement.

Upon the intellectual plane, Capricorn signifies external form, and those dominated by its influx are among the lowest on a scale of true spirituality. The brain of this influence is ever on the alert to seize and take advantage of circumstances. The Sign rarely denotes a purely scheming mentality, but the intellectual nature is directed to the attainment of selfish ends, and the penetrating power of the mind is great.

The natives are quick as lightning to see others' weak points, that they may work to their own advantage. They are indisposed to do any hard work unless they see some great benefit there-from in the immediate future.

The average Capricorn personality is pleasing to meet. Capricornians present a neat and attractive appearance. They possess charming manners. They are not easily excited, and show up well in emergencies. The indications ascribed to those of this Sign are thoughtfulness, diplomacy, caution, and reserve. Their personalities become dynamic when they are able to overcome a certain timidity. Once sure of themselves, they become expressive, aggressive, and show an attractive personality. Their timidity is not due to an inferiority complex; it is the result of the serious nature of these natives. They can be trusted with responsibilities, and will carry out important missions. Ordinarily they are very sensitive. They are mild-tempered, proud, loyal, and sympathetic. When their feelings are aroused, they show a strong temper, and can become exceedingly critical. They speak their mind so fast that they are not always aware of what they are saying. Fortunately, their natural patience helps to keep them from getting temperamental too often. They may not always be right, but they have their own ideas about fair play and justice. They are more apt to get angry at little things than big things.

On the whole they have good dispositions. It is up to them to study their characteristics, and to make the necessary adjustments and improvements in themselves. All of this may not be easy at first, but they have the type of mind that will help them if they so desire. They have the ability to concentrate. Under ordinary circumstances, they possess a great degree of self-control. They must do their best to guard against reasoning only according to their personal feelings, preconceived notions, and prejudiced ideas. It is an unfortunate fact that a number of people born in this Sign fall into this habit. They have a keen perception when not influenced by their inner feelings. They have the ability to overcome their natural reserve.

Many of their impulses are merely the result of personal desires or fancies. Much unhappiness is caused by acting upon impulses without recourse to reason, analysis, and careful judgment.

They should listen to the voice of their intuition. It will enable them to have a better insight into human nature and the motives of other people. Intuition should not be confused with the apprehension and fear which these natives often feel. Intuition, like inspiration, is not based upon previous association. It will prove advantageous to learn about this interesting power and faculty. It will help them to have unusual foresight in many things.

Capricorn people have the types of minds that enable them to be efficient in ferreting out facts and knowledge in instances where others fail. They have the ability to concentrate, meditate, and work many problems to successful conclusions. Under ordinary circumstances they show reliable judgment. They should learn to do the same thing in regard to their intimate feelings.

Indications point to a fairly good physical constitution. With reasonable attention to diet, they should enjoy good health.

This Sign presides over the knees. Saturn is the ruler of the Sign, and is known to rule the bones. It is advisable to guard against broken bones. These natives are more or less susceptible to digestive and intestinal disturbances as well. They should interest themselves in some form of light exercise in order to keep their bodies in good condition. They should always do their best to avoid the common cold. If they do get a cold, they should take measures to break it up as soon as possible.

They must avoid worry and periodical moodiness. Though

they are serious minded and prudent, they desire the good things of life. They enjoy pleasure and travel, as well as sports, games, and social activity. They have a fine sense of artistic appreciation.

The Capricorn-born derive a certain amount of pleasure from travel, but they are not inclined to travel extensively. They are sensitive, reserved, and somewhat timid in their amours, but they are loyal to the object of their affection. Their ideals are quite high, and this occasionally causes Capricornians secret hurt and disillusion. At times they are affectionate, but, for the most part, they appear reserved to the point of indifference. This attitude on their part is apt to lead to misunderstanding between them and their loved ones.

Since they are intellectually inclined, they tend to select their companions with an eye to purely intellectual compatibility.

The Capricorn-born possess an idealistic love nature and are inclined to be selfish as regards the object of their affection. Capricornians should curb unreasonable jealousy. They need to learn that love and life are practical matters as well as ideals, romantic dreams in a world of fantasy. There is a need for self-understanding for a Capricornian to accept the intellectual, emotional, and physical qualities of both himself and a loved one. If these above-named qualities do not blend to a reasonable degree, the union will not be harmonious.

Marriage will develop the more expressive side of the personality of these natives. They enjoy having a bright perspective on life, and marriage proves a source of inspiration for their progress.

Indications for this Sign show a great love of children, and give promise of many. These natives have a deep parental love, and may prove too indulgent in the care of children. Capricorn people also manifest this same type of love in their friendships and associations with others. Though they are patient and have considerate understanding, they should do their best to avoid becoming possessive. They have a fondness for home life, particularly if they have congenial companionship and understanding. If they live alone, home is but four walls to them. Their home life during youth was probably filled with unstable conditions. They and their parents may often have been at odds and this may have had an adverse effect on their early life. Nevertheless, they are usually devoted to their parents and family.

Capricornians should choose work that affords their minds and bodies the greatest expression. These natives possess exceptional financial and executive acumen. This shows that they can be successful in their own businesses. Capricorn nativity gives industry, conscience, and efficiency in business or profession. These natives are loyal to their employer. There are some Capricornians who become shiftless, but this is usually the result of discouragement. Once such a habit is formed, only the pressure of circumstance will change it.

They are trustworthy, and capable of doing anything easy that they set out to accomplish. They have a good degree of determination and patience, which will help them to progress.

It is true that many of this Sign do not appear to get anywhere for years, but, in time, recognition comes, and often very suddenly.

They have the type of personality that will enable them to get along fairly well in partnerships. They usually have a deep sense of appreciation and are capable of true co-operation, and they will accept their share of responsibility gracefully. The superficial Capricorns usually possess a conservative quality, which, if properly applied, will enable them to save a little money. This is truly the secret of their financial success. Money, like everything else in life, responds to the treatment given it. Many of the world's greatest fortunes have been built from small beginnings and trivial economies and the exercise of conservative principles.

Good profits will be made from investments in real estate, government bonds, and the stocks of large corporations. The Capricorn-born should endeavour to use their judgment in financial affairs and should curb their speculative impulses. Financial indications during the latter half of their life appear to be quite favourable. They will, no doubt, attract many people to them, but their actual choice of intimate friends will be limited, and those will be mainly of the social, surface type. There are times when they are socially active; at other times, they desire to be alone or with a close friend who seems to understand them. Their emotional sensitivity and intellectual moodiness are their greatest handicaps, and proceed from trivial causes.

They try to be serious thinkers, but there is no reason why they should permit this effort to preclude frivolity. This is the common error of serious-minded people who have no real understanding of life.

The Capricorn Child

The children of Capricorn are usually bashful and timid in the presence of strangers. Among their friends, however, they have a tendency to be very bossy.

A great deal can be done by the parents in the early years of the Capricorn child to eliminate some of the adverse tendencies by training them to stop worrying over trifles and trivialities. The vitality in infancy is rather low, but once infancy is past, the persistence of this Sign makes itself felt. The principle source of danger is from falls, bruises, and sprains. Change of scenery, cheerful society, and comfortable relaxation are all excellent cures for the Capricorn child. It is important for the parents to consult a competent physician at the first sign of illness. Rheumatism, cramps, hysteria, skin disease, and broken bones are common ailments. Remember, the Capricorn child should be watched carefully in infancy as this is the most dangerous period.

Capricorn children are born leaders and organizers. They chafe under restriction and dislike taking orders from others. They are capable of attaining great heights through the ability to make the most of their opportunities. They achieve a good measure of success in occupations connected with the earth and its products—Capricorn is an earth Sign. They will do well in positions of responsibility and trust. Some of the occupations for which these children may be trained with confidence of success are: builder, farmer, miner, professor, and real estate dealer.

The characteristics of the Capricorn child tend towards conservatism. They are cautious and make good friends. Emotionally, they sometimes develop a coldness in their nature and become irritable. In this group, the head rules the heart completely, and the outside rules the inside. The disposition is usually thoughtful and dignified; they seize every opportunity to better themselves.

The Capricorn Wife

These women are usually sensitive and intuitive, but they are not at all submissive. The Capricorn woman makes an excellent hostess and housekeeper and is capable and dependable. She is also ambitious for the success of her husband and children.

Capricorn women lack that certain feminine quality that usually attracts men who are looking for the pliant and submissive type of wife. The Capricorn wife is easily misunderstood. Beneath her reserved exterior she is an admirable woman. She needs encouragement and sincere affection in order to call forth her deep sense of loyalty. Capricorn women are not swayed by their emotions. In love matters they sometimes appear to be practical, materialistic, and lacking in sentiment. The real trouble is that they have difficulty in expressing their more tender feelings. They are fond of the opposite sex and are attracted to them, but if their affections are not immediately reciprocated, they can become indifferent and resentful. They put a great deal of emphasis on worldly possessions. They love ardently, if not demonstratively, and hold a deep respect for their family.

Capricorn wives should avoid overbearance with those they love. Above all, they should not be afraid to give of themselves wholeheartedly, so that they become sparkling fountains of connubial love.

The Capricorn Husband

The Capricorn husband falls in readily enough with the domestic scheme but adds little to it. This type of man usually marries for selfish reasons; the basic nature of Capricorn is somewhat selfish, as Capricorn is both a superficial and connective Sign.

As husbands, these men are good providers, for they are ambitious and successful in business. They do not allow much freedom of action to their wives. Even though there is plenty of money in the home, the wife is not free to spend it. A

Capricorn husband is sometimes dictatorial as well as conservative—he lays down hard and fast rules for the spending of his money. The entire household is directed by him; his wife is a lieutenant. As commanding officer, he can be exacting, obstinate, and unreasonable in his laws for family routine. These laws may be in accordance with good discipline, but they are wholly unsympathetic.

He is generally a good emotional companion for his wife, and has the ability to give a part of himself to create an atmosphere of enjoyment and add to the real pleasure of the moment. He demands that everything be given to his family, but he examines whatever he gets with caution and suspicion. He believes that some contribution from himself is always necessary to heighten his own enjoyment. His passions are strong.

Naturally the tone that this powerful birth figure casts over a personality usually is tempered by other configurations. In that case, many of the negative Capricorn qualities are tempered with softer aspects, making a most agreeable person.

The Cusps of Capricorn

(If your birthday is not within the cusp of your Sign, the following does not apply to you.)

If the birthday is from December 22nd through December 25th

You were born in Capricorn with Sagittarius tendencies. Your ruling planets are Saturn and Jupiter. While you are very stern in your decisions, you are of a kind and sympathetic nature. You are thorough and persistent and work hard to carry out whatever plans you make. You are destined to meet with many obstacles and hindrances. You should be strong enough to overcome them so as to use them as stepping stones to bigger and better things. The varied experiences of your past life will form a good foundation for your success. A child born at this time will be particularly susceptible to beneficial parental influences, which will make for continued success in adult life.

Pay attention to your hunches and ideas, for you are a

born intuitive. You are progressive and find pleasure in self-improvement and development.

If the birthday is from January 16th through January 19th
You are born in Capricorn with Aquarius tendencies. Your ruling planets are Saturn and Uranus. This gives you understanding of mankind and makes you clever, intuitive, patient, loving, and sympathetic. You have artistic and musical ability which should be developed. You are cultured and refined and possess judgment that may be relied upon. When you enjoy good fortune things run unusually smoothly, but during adverse periods it seems that everything under the sun has gone wrong. You are generous and considerate of others. You are a loyal friend and a delightful entertainer. While you can adapt your talents to many lines, you will be most successful in the fine arts, in humanitarian work, in dealing with the public, or in the management of a large enterprise.

The Decanates of Capricorn

If the birthday is between December 22nd and December 31st
You have the double aspect of Saturn in your chart. Few real friendships are shown under this aspect, but those who are privileged to make the grade will be true and lasting. Saturn is the symbol of time and is restricting in its influences. This planet is concerned chiefly with the fixity of all affairs that may be classed as concrete conditions. Its powers lie in stability, endurance, tenacity, and perseverance. Gain through thrifty methods and careful investments is indicated. You possess a firm spirit and an enduring nature.

If the birthday is between January 1st and January 10th
Your personal planet is Venus, which makes you constant, reliable, industrious, and persevering. Venus is one of the most benevolent planets in the solar system. It indicates harmonious surroundings and favours pleasure and good cheer. It also brings out the idealistic, artistic, and musical faculties, and presides over the emotions and affections.

While the planet Venus has a decided influence of her own, she is greatly affected by aspects from other planets. Since Saturn is the ruling planet of Capricorn, it will naturally act as a restraining influence on the planet Venus and cause you to withhold your true inner emotions.

If the birthday is between January 11th and January 19th

Your personal planet is Mercury, which makes you rational and intellectual, though somewhat changeable. Your personal planet Mercury is considered a convertible planet; it is strongly affected by whatever planet it is in conjunction with. Mercury controls the brain and nerves, and makes its subjects excitable and active. This planet will play a prominent part in your life, since it controls commercial, intellectual, and family affairs. With Saturn acting as a restraining influence upon Mercury, you will tend to be practical and cautious.

The Degrees of Capricorn

December 22nd

You possess a resourceful, capable, and practical nature. You are commercially minded and interested in all phases of business endeavour. You are a born leader and possess the ability to command the respect of your friends and associates. Many of your difficulties can be avoided if you learn to overcome a quarrelsome and combative spirit. If you permit your negative tendencies to become habits, you may become designing in your social and business activities.

December 23rd

You possess a profound mind alternately swayed by principle and ambition. You show a great deal of determination and ambition. You have a great deal of adaptability, and unusual aptitude at reproducing and imitating. One aspect in this Horoscope indicates a tendency to become extremely temperamental and excitable when your plans and ambitions are interfered with. As a born leader you want to have your own way in matters.

December 24th

These Capricornians possess an ambitious and determined personality. They show a marked aptitude for dealing in financial affairs. Intense concentration of purpose will aid them materially in life, provided they can learn to overcome a tendency to display their strong likes and dislikes regardless of consequences. One aspect here indicates the possible development of an inferiority complex.

December 25th

Those of this degree possess an adventurous spirit and a desire to travel. They are fond of social activity. They show an aptitude for organizing and controlling others. They must avoid a tendency to do too many things at one time.

December 26th

These natives are endowed with a tactful, sympathetic, and proud nature. They show a great love for fine clothes, and have a desire to be well-dressed at all times. They attach great significance to outward appearances. One aspect in this Horoscope indicates difficulty in getting along with the immediate family because of a desire to impress outsiders.

December 27th

A bright, cheerful, and affectionate nature is indicated for this chart. Great generosity and a desire to help others is also shown. One aspect here shows a tendency to daydream. These natives must concentrate on one task at a time, completing each before starting another. A magnetic sex appeal will bring popularity with the opposite sex.

December 28th

Those of this birthday possess an adventurous, mystic nature, and a scientific trend of thought. A great love for travel and a fondness of the sea are also indicated. A desire to help those in less fortunate circumstances will lead this native into many strange experiences during life. Studies which can be used for the good of humanity and the alleviation of suffering may be the life ambition of this person.

December 29th

A sensitive, highly-strung nature is indicated in this chart. These natives have a tendency to be irritable and impatient when their plans and desires are not readily fulfilled. They possess progressive minds and vivid imaginations, but may develop tendencies to procrastinate. This may be caused by a desire to avoid assuming responsibility. If this is so, they should try to buckle down more!

December 30th

These Capricorn-born possess energetic, powerful, ambitious, and serious-minded natures. Versatile minds coupled with marked social instincts will enable them to gain success and recognition in public service. One aspect of this Horoscope indicates a tendency to be too apprehensive concerning the welfare of their loved ones and friends. Moderation of this golden virtue is advised, as it is apt to cause misunderstanding and misfortune. Much affection for the mother is indicated.

December 31st

Those of this degree possess a progressive, determined, and generous nature. They will succeed in life through their own merits and capabilities. They are clever with details, and may find marked success in any business or profession where intelligent application of detailed knowledge is essential. They should be surrounded by love and understanding, as certain aspects in this chart indicate the possible development of a selfish and materialistic character.

January 1st

A well-balanced mind, great determination of character, and an affectionate nature are bestowed upon the natives here. They have magnetic personalities, but, at times, may be somewhat temperamental and headstrong. They may have a delicate constitution, and should not overexercise or go to extremes in mental or physical exertion. Enlightenment will come through past experiences. They may expect many ups and downs, and are likely to suffer through deception. These natives should study the deeper side of life harder and more often.

January 2nd

These natives possess an amiable disposition, and have the ability to learn quickly due to a perceptive mind. An artistic temperament and a lovable nature brings the desire for the better things in life. One aspect in this Horoscope indicates the desire to get by with the least possible personal effort. They must not become self-indulgent.

January 3rd

Those of this birthday possess a highly magnetic personality. A strong, healthy body with very good recuperative powers will enable them to overcome their physical dangers. A charming, winsome disposition will bring many sincere friendships into the life. One aspect in this chart indicates disappointments due to misplaced confidence. Losses through financial schemes are shown.

January 4th

These natives are endowed with initiative, originality, and perceptiveness. They show a tendency to be contrary in a more or less mischievous manner. Good business ability and commercial foresight will greatly aid them in the attainment of success in the business world. A kind, sympathetic nature and a desire to help humanity may bring disappointments because of unappreciative attachments. This degree is not well aspected in romantic matters.

January 5th

An intuitive, artistic, sensitive, yet practical nature is indicated for the natives of this chart. They are also independent and have the ability to carry out their objectives in life without too much assistance from outside influences. They should never force themselves into vocations, but should permit their instinctive foresight to have full sway. By doing so, they will decide their true course in life.

January 6th

Those of this degree possess a determined, yet flexible nature, and a methodical, prudent, but gentle disposition. Marked capability in dealing with the masses, and success through association with influential and prosperous friends are indicated. They are not receptive to training that does not concur with their sense of justice and fair play. They must learn not to rely on their snap judgment, but to wait until they have attained knowledge and practical experience.

January 7th

These Capricornians possess a refined, artistic, and charitable nature. They are also gentle, prudent, and sensitive, but they may be lacking in confidence. A charming and affectionate disposition is indicated. They must learn to develop a greater degree of concentration in order to increase their self-confidence. While they are considerate and obedient to the wishes of their families, it would be unwise for them to bear the brunt of family responsibility, as this may eventually cause them to lead a retiring and lonely life.

January 8th

A profound mind and a reserved nature are bestowed upon these natives. Good fortune and much natural charm will bring many lasting friendships. Effort should be made to develop consideration for the feelings of others. Tact should be exercised in speech and action. These natives show great enterprise in acquiring the good things of life, and success will be attained mostly through their own efforts. Mental and physical overexertion must be avoided, except in exercise of the love-nature.

January 9th

The indications for those of this chart show an alert mind, remarkable intellect, and a keen sense of judgment. Much social grace and charm is evident as a result of an amiable and pleasing disposition. A fiery temper and an unyielding nature should be controlled. Great fixity of purpose and much skill in the performance of their undertakings will bring success in their endeavours. Care should be taken not to sacrifice home for social life.

January 10th

These natives possess a bold imagination. A keen mind, ever seeking knowledge and improvement, will aid in the attainment of spontaneous success in the business world. An extravagant nature and a decided flair for fine clothes and expensive companions is shown. This should be toned down. The development of a speculative impulse must be avoided as it can cause many embarrassing situations. The sensitive nature shown here flourishes in an environment of patience, tolerance, and consideration.

January 11th

Those of this degree possess a clever, critical mind, and a sympathetic nature. An obstinate temperament may give others some cause for concern. Keen interest in literature and art endow these people with the possibility of an intellectual personality. Their sensitive natures require an atmosphere of sympathy and fair play. They should develop the practical side of their natures in order to attain the greatest measure of success and happiness in life.

January 12th

These Capricorn-born possess a clever, perceptive mind, which coupled with great intensity and sincerity of purpose tends to make them critical and sarcastic when their plans and ambitions are interfered with. They can avoid the overdevelopment of this aspect by realizing the consequences of such an attitude. Physical activities should be indulged in as much as possible in order to offset the possibility of overtaxing the mind by too much study. These natives must not permit themselves to become too cautious, suspicious, or cynical.

January 13th

The indications for this chart show an imaginative, energetic, and aggressive nature. An experimental and scientific mind with a leaning towards the mystic and occult sciences is also indicated. The study of science may lead to a professional life. One aspect here shows ability to achieve fame in the humanitarian pursuits. These natives will succeed best if they choose their own vocations. They may meet with sorrow and disappointment in their domestic affairs.

January 14th

These natives are endowed with a magnetic personality and

a pleasing, affectionate disposition. They are fond of music and art and enjoy the beautiful, refined, and esthetic things in life. One aspect here indicates a tendency towards self-indulgence which should be discouraged. They must not allow themselves to be spoiled and pampered as this would only add to their difficulties. They should refuse all unnecessary indulgences and conserve their strength and resources.

January 15th
Those born on this day possess an inspired and artistic nature. They are quick in their emotional reactions and should practise self-discipline and restraint. Their natural ability, intuition, and keen foresight suggests training for a business career where they may be assured of success. One aspect of this Horoscope indicates that they must be cautious while travelling.

January 16th
These natives possess artistic, inspired, and intellectual minds. Unless they have the proper companions and surroundings, their sensitive psyche can easily develop an inferiority complex. Marked introspection, with an inclination to become moody and despondent at the slightest provocation, should be eliminated by pleasant, physical satisfaction. One aspect in this Horoscope indicates that a career combining both executive and artistic abilities will bring great success.

January 17th
Those of this degree possess a determined and forceful nature. Self-discipline will be valuable in order to combat possibility of a monstrous temper. One aspect of this chart shows a level-headed, judicial, and perceptive mentality coupled with a high-strung nervous system. It is, therefore, necessary to avoid too much mental exertion as this may result in serious consequences. Because these natives are studious and ambitious, they may become moody and unruly when their progress is impeded.

January 18th
An agreeable, thoughtful, studious, and retiring disposition is bestowed upon those of this birthday. They may display

great prowess in outdoor sports and physical activities, and there are indications of possible fame in athletics. Their strong wills enable them to overcome many obstacles in life.

January 19th

The indications for this chart show a courteous, pleasing, and sociable disposition. The magnetic personality of these natives will attract many friends. One aspect here shows a tendency to look upon the gloomy side of life. These people should train themselves to instil self-confidence, and help themselves to overcome a dark attitude. Undue excitement and too much dissension will have an adverse reaction on the nervous system.

Compatible and Incompatible Signs of Capricorn

Capricorn is not considered a very sexual Sign, but there is no doubt that it can exhibit a considerable degree of lustfulness. It is a narrow Sign, lending itself easily to excesses. Generally, personal ambition influences matrimonial affairs to a great extent, and the Capricorn native usually seeks some material advantage through marriage. At the same time, there is great sex drive, and the relations of a Capricorn native with members of the opposite sex are quite free.

The men have a strong, protective instinct, while the women, though perfectly capable of looking after themselves and their affairs, affect an appealing air to seek protection.

Capricorns are born managers and seek to manage the lives of everyone with whom they come into contact.

The women use every effort to advance the careers of their husbands and relatives, and are frequently strikingly successful in making something out of quite unpromising material. Many prominent politicians and businessmen owe their positions and successes almost entirely to their Capricorn wives.

When afflicted, Capricorn can be selfish, grasping, and miserly. At the best, it is not an affectionate Sign and makes a much more dutiful than loving partner. The rigidity of outlook and the Mosaic sense of justice (an eye for an eye, and a tooth for a tooth, and so on) makes Capricorn a vindictive Sign. Capricorn people set great store by their rights, and are usually unforgiving. An offence must be expiated by just an adequate amount of punishment.

In matrimonial life, lapses on the part of the husband or wife are rarely forgiven and never forgotten. There may be no second chance for the partner of a Capricorn native. Capricorn marriages, however, are usually lasting, perhaps because Capricorn rarely marries in haste, and is more likely to err through over-caution in choosing a partner than by careless or impulsive love affairs.

Capricornians have a certain ruthlessness about them which may, perhaps, be attributed to overambitious tendencies. They like to appear practical and business-like, and those factors combine to make them materialistic. Marriage for them may, therefore, be viewed more from the standpoint of necessity than from any romantic or sentimental reason. They can be decidedly possessive. They assume an ownership in love that resembles ownership of property.

Though they may be externally undemonstrative, they inwardly have a deep craving for love and affection. If they don't get it (which more often than not is their own fault), they feel lonely and misunderstood. Theirs is a rather complex nature where love or romance is concerned, and the situation is not made easier by their mistrustfulness. As they are realists, there is not a great deal of room for optimism in their nature. They are frequently sticklers for outward convention and appearance.

Capricorn and Aries

The impetuous and aggressive Aries will not have the patience to fall into slow and methodical step with Capricorn. The Capricorn would not be too pleased with the Aries manner of leaping forwards into whatever proposition appeals to him, for Capricorn likes to think things over. Not a good combination as the Ram (Aries) and the Goat (Capricorn) would not make good life partners. There is a compatibility of sorts in sexual affairs, but they are not suited temperamentally or emotionally to each other.

Capricorn and Taurus

There is a fair degree of compatibility for these two IF Taurus will give Capricorn the encouragement and flattery needed. To the warm, Venus-ruled Taurus, Capricorn may seem a little cold and aloof, but if anyone can melt the iciness of Saturn, it is Venus. With mutual understanding of the little quirks in each other's nature they could make a good "go" of a partnership.

Capricorn and Gemini

Here we find too many opposite qualities to be overcome to regard this as a good partnership. Patience is an integral part of the Capricorn nature—it is nonexistent with Gemini. Methodical procedure is a MUST with Capricorn—Gemini would lose interest in anything that takes too long. The solidarity of Saturn would not look kindly on the changeable Gemini Mercury. If Gemini could settle into a slower gait and fall into step with Capricorn, it might work for a while. Fixity is utterly foreign to the Gemini nature, and partnership just doesn't look good for these two.

Capricorn and Cancer

Here are two Signs that could meet on common ground since each has what the other needs. Sympathetic Cancer, with love and understanding, would be a healing balm to the somewhat cold and suspicious Capricorn. Cancer's utter absorption with home and family would also be pleasing to Capricorn. Both are fitted to plod along together until their goal is reached, for Capricorn can make Cancer's dream of security come true.

Capricorn and Leo

These two would not see eye to eye. The outgoing Leo, with freedom of action in social activity, would keep the faucet of Capricorn's suspicion running full blast. Leo just couldn't be long satisfied with Capricorn's plodding nature. Leo is open and carefree, and will leap first and look (maybe) later. Leo forgives and forgets, but Capricorn is slow to forgive, and never forgets. This would not be a good combination.

Capricorn and Virgo

There are many qualities in these two Signs which would make them compatible. With Capricorn's insistence on exactitude and Virgo's demands for perfection in herself and everyone else, the two Signs should get along well. Much of Virgo's carping and criticism would be eliminated, and they could weep a duet when the world gets too rough for them. Mercury, as Virgo's ruler, is quite different as Gemini's ruler. Here he would blend well with Saturn, Capricorn's ruler. Both these Signs bestow great pride upon their natives, and Virgo and Capricorn show this in their personal appearance and in their home. This is basically a good combination.

Capricorn and Libra

It is true that Libra can attract and intrigue Capricorn, but it is likely that Libra may become bored with the steady, non-varying Capricorn. Capricorn would have to put the damper on social activity, and it would be subject to Capricorn's dictum. Capricorn is far more liberal in sex matters before marriage than after, so Libra would have to learn to walk the tight wire of Capricorn's behaviour patterns. If Libra can do this, there is a good chance for a marriage between these two.

Capricorn and Scorpio

This does not look too rosy. Scorpio is there with a swift sting and a temper that can lash violently and effectively. Capricorn meets this with the stubbornness that is his own brand. Both are very disagreeable when frustrated. Not a good combination unless softened by other aspects.

Capricorn and Sagittarius

Here is a study in extreme opposites. One is free, open, jolly and optimistic; the other is sober, restrictive, and suspicious. Sagittarius would go far to overcome the unpleasantness that could result from Capricorn's taciturn and cold exterior, but would probably get rather weary of agreeing, complying, and conceding all the time. Unless Sagittarius is so benumbed by love that he—or she—will give up all freedoms and stay pinned to the hearth, there is not much chance for happiness here.

Capricorn and Capricorn

These two should have an enduring marriage, for there is much compatibility between two Capricorns. Both have the same long-range aspirations and the basic qualities to attain them. One cannot find too much fault with the other as they have much the same faults. In important things, they would both have what it takes to overcome all obstacles. Fine ingredients for a happy partnership.

Capricorn and Aquarius

Here we have a difficult combination to analyse. The sure-footed Capricorn may not be able to keep up with the nimble water-bearer Aquarius, who aims to make the world a better place to live in. Capricorn wants all effort—and anything else Aquarius has to give—to be centred at home for their mutal good. Capricorn will not tolerate the Aquarian's interest in other people. Aquarius can't abide confinement or restriction of any kind, and may pack up and go out into the world to find bigger and better goals to conquer. A doubtful combination.

Capricorn and Pisces

Capricorn will find a sympathetic and understanding mate in Pisces, and the steady-going temperament of Capricorn is just what Pisces needs for a sense of confidence and security. The sexual needs are compatible, and the social goals are similar. Capricorn is more practical than Pisces, but this is one of the many things Pisces will admire. Too, Capricorn will be happy knowing that Pisces' dependence will increase each year, for Capricorn is happiest when needed.

Some Famous Persons Born in the Sign of Capricorn

Konrad Adenauer—German Statesman
Clement Attlee—British Prime Minister
Marlene Dietrich—Actress
Barry Goldwater—US Senator
J. Edgar Hoover—FBI Administrator
Joan of Arc—French Martyr
Danny Kaye—Comedian
Johannes Kepler—Astronomer and Astrologer
Rudyard Kipling—Author
Robert E. Lee—Confederate General
George C. Marshall—US General and Statesman
Tony Martin—Actor
Ethel Merman—Actress

Gamal Abdul Nasser—UAR President
Sir Isaac Newton—Physicist and Philosopher
Richard M. Nixon—US President
Carl Sandburg—Poet and Biographer
Albert Schweitzer—Physician and Philosopher
Maurice Utrillo—Painter
Daniel Webster—Statesman
Woodrow Wilson—US President

II

AQUARIUS

January 20th–February 18th

THIS SIGN symbolizes judgment. This constellation forms the starry Urn of Minos, from which flow wrath and condemnation or blessings and rewards, according to work done in the body regardless of theological faith. The earlier baptismal urns of the primitive Christians and the elaborate stone fonts of the later churches are relics of this great astral religion.

The Sign Aquarius signifies the legs of the Grand Archetypal Man and, therefore, represents the locomotive functions of the human organism. It is the natural emblem of the movable and migratory forces of the body.

The Water-Bearer, upon the esoteric planisphere, is occupied by Reuben. "The excellency of dignity and the excellency of power," says Jacob, "unstable as water thou shalt not excel." A simple but magnificent astrological description of the Sign has, from time immemorial, been two water lines, like the ripples of running water.

The Sign not only contains the rites and mysteries of consecration, but will reveal the potency of all sacred and dedicated works.

The mystical gem is the garnet.

The fortunate day is Wednesday.

The fortunate numbers are eight and four.

The fortunate colours for this Sign are pastel shades of blue and green.

Best locations for success are around busy places and in large cities.

Aquarius is the lowest of the airy Trigon, and the constellation of Uranus.

Upon the intellectual plane, Aquarius represents the truth

of material phenomena. Those dominated by its influx constitute the school of inductive philosophy—the grand basis of all science. They represent the intellectual and scientific spirit of their age and generation, and cannot advance far beyond those classes of facts which are demonstrable to the senses.

The Aquarius personality is hard to define precisely, because it is changeable. This makes a personality at one time active, expressive, interesting, and attractive, and at other times moody, indifferent, and indolent. The latter are reactions to the intense activity of an unusually serious mind.

Aquarians are remarkable people to meet. They have naturally charming manners, and though somewhat reserved or timid in some situations, they can be expressive, and create a good impression upon all they meet. Aquarians are honest and make loyal friends. Altruism is one of their chief characteristics, but this does not always mean they are absolutely right in their humanitarian views. They are self-willed and can be most obstinate and independent.

They possess a good degree of the spirit of adventure.

Emotionally, they are sensitive and easily hurt. They are apt to show a temper ranging from a simple manifestation of hurt feelings to downright anger. In the latter mood, they can speak most unpleasantly. It is fortunate that they usually get over it quickly and are not inclined to hold a grudge for long. The women of this Sign are apt to hang on to unpleasant ideas much longer than the men.

Aquarians dislike pettiness in others; they should examine themselves and apply the same critical appraisal. They have a great deal of courage and are often daring to the point of rashness. They are ambitious, and unusually persistent in anything that interests them. They are dreamers, and have the power to make many of their dreams become realities. Few people realize it, but if others would understand and leave an Aquarian alone when he or she happens to be temperamental, they would find that such an individual will get over it quickly. If one has a tendency to argue with an Aquarian at the wrong time, that argument can continue for quite a period. There are times, however, when one cannot get an argument out of them no matter what is said.

When influenced by good feelings, they are among the world's most thoughtful and gracious people.

Those who reflect the best qualities of this Sign possess an intensely active mind. They are always busy at something or other, even though it is but a daydream. Usually they show good judgment, but when they are influenced by their emotions and prejudices, their judgment is poor. They should do all within their power to avoid this form of fallacious thinking.

They have unusually keen powers of observation. They are apt to note details without apparently paying much attention. Their powers of analysis, synthesis, and classification also function rapidly. They are capable of action before many people have had an opportunity to think! This quick action is all right, except in instances where it applies to their own emotions. In such cases, they are likely to act without logical analysis. In their imagination they are free to enjoy all sorts of flights of fantasy. They are also capable of using their imaginations in practical ways when they so desire. Imagination is the only faculty that enables one to visualize the creation of new things essential to progress. In musing or daydreaming, one toys with whatever thought, idea, or fantasy is in the mind. The imagination enables these natives to review the past with clarity, and helps them construct ideas as to their future progress.

They have exceptionally good memories. The power of memory depends upon the amount of attention devoted to acquiring knowledge or information. They have the ability to learn most things easily, and they are apt to be satisfied with just being aware of what they know and letting it go at that. They may forget the name of someone to whom they were introduced, but they will remember some details of that person for many years.

These natives are inclined to classify all knowledge which comes to them from external sources. They should apply the same principle to the ideas that arise from within in order to determine their true value before acting upon these musings.

In considering inspired ideas, it must be borne in mind that such thoughts come without any apparent cause, though they may be responses to certain stimuli. An impulse, on the other hand, is a personal desire or wish, and is always connected with a recent association or activity. Aquarians should learn the art of recognizing the value of their inspired ideas, for Aquarians have remarkable intuition which gives them an unusually keen insight into the motives of others. Aquarians are individualists and no one can help them in any manner until they are willing to help themselves.

Indications for this Sign show general good health if its natives will prevent their moods from causing them to become negligent. They have good constitutions, even though they have emotion-wracked nervous systems. They must guard against carelessness in diet, and avoid excesses of any kind. They must learn what agrees with them. This Sign rules the calves and ankles, and also has much to do with the glandular and circulatory systems of the body. Persons born under it must not neglect to take exercise in order to keep their bodies in good condition. Aquarians usually possess a fondness for sports and entertainment. They find pleasure in many things that other people do not seemingly enjoy. They have an appreciation of artistic things—music and the beauties of nature. They take a keen delight in all sorts of travel, and will, no doubt, travel much in the course of their lives. Travel affords an outlet for their adventurous and enterprising nature, and adds much to their store of knowledge.

Love plays an important part in the Aquarians' lives; their sensitivity in love and romance is proverbial. Their wooing is idealistic, devoted, considerate, and intensely affectionate. They are quite sensitive regarding the object of their affections, in fact, inclined to almost unreasonable jealousy. Fortunately, if they are among the more thoughtful Aquarians, they will get over the predisposition to jealousy in time. This attitude occurs because they are not conscious of the intensity and depth of their own emotional natures. They are apt to misinterpret their impulses. They are so sensitive about love that they notice the slightest inattention, even though it may be entirely inadvertent. It is their sensitivity that causes disillusionment. It is true that these natives' affections are sincere and deep, but it is also true that they react against themselves in such matters because they are oblivious to their own motives. Love proves a stimulus to them and affords a powerful source of inspiration. They have the sort of mind and personality that enables them to get along with any particular kind of person they choose. Aquarians need to take into consideration their own sensitivity, and attain a measure of self-mastery. The sensitive, affectionate, and ardent nature of Aquarians requires expression—they crave love, affection, and tenderness. Try as they will to hide their feelings, desire is still there. They require devotion as well as the companionship of an active intellect that preferably has patience and understanding.

Indications for this Sign show that its natives have considerable love for children. Aquarians make devoted parents, and desire to give a child great advantages. Although these people possess an active and adventurous nature, they are fond of home life and its comforts. They enjoy having a place to which they may return from their escapades.

It is indicated that the temperament of these natives is adapted to intellectual rather than physical labour, although they are capable of doing any kind of work they set out to do. They are versatile and adaptable; they often take an interest in new projects, for Aquarians enjoy the unusual. They are efficient in anything they do, and are to be found in a variety of occupations. They make good salesmen, aviators, electricians, organizers, and inventors. They are found in all sorts of uncommon pursuits such as exploring, research, and experimental work, and they usually are intensely interested in the occult. They have minds which enable them to rise and progress in life, regardless of education. This is because they are *natural* students and thinkers, and possess the courage and perseverance to succeed in anything they undertake. When it is necessary to make an actual choice of vocation, they are apt to experience difficulty in coming to a decision as to exactly what they should do. This hesitation happens because Aquarians have so many talents.

In partnerships, they can be most successful, as they have a deep sense of co-operation and are enterprising. They are more successful in partnership affairs when there is someone backing them. Though they are self-sufficient enough to be in business for themselves, they must learn to be patient with themselves and to face early discouragements. It usually takes a variety of experiences in life to make the average

Aquarian see things this way, but once they do, the business usually grows and is financially successful.

According to indications, many of these natives are not as careful in their financial affairs as is prudent. They are, on occasion, too generous and are oft-times unwise spenders. Once they are able to control this extravagance to a reasonable degree and apply a more conservative principle to their natures, they may build towards financial security. They will not have much success in speculation, and it is advisable to be extremely conservative in such ventures. Practical investments in electronics industries and aviation stocks usually prove to be advantageous. They have a liking for get-rich-quick propositions, and usually succumb to clever sales appeals.

Aquarians will attract many people, for they are loyal in their friendships and do all they can to help those whom they love. The Aquarian natives lead active and interesting social lives because they are so capable of understanding human nature. In summary, they have an extremely sensitive emotional nature. This often proves to be their only stumbling block to progress.

The Aquarius Child

These children are of a rather shy and retiring nature. They enjoy solitude to an extreme degree, and this causes them to withdraw into themselves. They are naturally affectionate and of sweet and kind disposition. They are usually pliant to the opinion of a loved one, and will readily yield for the sake of harmony. Aquarius is an intellectual Sign, and its children usually have active minds. They are persistent and usually successful.

The principal bad habit of the Aquarian child is worry. This trait reflects on their physical well-being; it is advisable for the parents to see that they do not come into contact with inharmonious companions who might worry them.

The fundamental vitality of the Aquarian child is moderate; the pathology denotes that super-sensitivity and depressive moods may develop into an inferiority complex.

Defective circulation will contribute to illness, therefore, an orderly life is necessary. The best medicine for them is harmonious surroundings. Places outside the city on high ground would be the best location for success. Diseases peculiar to this group include anemia, blood poisoning, spastic nervous diseases, swollen ankles, and varicose veins. They are subject to psychic disturbances, and obscure diseases of a nervous origin. They should never live in an environment where they will become apprehensive, as an acute nervous condition may develop. They are naturally adapted to buying and selling, as they are born traders.

Literary ability and inventive genius are two talents which, if properly developed, can lead them to occupations connected with scientific research.

The Aquarian Wife

The Aquarian woman does not slip into matrimony with ease, although she is well-equipped in that she is capable, intellectual, discerning, adaptable, and often very talented. She has the ability to accomplish a day's work without grumbling or fatigue.

Her interests are apt to be wide, and it never occurs to her to watch her husband's actions with suspicion or to check up on how he spends his spare time. She naturally trusts him. Her own behaviour is above reproach. Aquarian women are the kindest in the world, and they would rather suffer themselves than create a condition which could cause someone else grief or sorrow. Basically, however, the Aquarian woman is temperamental, and should her urge for a change of partner be sufficiently justified, she would make the change without regret. Emotionally she is responsive, but her intellect rules her, and she is most appreciated as a wife when married to a successful man whose work she can share.

The Aquarian Husband

The Aquarian husband is the kindest and most generous of all types. The generosity of Leo and Aries is well known, but it is nothing compared to the openhanded giving without thought of reward that is part of the character of the Aquarian husband.

Aquarian men are not ardent lovers unless some other

planetary configuration stimulates this urge. They are gracious and sociable; they accept marriage as part of the domestic scheme. They are perfect gentlemen in every way, and treat their wives and family with the same consideration and courtesy that they accord to strangers.

The drawback in their marital relationship appears to be their impersonality. Women seem to prefer possessive, dominant types to the broad-minded Aquarian husband. His impersonality appears to many women as a lack of interest; as wives, they want the whole attention of their husbands.

It has been said that the Aquarian's universal interest will one day be the attitude of the entire world. Such men are happy when married to highly intellectual women whose humanitarian outlooks coincide with their own.

The Cusps of Aquarius

(If your birthday is not within the cusp of your Sign, the following does not apply to you.)

If the Birthday is from January 20th through January 23rd

You were born in Aquarius with Capricorn tendencies. Your ruling planets are Uranus and Saturn. This denotes that you are versatile, methodical, exacting, and practical. You have a good memory and quick perception. If you develop your magnetic power, it will be possible for you to become a miracle worker. You investigate every venture and do not let criticism alter you from your course.

You are always helping someone, and are often discouraged because you are not in a position to do more. Remember, self-preservation is the first law of nature. After you have provided for your own needs, you can help others to better advantage. You like to fight your own battles and seldom bother others with your worries or problems.

If the birthday is from February 15th through February 18th

You are an Aquarius with Pisces tendencies. Your ruling planets are Uranus and Neptune. This indicates that you are inclined to be somewhat jealous and reckless in love affairs. You can easily fit into any environment.

You are likely to be successful in any undertaking along

scientific lines. Your experiences in life may make you seem petty and cynical, but in reality you will always be liberal and broad-minded. You are usually suspicious before you investigate a proposition. You have a personality that attracts many friends who respect your opinions and follow your advice. You are fond of travel and will take some long journeys. Yours will be a long, prosperous, and useful existence.

The Decanates of Aquarius

If the birthday is between January 20th and January 31st
The personal and ruling planet is Uranus, sometimes considered the Spiritual Awakener. It is the planet of change and energy. It may bring these natives before the public early in life and endow them with a magnetic psychic personality. The double influence of Uranus will aid them to offset some of the more negative aspects of their Sign.

If the birthday is between February 1st and February 9th
The personal planet is Mercury. It is considered a convertible planet; it greatly affects whatever planet it is in conjunction with. Mercury controls the brain and nerves, and makes its subjects excitable and nervous.

This planet is known to be the great mental ruler. Mercury will play a prominent part in the lives of these natives, since it controls commercial and literary affairs. With Uranus and Mercury as the guiding stars, there is every indication that these natives will excel in all endeavours where concentrated intellectual application is an important factor.

If the birthday is between February 10th and February 18th
The personal planet is Venus. Venus is one of the most benevolent planets in the solar system. This planet indicates harmonious and fortunate surroundings. It favours pleasure and cheerfulness. It also brings out the artistic, idealistic, and musical faculties. While the planet Venus has a decided influence of her own, she is greatly affected by aspects from other planets. Since Uranus is the ruler of the birth Sign, the influences of Venus will be greatly expanded by the profound mental activities which Uranus governs.

The Degrees of Aquarius

January 20th

You are good-natured, hospitable, and diplomatic. You have a natural affinity for the sea and could be successful in maritime affairs. Some trouble through relatives, wills, or financial documents is shown. Your somewhat sensuous and artistic nature will attract many unusual friendships throughout your life.

January 21st

You possess a highly emotional disposition. You will gain through the experience of those who may put obstacles in your path from time to time. Although deception and troubles through friends and relatives may retard your progress, you will make some unexpected financial gains despite your difficulties.

January 22nd

You are an idealist. Being diplomatic and versatile, you will make many important friendships throughout your life. One aspect in this Horoscope shows a tendency to fly off the handle at the least provocation. This will make you liable to accidents and sudden reverses, especially through marriage, law, and property. Since you are fond of learning, use your knowledge to overcome your inherent negative qualities.

January 23rd

There will be many influential friendships in your life. You have an inventive turn of mind and can be successful in scientific endeavours. Some persons born in this degree will gain fame and fortune through sheer ability. You have great love of travel and will move around from one place to another.

January 24th

You may experience much sorrow and suffer many trials and tribulations. You need a great deal of love and affection to help you fight life's battles. Your strange moods will make you somewhat eccentric and contrary in your ideas and actions. Do not try to buy your friendships but earn them through good deeds.

January 25th

You are fond of writing, reading, change, and novelty. You can be successful through your interest in new fields of endeavour. For this reason, success may be found in some ultramodern activity. One aspect in this Horoscope indicates possible trouble with the law. Some help will come to you from an elderly relative.

January 26th

You may earn money easily, but you will be inclined to be extravagant and squander your money on pleasure. One aspect in this Horoscope indicates the possibility of injuring your health through overwork or study. Trouble from the opposite sex may cost you a considerable sum of money. Beware of false promises and secret intrigues.

January 27th

You are dignified, ambitious, intuitive, and generous to a fault. You seek and give much pleasure to others and may, thus, suffer imposition. Nevertheless, money should be plentiful. You are liable to suffer from inflammatory ailments from time to time. Marriage is somewhat unfavourably aspected, so look before you leap, and don't be taken in by outward appearances.

January 28th

You have a strong character and show much talent, but you are liable to impair your health due to mental and physical over-exertion. You are clever and fond of debate and politics. You can be successful in municipal government work. Excellent judges, lawyers, and law enforcement officers are shown here.

January 29th

You will be fortunate in most things. You are ambitious, strong-willed, argumentative, clever, and worldly-wise. You have the ability to rule and direct others. You will enjoy life in your own way. You have strong love for the home and will most surely own one during your lifetime. Honour through children and a happy married life are also indicated.

January 30th

You are sympathetic, impulsive, yet practical and tenacious. You will have good fortune with your relatives. You will have a tendency to become brusque and irritable when your plans go astray. One aspect in the Horoscope shows the possibility of success and recognition in the artistic world.

January 31st

You will be somewhat stubborn and abrupt at times. This attitude will cover up some of your sterling traits of character and excellent intellect, which will insure a successful career. Curb a tendency to be bold and venturesome, with a tendency towards waywardness. You will go far in the business world when you learn to control your negative emotions.

February 1st

You are strong-willed and obstinate, courageous and venturesome, impulsive and affectionate. You are fond of music, the arts, travel, and the good things in life. Success in a maritime career or in the artistic world is shown by this degree.

February 2nd

You possess a generous, independent, enthusiastic, and optimistic attitude. You love freedom and open-air life. Your love for the great open spaces will make for a good deal of good fellowship, and public recognition in the sporting world. You are blessed with a strong constitution and, seemingly, tireless energy.

February 3rd

You are original and persistent and have an intellectual mind. You are fond of study and may have outstanding scientific ability. Curb a tendency to be too bold and venturesome. You are liable to suffer from overstrain and accidents. Moderation should be learned and a quick temper curbed.

February 4th

You possess powerful emotions with the ability to sway others. You should guard against nervous tension, colds, and chills. Your health may not be too robust. Trouble through property, documents, and superiors is probable. You should be successful in the legal profession. One degree in this chart shows success in banking and insurance.

February 5th

You possess a sensitive and responsive disposition that is highly strung and irritable at times. Unexpected changes may affect your fortunes, but secret help will be forthcoming when you least expect it. This degree shows aspirations towards travel, and success in foreign lands.

February 6th

You possess force of character and some specialized talents. You have an ambitious disposition and are always looking for perfection. There will be a friendly relationship with relatives and a possible inheritance of a considerable amount. There is also possible success in the field of electronics and modern scientific research.

February 7th

You possess a somewhat suspicious and distrustful nature and may be given to intrigue and eccentricities. Curb a tendency to be critical of your friends and associates. One aspect in this Horoscope shows that you are receptive to great ideas but incapable of effectively carrying them out.

February 8th

You may have many trials to contend with in business and domestic matters. You may be changeable and vacillating, and inclined to be querulous. You are unsympathetic and not receptive to the misfortunes of others. You may lead a humdrum life, experiencing little good fortune, unless you develop the more positive side of your character.

February 9th

You possess considerable enthusiasm and some practical ability for public work. You are the type of person who will carve out his own fortune, but is liable to sudden losses in business due to unscrupulous persons. Take care and use good judgment when signing documents. You must continually be on guard against deception both in your business and personal life.

February 10th

You may experience many vicissitudes of fortune as you are liable to unexpected reversals through ill health, treachery, and deception in business. You are brutally frank at times, yet, by nature, you are fundamentally kind and sincere. You have what is known as a complex nature.

February 11th

You possess a hospitable temperament with some capacity for organization. You will find great inspiration in writing. You will be liable to occasional upheavals in business. You must guard against deception, both practised and suffered. You should continually be on the alert to successfully combat a tendency to create an argument for the sake of mental stimulation.

February 12th

You possess broad sympathies and strong emotions. Strong love for the mother is shown by this degree. You are fond of the opposite sex and will be generally successful in both love and business. You must curb fits of depression or you will miss much of the fun in life.

February 13th

You possess an erratic and impulsive nature. You have a vivid imagination and love novelty and change, and are easily influenced by others. However, when your temper is aroused, you can become stubborn and unforgiving. You are capable of great success in any of the intellectual vocations.

February 14th

You are artistically, musically, and scientifically minded. You are also impulsive, quick tempered, aggressive, and high strung. You have a mystical temperament with a turn for philosophical study. You are often extravagant, but you have profound understanding and possess good business ability.

February 15th

You must learn to not be extravagant. You are clever, but inclined to be critical of others less gifted. Ups and downs of fortune will result from your impetuous nature. Curb this tendency or ill health may retard success and happiness.

February 16th

You possess a keen intuition and a spiritual outlook. You have a kind and generous disposition, but are liable to sudden outbursts of anger and resentment. You must overcome the habit of being too pessimistic in your point of view. You will be successful in secret matters and associations. The possibility of a wealthy marriage is indicated.

February 17th

You will be generally successful in business and love and will gain through elderly relatives and friends, especially females. You are very witty and blessed with considerable literary ability. This degree promises much good fortune and domestic joy. You have strong socialistic tendencies and are militantly democratic.

February 18th

You possess the power to turn adversity into triumph. You will make or break your own destiny. You will be successful in business and love despite occasional disappointments through strangers. Your intellectual faculties and abilities are outstanding and your ambitions will be realized.

The Compatible and Incompatible Signs of Aquarius

Aquarians belong to the idealistic group of Signs and are not particularly concerned with sexual matters alone. It is a contemplative, philosophical sort of Sign, with great interest in life and humanity.

The Aquarian outlook is a friendly one, and friendship largely replaces possessive love and sexuality. In spite of a progressive outlook, Aquarius is rigid in matters of morality, and tends to have old-fashioned and Victorian ideas.

Under affliction, Aquarians can become ineffective muddlers and shiftless wastrels. On a low plane they are clumsy, blundering, and harmless. They mean well and have little backbone and less common sense. The positive Aquarian is friendly, helpful, and susceptible to praise and flattery. The idealism of the Sign, however, does not altogether favour happiness or contentment in marriage—especially in the men—and this may lead to wandering affections.

Aquarians are original in their ways, and have the pleasing habit of anticipating the likes and dislikes of those with whom they come into contact. Hence, they are invariably well liked, and for this reason can become social successes. In many ways they are eccentric. For example, they may have eccentric ideas on art in an attempt to appear original. They may become snobbish in an attempt to establish an air of social pre-eminence.

Because of this eccentricity it is often an exceptional task to please them. The exterior inevitably displays no emotion and maintains a consistently impassive front. Nevertheless, their form of temperament is very pleasing to many who admire and envy the trait.

Do not confuse "excitement" with "enthusiasm," however. Certainly Aquarians are capable of unprecedented enthusiasm. Furthermore, they do not intend to hide their light under a bushel basket if they can help it. They have special qualities, and intend to let the world know about them.

In courtship and love-making they can be quite artistic. They have the ability to turn a pretty compliment; they know how to select sentimental mementos. Those of this Sign should study well the basic qualities of those whom they select as life partners. Many heartaches and much disillusionment can be avoided by doing this.

The general comparisons are as follows:

Aquarius and Aries

The instability of Aries and the unpredictable quality of Aquarius would be provoking to both of these persons. The whole partnership would be a gamble, and Uranus (ruling

Aquarius) and Mars (ruling Aries) make a rather explosive combination. Aries is exasperated by the Aquarian's changeable qualities (Uranus is the planet of change). Aries might be somewhat chagrined at the Aquarian habit of pouring water on some of his enthusiasms. Not a good chance to take.

Aquarius and Taurus

If these two expect sweetness and compatibility to come from this combination, they are both in for shock. The unpredictable Aquarian is too much for easygoing Taurus. The conservative Taurus habits will soon get on the high-strung nerves of dynamic Aquarius, and the battle is on. Both of these natives love ease and comfort, but there is wide divergence of views as to how to obtain them. The Taurus lover is not going to take kindly to the Aquarian's unwillingness to share secrets. Better look long and hard before taking this leap.

Aquarius and Gemini

These two should have a satisfactory basis for compatibility. The Mercurial Gemini will love the "surprise" quality of Aquarius, and both adore change. The dual personality of Gemini can find its complement in the many faceted personality of Aquarius. Neither are overly ardent in their sexual impulses, and both are intellectual. Should a union between these two take place, Gemini must not feel shut out or offended when Aquarius wants to be alone. It is a passing mood only.

Aquarius and Cancer

This does not look like a good chance to take. Aquarians love to keep whirling on the social scene, which will wear the quiet, home-loving Cancer to shreds. Aquarians want to share their good things with the world, while Cancer believes personal obligations should come first. Cancer is conservative in taste and Aquarius more forward looking. What with the eccentricity of Aquarius and the moods of Cancer, the odds here are too great for this combination to prove successful unless one becomes entirely subservient to the other.

Aquarius and Leo

The Sun (Leo) and Uranus (Aquarius) make a really good

combination. Leo likes surprises and Aquarius will certainly supply them. There is mutual respect for the talents of the other. Both are much interested in helping others. This combination would also be ideal for a business partnership dealing with the public. They are each aware of the other's needs in intimate matters, and this could be a happy combination for both Signs.

Aquarius and Virgo

The Virgo nervous system is in for an increase of jittery moments with the bang, bang of the Aquarius surprises. Virgo must have a precise, well-ordered existence, while Aquarius couldn't care less for "set" systems—or order—when he doesn't want it. Aquarians will not tolerate restraint, and Virgoans seek to change things to their own way of liking by criticism. Unless these two have the same cultural background and educational level, the basic differences between them would be almost insurmountable. There may be a glimmer of hope should they be college sweethearts or if they both work in the same business—but it would be well for both to shop around a little longer before taking the leap.

Aquarius and Libra

There can be rare perfection in this combination. Both like the same thing—beauty, society, and people. Venus (Libra) and Uranus (Aquarius) will give each other all things they seek, for they are perfect affinities. One tiny shadow falls across the Libran's path. They must learn to accept Aquarius' need for solitude at times, and not question it or demand any explanation. It is a basic need of Aquarians and it soon passes—Libra must take it in stride. Otherwise, this is a wonderful combination.

Aquarius and Scorpio

Here are two who will do much better just staying friends. Marriage would probably create a battle of nerves for both. Aquarians with their flitting hither and yon would set the solid Scorpio into a tizzy. Aquarius' reserve in love-making would not fill the passionate demands of Scorpio. The "fixed" Scorpio could not feel sure of his own name after a month of

Aquarian unpredictability. They both admire a lot about the other, but marriage would bring out the possessiveness of Scorpio and Aquarius would rebel. Better keep it outside the fence of marriage.

Aquarius and Sagittarius

These two could have a pleasant life together, for there is much in common in their basic make-up. They are both social, and go in for large groups and public-spirited associates. They both like the change that travel gives and they both like excitement. Sagittarius is one of the few Signs who will understand the idiosyncrasies of the Aquarian temperament and will treat them considerately. He wants the same indulgence regarding his own little quirks. Could be a happily-ever-after affair for both.

Aquarius and Capricorn

This is an unlikely combination. These two are simply too different to resolve their divergent qualities. Aquarius' interests are wide-spread—the home alone is not enough to keep an Aquarian spellbound. Capricorn expects home interests to come first. Aquarius is likely to make up new definitions for boredom after a steady diet of the slow, plodding Capricorn, and is likely to flee to the big wide world to conquer.

Aquarius and Aquarius

At last we have just the right mate for an Aquarian—another Aquarian! No one on earth could be so in harmony with either of these as they are with each other. They can well understand the qualities which baffle, bewilder, and madden others. This is the type of couple one meets in the out-of-the-way places of the world doing research together. Many of the early missionaries were Aquarian couples or those who had strong Aquarius aspects in their Horoscopes. Yes, here is the perfect combination of the Aquarian age, the torchbearers of human dignity.

Aquarius and Pisces

This may not be a bad combination if Pisces will study the Aquarian Horoscope. Here are tolerance and human sympathy coupled with the need for human understanding by the Piscean partner, who is willing to go all out to find that elusive cup of human tolerance and dignity. He will surely find it in his Aquarian mate. All Pisces has to do to make the marriage a happy and lasting one is to give Aquarius the benefit of the doubt.

Some Famous Persons Born in the Sign of Aquarius

Marian Anderson—Singer
John Barrymore—Actor
Jack Benny—Comedian
Omar N. Bradley—US General
George Burns—Comedian
Charles Darwin—Naturalist
Charles Dickens—Author
Jimmy Durante—Comedian
Thomas A. Edison—Inventor
William Randolph Hearst—Publisher
Jascha Heifetz—Violinist
Fritiz Kreisler—Composer and Violinist
Charles Lindbergh—Aviator
Abraham Lincoln—US President
Douglas MacArthur—US General
Harold Macmillan—British Prime Minister
W. Somerset Maugham—Novelist
James A. Michener—Novelist
Franklin D. Roosevelt—US President
Ann Sothern—Actress
Adlai Stevenson—US Statesman

12

PISCES

February 19th–March 20th

THIS SIGN symbolizes the flood because when the Sun passes through this Sign the rainy season commences, and the snows of winter melt, flooding the valley below. This Sign is also the terminus of Apollo's journey through the twelve Signs.

The Sign Pisces signifies the feet of the Grand Cosmic Man, and, therefore, represents the basis or foundation of all external things, as well as the mechanical forces of humanity. It is the natural emblem of patient servitude and obedience. It signifies confirmation, also baptism by water. It indicates to us the divine purpose of the great cycle. This cycle commences with the disruptive, flashing, dominating fire of Aries and terminates with its polar opposite, water—the symbol of universal equilibrium.

Pisces is the last emanation of the watery Trigon, and is the constellation of Neptune. Upon the intellectual plane, Pisces represent mental indifference. It is the polar opposite of the head. Those dominated by its influx express a peculiar indifference to those things which generally interest others. They take all things as they come and pay no serious attention to any.

The mystical gem of Pisces is the bloodstone.

The fortunate day is Friday.

The fortunate numbers are five and eight.

The fortunate colours for this Sign are all shades of lavender.

Best locations for success are the seashore and cities near water.

There are two distinct types of Pisces personalities. One is very charming, magnetic, attractive, and pleasant to meet.

The other has all of these qualities, but possesses a great degree of reserve that borders on bashfulness, and does not give any positive expression to the personality. This reserve often causes misunderstanding. If you have the latter type of personality it is up to you to make the necessary corrections and endeavour to become more expressive and self-confident.

You must bear in mind that some very great people have been born in your Sign and that they, too, had to overcome sensitivity and timidity and instil within themselves self-confidence, determination, and courage. *Study yourself, know yourself, and then set out to bring out your personality to the best of your ability; and you will be happy.*

You have a naturally kind, generous, sympathetic, patient, and reserved disposition. From an intellectual and emotional point of view, you are quite sensitive in your reaction to the spoken word and the general attitude of people around you. By nature you are peaceful. You have an extremely sensitive, yet not necessarily quick, temper. Anger and peevishness have a tendency to upset your nervous system.

It is well within your power to overcome any timidity or unbecoming reserve. By making an effort to cultivate the positive and expressive qualities of your personality, you will make yourself attractive and interesting and greatly enhance your prospects of success in life. You are faithful to any trust or commission. You have a fine and deep sense of appreciation for any kindness shown you, whether it be in thought or action. Take stock of yourself and do all within your power to build up your self-confidence, natural courage, and power of self-expression. Master your timidity and extreme sensitivity and you will do much towards making yourself happier and more successful. It is true that your mind is the power behind your personality and its expression.

You have good powers of observation, perception, and judgment. However, it would be wise to take stock of yourself and see how great a part your emotions play in the process of reasoning along certain lines, particularly in relation to matters which affect your prejudices and pet notions. When you reason according to these, your judgment is apt to be erroneous.

It it true that each and every one of us has a mind of our

own and that we have the right to use it as we desire. But personal prejudice often precludes the possibility of one arriving at an intelligent understanding of a subject. In any discussion, when all facts are considered only one side can be right. With some Pisces, however, both sides can be wrong, because of their preconceived notions. Do your best to avoid this type of reasoning and you will attain true knowledge and understanding in the course of your life.

You have a keen perception and are able to grasp many details of a proposition that some others are apt to miss. You have the ability to learn things quite easily. In most instances you retain what you learn.

You have a vivid imagination and may be fond of romantic daydreaming. You enjoy the realm of fantasy to such an extent that you may experience disillusion in some of your personal affairs and romantic ventures. This is due to the fact that through your imagination you have developed a romantic ideal which is beyond the realm of possibility. It is only natural that disillusion follows. Your imagination is given to you for practical purposes. Some of the world's memory wizards belong to this Sign. They are able to recall facts with a great degree of accuracy. The original impression on the memory depends upon interest and attention. The people of your Sign, however, are highly impressionable and apt to retain this first impression.

You have the ability to learn anything that you set out to learn. Your memory enables you to retain and recall knowledge to consciousness without difficulty. You have good reasoning power. You are inclined to consider ideas until you are sure of them.

Travel affords you much pleasure and relaxation from the routine monotony of everyday life. Many minor travels, and several rather extensive journeys, usually come into the lives of the average Pisces.

Your feelings are deep and intense. Once you have overcome your reserve, you can be very demonstrative in your affection. You are devoted to and considerate of the object of your affection. You must, however, guard against unreasonable jealousy. One of your nature desires much attention and affection, and if this is not forthcoming you are apt to be deeply hurt, and you usually show it. You are extremely sensitive in love and often try to disguise your feelings. Your romantic fantasy may often lead you to lofty, but impractical, ideals; it is likely that reality will bring you back to earth with a thud. To one of your nature, love and companionship are essential to true happiness. Love inspires you and brings you renewed courage and self-confidence. You can get along with anyone that you love.

In selecting a mate, you should guard against emotional impulsiveness. If there is not a reasonable blend between your intellectual, emotional, and physical qualities and those of your mate, the marriage will prove to be discordant. Do your best to overcome unwise emotional sensitivity and you will do much to enhance your prospects of happiness.

Your birthsign shows a great love for children. Your Sign is known as a fruitful Sign. You are a fond and somewhat indulgent parent. You possess a great love of home life. A harmonious home life is most essential to your welfare and happiness. Ordinarily, you take good care of your home and show taste in its furnishings and arrangement.

Pisces are well suited for positions in the healing arts. They also make good instructors, mechanics, designers, florists, pattern makers, machinists, religious workers, authors, actors and actresses, agriculturalists, and ranchers. The average Pisces is industrious, conscientious, and faithful to his vocation. He is attentive to details, and capable of performing exacting work, such as pattern making and designing scientific instruments. Pisces may be trusted with important commissions and responsibilities.

Those born under Pisces are capable of originality in their work, and often develop new ways of doing things more efficiently and at less cost. Pisces people are inclined to be apprehensive when in business for themselves. They create their own obstacles to economic progress. They represent the type of personality that can make a success of partnership ventures. They are naturally co-operative and the right type of associate will bring out their natural ability.

In financial matters you are occasionally conservative and occasionally an impulsive spender. You have natural conservative principles but you react against them. The true secret of financial success and security lies in your making money work for you. This can only be accomplished by saving and investing wisely. Some Pisces are inclined to delve into speculative ventures with a fair degree of success.

Your generous and sympathetic nature will bring you many friends and acquaintances. Your choice of friends will be the intellectual and spiritual types. Sometimes you are apt to be slightly jealous in matters pertaining to friendship, but you have the ability to hide this feeling from others. You are loyal to your friends and often willing to make sacrifices in order to help them. By bringing out the positive and attractive qualities of your personality you can lead an active and interesting social life.

The Pisces Child

The children of Pisces are of a pronounced negative disposition and subject to varying moods. They are sensitive to their environments, and for this reason it is of the greatest importance that the parents of these children guard against the influence of evil companions. The old saying about bad company corrupting good morals applies to these children, since they absorb good or evil with equal facility. Until they have learned to choose the right path for themselves, it is important that the parents guide them. They also have a strong tendency towards hero worship and there is great danger that they may become obsessed with some undesirable ideal. It will be difficult to free them from such an influence. The children of Pisces are kind and sympathetic. They are fond of rich foods, thus great care in diet is essential.

The fundamental vitality of the Pisces child is weak. Neglect may cause throat or lung disorders, while digestive disturbances result from apprehension and restlessness. It is good medicine for the Pisces child to spend as much time as possible near water. Pisces children are liable to diseases involving mucous discharge and secretion. They are also subject to somnambulism and hypochondria.

Pisces children usually learn quickly and have the ability to specialize in almost anything they choose. Though they are capable, they sometimes lack confidence in themselves and oft-times miss opportunities. They can be successful in any line of work connected with the sea or its products. These children have a mental capacity beyond that of the average.

Emotionally, they respond to their environment, as they are so compassionate.

The Pisces Wife

The Pisces woman is ideally adapted for domestic life. She is not as active as many of the other types, but her spiritual qualities and emotional responses are excellent. For this reason, many men are willing to sacrifice personal advantage for the spiritual and emotional companionship provided by the Pisces woman.

This woman is competent and thoughtful of others. Her home is a restful and luxurious place of refuge. The negative Pisces woman may be self-indulgent and tend to idle away the days by seeking entertainment and personal pleasure among the so-called artistic and literary set. While a reasonable amount of socializing is good, an excess becomes a major cause of family dissension. When the health of the Piscess wife is on the wane, encouragement and considerate attention on the part of the husband and her family is essential to her recovery. The negative side of the Pisces feminine nature is not inviting, but when the Sign has favourable planetary support, these women make devoted and sympathetic wives and mothers. They are extremely responsive and very good mates in the physical sense. They are adaptable and lovable, and their concept of sex is high and beautiful. Because of her supersensitive nature, the native of this Sign should take care when choosing a mate.

The Pisces Husband

The Pisces husband brings many benefits to the home. He is loving and attentive, considerate and thoughtful. He has a strong sense of dignity with a charitable and benevolent disposition. The negative Pisces type is not always a good provider. He gives his family all that he has, but because of his uncertain and diffident nature, he is not always able to obtain much in a material way. He also has a tendency to put off until tomorrow things he should do today. He dislikes facing the hard, cold facts of life. The positive Pisces husband has more than sufficient direction to guide him to success in any undertaking he chooses. He appreciates the finer things in life and does everything to attain them. His eyes are one of his outstanding features and they have the power to instil confidence and trust. In personal appearance he is fastidiousness, refined, and magnetic. He is sensual and seeks a sympathetic response to his love-making; he is the type of man to whom sexual satisfaction is important. His greatest weakness lies in his tendency to be careless of personal welfare due to a desire to please and help others, even at a self-sacrifice.

The Cusps of Pisces

(If your birthday is not within the cusp of your Sign, the following does not apply to you.)

You were born in Pisces with Aquarius tendencies. Your ruling planets are Neptune and Uranus. This indicates that you are a person of high principle. You have executive ability and capacity for accumulating money. Your experiences are different from those of the average. You are quiet, refined, and a good conversationalist. While you are not careless, you are inclined to be hasty. You have odd tastes and strong likes and dislikes. You are neat in appearance and dislike untidiness in others. Your fondness for travel will bring you many advantages and some unusual opportunities. Unless you are careful, you will contract an unhappy marriage. You have an ideal character but become bored and restless easily as the commonplace things of life do not appeal to you. Among your interests are science, philosophy, religion, and invention. You are promised a long and eventful life.

If the birthday is from March 17th through March 20th

You were born in Pisces with Aries tendencies. Your ruling planets are Neptune and Mars; this shows that you are intelligent and enterprising. You can execute important commissions with ease and accuracy. You are a keen observer and often benefit from mistakes of others. You frequently devise ways and means to accomplish things that others have given up as impossible. In your method of work you are original, and refuse to follow the lines of least resistance or to cling to an obsolete system. You like to keep your affairs to yourself and to be secretive about your plans until you are ready to execute them. A secret is perfectly safe with you, as you regard the confidence of others as something to be respected. You will travel extensively and can achieve a prominent place in life.

The Decanates of Pisces

If the birthday is between February 19th and February 29th

The ruling and personal planets for this decanate are Neptune and Jupiter. Jupiter is known as the harmonious planet of good fortune, while chaotic Neptune, the spiritual awakener, governs the scientific, inventive, and artistic faculties. This would indicate that the native possesses dualistic tendencies and a very changeable and unpredictable nature. Negative and positive tendencies will be definitely marked. This should give those of this decanate an opportunity to overcome and eliminate their adverse qualities, and to constructively develop the more positive ones.

If the birthday is between March 1st and March 10th

The personal orb for those of this decanate is the Moon—Ruler of Night and a symbol ol life's forces. It is the natural reflector of the Sun and governs the domestic, idealistic, and home-loving tendencies. The natives of this decanate may be changeable and temperamental. They are, also, democratic and imaginative and have pronounced domestic tendencies. There are indications of a dislike for dissension and combative activities as well. These natives will be apprehensive and occult. In its aspect with the planet Neptune, the Moon will cause them to be secretive in many of their thoughts and activities.

If the birthday is between March 11th and March 20th

The personal planet for this decanate is Mars, which is the symbol of war and the centre of divine energy. It influences the energetic, active, and constructive tendencies. Mars will materially aid these natives to overcome some of the weaker and more negative aspects of the spiritual planet Neptune.

It will give them the necessary impetus to bring about the successful conclusion to most of their endeavours. Without this force, it would be difficult for them to realize many of their cherished ambitions.

The combination of Neptune and Mars is indeed a fortunate one; the aggressive and powerful Mars strives to force its natives to attain their objectives.

The Degrees of Pisces

February 19th

You possess a retiring, studious, and chaste nature. An envy streak, which may become apparent from time to time, should be curbed. You are fond of literature, music, and art. Make maximum use of your intellectual and commercial training. Learn self-confidence and cultivate the ability to see the viewpoints of others. Due to a lack of emotional stability you may be hard to understand at times.

February 20th

Great ambition and a perceptive mind is indicated here. A highly magnetic personality and an enterprising, forceful disposition will bring many respected and beneficial friendships in life. You must try to overcome an exaggerated sense of self-importance. A wayward spirit and a desire to make changes frequently indicates travel in many lands. This aspect should be moderated to attain a more modest and stable point of view.

February 21st

You possess strong will power and a commanding, energetic personality. Initiative and good business acumen will enable you to progress rapidly in the commercial world. There is a tendency towards extravagance which should be curbed. Learn to appreciate the value of personal possessions, and to cherish them. An emotional nature full of adventure and wild dreams should be moderated. You must learn that life's greatest rewards come from well-directed personal efforts.

February 22nd

You possess an original, daring, and masterful nature. A strong will power coupled with a desire to have your own way should be curbed. A diversified education along commercial lines will be of great advantage. Much success is indicated in the business world. By exercising tolerance and patience, you can temper an overly energetic disposition. Money troubles are likely because of a good naturedness, and unwise investments.

February 23rd

You are endowed with a bright, cheerful disposition. Material success is indicated through the ability to make and hold influential and beneficial friendships. Marked originality and a good sense of humour will make for a position of prestige in the social world. A vivid imagination coupled with excess energy may cause you to be impatient, restless, and fretful at times...

February 24th

You of this birthday possess a resourceful mind and natural executive ability. Marked determination to succeed in all undertakings may cause you to work alike for good or bad. Discrimination between right and wrong should be carefully exercised. A liberal education will be an important factor in overcoming many of the negative qualities of your nature. Moderation should be the keynote throughout life.

February 25th

An impulsive and somewhat radical disposition, a brilliant mind, and excellent intuitive powers are indicated for you. This combination of mental qualities is usually found in persons who attain outstanding success and recognition in public service. Effort should be made to curb a tendency to be too impulsive and erratic. Such characteristics, if permitted to develop, can prove most detrimental.

February 26th

You possess a keen, shrewd, and alert mind. You will be deeply moved by your sympathies and will become a champion of human rights. There may be a tendency to meddle in the affairs of other people. While the intentions are most charitable, many misunderstandings and disappointments are indicated, unless you learn to mind your own business first. Success is intimated in the fields of arts, letters, and sciences.

February 27th

An adaptable, versatile, and intuitive mind is implied in this chart. The value of concentration should not be underestimated. One aspect of this Horoscope indicates a tendency to tire easily and drift rather aimlessly from one thing to another. A charming personality coupled with a good sense of humour will attract many friendships. Diligent application of the many fine capabilities shown here will aid you to attain success and happiness.

February 28th

You possess a sympathetic nature and a pleasant disposition, and should develop a sense of independence and diplomacy to curb an adventurous spirit. As a result of an inquisitive, aspiring, and perceptive mind, success is apparent in the professional world. You may be attracted to the study of medicine. An ability to get along with all types of people will aid materially in attaining success.

February 29th

Those of this degree possess a pleasing and courteous disposition, and an alert and intuitive mind. A tendency to dominate others and assume leadership regardless of consequence should be carefully checked. You are industrious and self-reliant, and possess a highly ambitious and determined nature.

March 1st

Wholesome charm and great magnetism are bestowed upon those of this chart. You have an inventive mind, and show originality in your ideas and undertakings. Beware of colds; and it is necessary that all precautions be taken to avoid draughts and sudden changes in temperatures. A desire to speculate should be curbed, as many disappointments are shown if this characteristic is permitted to develop. This birthday does not indicate an easy passage through life.

March 2nd

Those of this birthday possess a gentle and sympathetic disposition, and a good mind coupled with a charitable nature. Your magnetic personality and ability to attract staunch and loyal friendships may result in a dependent attitude. Excess attention on the part of the parents and relatives may develop a clinging-vine disposition.

March 3rd

A flexible, happy nature, and a clever, imaginative mind are the indications for you. You may become too generous and agreeable for your own good, and should learn that caution is the better part of valour. You are fond of mimicry, and possess a great fondness of the stage and theatre. One aspect in this Horoscope shows a tendency to take good fortune too lightly. This may result in taking things for granted.

March 4th

You possess a calm and peaceful attitude towards life. An open-minded manner coupled with humanitarian principles will endear you to your friends and associates. Gains are indicated through influential associations. One aspect in this Horoscope shows a tendency to take good fortune as a matter of course. This attitude should be corrected.

March 5th

You possess a benevolent, charitable, and sympathetic nature. A desire to help all those who ask assistance may result in expenditure beyond your means and cause financial embarrassment. You are subject to flattery and can easily become prey of designing friends and associates. One aspect of this Horoscope shows a tendency to become conceited.

March 6th

This chart shows an energetic nature and great skill in the execution of duties. Persistence and determination, even in the face of difficulties, can bring you success and financial independence during the middle years of life. Tolerance and consideration for the feelings of others must be learned. One aspect in this chart indicates a tendency to be somewhat impulsive.

March 7th

A sensitive and idealistic nature and a friendly and kind-hearted disposition is your good fortune. Certain planetary aspects indicate a tendency to be too generous. Learn to recognize the true from the false; remember that charity should begin at home. Fondness of travel by water and signs of a long sea voyage that may result in a profitable business connection are evident.

March 8th

You possess an intelligent, scientific, and experimental mind. Excellent conversationalists are found in this degree; you should enjoy great popularity. An independent, orderly spirit coupled with a magnetic personality is shown. The fine qualities that come with this birthday will make it rather easy for you to get what you want from parents, friends, and associates.

March 9th

You are endowed with a pleasing personality and splendid intuitive powers. A highly emotional nature may develop into an uncontrollable temper unless effort is put forth to overcome this negative aspect. You have an imaginative mind, and there is a tendency to brood and daydream too much if left alone for any great length of time. Associate with persons of your own age. Above all you must resist becoming the victim of a parent fixation.

March 10th

Those of you born on this day possess a serious and aspiring nature coupled with strong mental capabilities. You are profound and practical. A strong sense of independence and a desire to help others in less fortunate circumstances is also indicated. At times you may become too magnanimous for your own good. You show a marked respect for your elders. You will create your own destiny. Success in life is intimated through dealing with new enterprises and large institutions catering to the public welfare.

March 11th

An original and enterprising mind, and a harmonious disposition are indicated for you. One aspect in this Horoscope foretells that you are easily satisfied and may lack the incentive to overcome obstacles. Learn self-confidence and the practical methods of achieving success. Cheerful companions of your own age rather than older persons are essential. You must learn to temper your high hopes and ambitions, and remember realities.

March 12th

Your splendid character and sympathetic nature are coupled with deep emotions. Instinctively intellectual, you will mature early, but show a tendency to become overly reserved and studious. It is essential that you have a happy environment. Pursuit of outdoor activity and athletics is strongly advised. Your emotional temperament needs patient and understanding treatment.

March 13th

You are endowed with an expansive and genial personality. You can attain much popularity in your social life through charming manners and interesting conversation. Love of travel is indicated. Your emotional nature is stable. An artistic temperament coupled with a magnetic personality will make for success in a professional rather than a business career. Public recognition through literary ability can be assured by proper education.

March 14th

This chart indicates an astute, practical, and intuitive mind. An artistic temperament with marked humanitarian principles will bring many lasting and influential friendships into your life. You are generous, of good appearance, kind-mannered, and athletically inclined. One aspect in this Horoscope indicates a tendency to shirk responsibility and a desire to get by with little personal effort. The diligent application of your many natural talents is for success.

March 15th

A keen intellectual mind is in you coupled with excellent powers of concentration. Avoid a tendency to assume a too serious outlook upon life. A bright, cheerful atmosphere and the company of congenial friends will greatly aid in eliminating this aspect. A highly magnetic personality and an independent nature can make for great success in the business world, especially if you exert effort to overcome some of the more negative tendencies shown in this Horoscope. You are fond of music and travel.

March 16th

You of this degree possess unusual intellectual qualities and the ability to develop your mind along scientific lines. There is an indication that you can develop a steady and forceful disposition. One aspect in this Horoscope indicates a desire to defy convention and become a bold innovator. Refrain from making radical changes in love and business; you are liable to suffer through fraud and unwise speculation.

March 17th

A sensitive, impressionable, and inquisitive nature is indicated for you. Love of travel to distant lands is shown. At times you may become difficult because of a cross temper. One aspect in this chart shows a rather extravagant nature, which should be curbed in order to prevent serious financial embarrassment in later years. A marked interest in humanitarian activity should be encouraged by proper educational training.

March 18th

You possess a romantic nature. A rather "hard to please" complex is due to a self-centred viewpoint. You show a decided tendency to associate with persons older than yourself; try to make friends of your own age. Tolerance and understanding should be practiced. Fondness for the good things of life, which results in depletion of health and finances, should be curbed.

March 19th

If you were born on this date, you possess a bright and cheerful disposition, and a generous nature. You will be righteous in both personal and social matters. Pursue a career where your mental faculties will be demonstrated to the best advantage. A strong attachment for the home and parents is also indicated. One aspect in this Horoscope shows a desire to be well-dressed and in the height of fashion at all times.

March 20th

An unselfish and charitable disposition is the endowment of this birthday. You must learn the value of concentration, to overcome a tendency to do too many things at one time. You can be a fluent conversationalist and prolific writer. Train yourself towards some definite goal or profession where your many natural talents will be an asset. Once you learn to control your emotional nature, success and public recognition will be assured. You should experience more than average good fortune.

Compatible and Incompatible Signs of Pisces

At its best, Pisces is a well of sympathy, charity, benevolence, and hospitality. As a rule the natives of Pisces are kind, sympathetic, imaginative, and highly emotional. They are intuitive, receptive, and mediumistic, but are not generally very practical. The Sign is a sentimental one that tends to be swayed by every emotion, and puts up little resistance to temptation.

Petulant irritability, incessant chatter, and the habit of "dissolving into tears" at the slightest provocation are some of the feminine weaknesses of Pisces.

The vices of the Sign, however, are based upon weakness rather than any depravity, and much will depend upon upbringing, and choice of associates.

While the negative side of Pisces is not inviting, the more robust and positive type make the kindest, most loving, devoted, and sympathetic mates. They are extremely responsive, and this tends to make them good partners in the physical sense of the word.

They are adaptable and experimental, and their concept of sex is on a high plane.

Yes, Pisceans are sentimental souls, easy to get along with as a rule, though they are subject to moody periods during which they are difficult to understand.

They have an apparently inexhaustible fund of sympathy and good fellowship, but their variety of moods may make contentment in marriage hard for them. They are somewhat unsure as lovers, for they seem to have a need for "atmosphere" in the emotional field, even though they are inwardly full of affection. The trouble seems to be the dual nature which produces a series of psychological contradictions. Thus, while they experience a strong desire for romance, a force within seems to form a brake on their emotions. They want to say the nicest things—instead they may say just the opposite.

Pisceans, more than any other Zodiacal types, need to be careful in the selection of a matrimonial partner. They are so easily persuaded that they may find themselves married to the very partner they should be at pains to avoid!

Pisces and Aries

Aries may prove too fiery and too aggressive for the sentimental and gentle Pisces. Though Pisces is quite romantic, he desires a more delicate and refined approach to love-making than the impatient Aries cares to take time for. Neptune, the planet of the higher mind, gives Pisces an ethereal quality. Unless Aries is willing to take a trip to the clouds now and then, he'll probably have to change his mind.

Pisces and Taurus

This is usually a happy-ever-after combination. Both natives will find just what they are looking for in each other, and their compatibility is strengthened by the fact that Neptune, ruler of Pisces, is the higher octave of Venus, ruler of Taurus. Pisces is romantic and imaginative; Taurus will like that. Taurus is steady, strong, and loving; Pisces will adore that. Both are home-loving. This combination would be a good one, indeed.

Pisces and Gemini

This does not look good. Gemini loves to flit in the pursuit of happiness, or in the happiness of pursuit. Pisces will not like that and will probably seek retreat in a cloud of gloom. Few people can change their basic make-up and adopt an entirely new character, but that is what Gemini will have to do if he marries a Piscean. Not good at all!

Pisces and Cancer.

These are real affinities. Both like home, possessions, and friends. Both will pull together for their mutual interests. Both are sentimental and loving, and each likes to possess and hang on to what he cherishes. Certainly there will be moments of gloom and doom when both of them will feel hurt at the same time. They may wrangle all over the house, but even with these little momentary "storms", they will have happiness together.

Pisces and Leo

Leo likes to have someone dependent on him, but he won't like the possessiveness of Pisces, or the tears; neither will Pisces' pouting appeal. This does not look like a good match. Leo's bold and vigorous temperament may be a little too much for sensitive Pisces. Better not chance it.

Pisces and Virgo

There is a marked contrast between these two—and while "opposites" are supposed to attract, if there is too much opposition or contrast, it may not be a combination. Virgo's criticism and bossiness may break down the sensitive spirit of Pisces. Pisces' sentimental tearfulness might be just too much for Virgo to take for any length of time. There would be too much "alteration" to make on this outfit.

Pisces and Libra

These two can like each other very much, but marriage would prove an acid test to any affection they felt. Libra is very social and Pisces is a "togetherness" person. Libra could not tolerate jealousy and suspicion; Pisces would want Libra to be exclusively his or her own at all times. Not a good bet.

Pisces and Scorpio

This is a "love-at-first-sight" affair; but it is not likely to stand up for any length of time. Scorpio will always have an ear and perhaps will want to rove when compliments are proffered. Pisces wants exclusive ownership. Scorpio, too, is possessive, but will not tolerate that characteristic in another for long. Pisces will pout and scold while Scorpio shouts, and another marriage becomes a has-been.

Pisces and Sagittarius

These two can enjoy a beautiful friendship so long as Pisces doesn't presume on the other's boundaries, but it would not prove to be a good combination for marriage. Sagittarius, free and easygoing, couldn't stop to lug the clinging, possessive Pisces along the road of life. Nor could he stand the abused attitude of Pisces. No matter how much Sagittarius loved Pisces, pity would soon supplant love, and it would be duty and conscience battling within. He couldn't stand the confinement of being married to a Piscean, and Pisces couldn't take the varied interests of Sagittarius.

Pisces and Capricorn

These two have a very good chance for happiness. Capricorn, so much misunderstood, will find sympathy and understanding in the Pisces mate. Pisces will find the practicality of Capricorn admirable, for it will increase the Piscean's feeling of security. Capricorn is never happier than when someone who needs him clings fast. They are entirely compatible sexually, and there is every chance of an enduring union between these two.

Pisces and Aquarius

If Pisces will try to understand the Aquarian mate, there will be a good chance of happiness here. Pisces can give tolerance and sympathy, and these two qualities coupled with human understanding can be the Piscean contribution. Aquarius must learn to give Pisces the benefit of the doubt; then Aquarius will help Pisces to build up self-confidence, so that the Piscean fears, which seems to be based largely on insecurity here, will prove groundless.

Pisces and Pisces

Since these two seem to have the same virtues and vices, they should get along well together, for at least there will be understanding and sympathy for each other. Both have the same love of home and possessions, and the same basic interests. The only drawback is a possible drifting too far from practical realities. Both at least can be anchored to each other, so that they can put their shoulders to the wheel and face the responsibilities that reality demands. They have the refinement and delicacy that each desires in love, so all in all, this should be a good union.

Some Famous Persons Born in the Sign of Pisces

Alexander Graham Bell—Inventor
William Jennings Bryan—Statesman
Luther Burbank—Naturalist
Enrico Caruso—Singer
Grover Cleveland—US President
Albert Einstein—Physicist
Geraldine Farrar—Opera Star
Jackie Gleason—Actor and Musician
Ben Hecht—Novelist and Dramatist
Henry W. Longfellow—Poet
James Madison—US President
David Sarnoff—Communications Executive
Dinah Shore—Singer
John Steinbeck—Novelist
Elizabeth Taylor—Actress
Ellen Terry—Actress
Earl Warren—US Chief Justice
George Washington—US President
Rex Harrison—Actor

13

THE PLANETS

IF THE twelve Signs constitute the innate, latent possibilities of the organism, and, as such, represent the constitution as a whole, the planets comprise the active forces which arouse these latent possibilities. In this duplex action of Sign and planet, both natures come into play and produce the varying results of external life. Man, the microcosm, is merely the sounding board, so to say, the reacting point for this ethereal and magnetic vibrations. Furthermore, while the twelve Signs represent the human organism as a form containing possibilities, the Sun, Moon, and planets represent the spirit, soul, and senses of that organism. Man consists of body, soul, and spirit. As at present manifested, he has five physical senses. The constellations are the body; the Moon is the soul; the Sun, the spirit; and the five planets, Saturn, Jupiter, Mars, Venus, and Mercury, represent and express the five physical senses. It is in this light that we must consider the various natures of planetary influx.

The Sun

Ruler of Leo, centre of the solar system, and Giver of Life. It rules the Individuality.

In good aspect it influences: ambition, loyalty, faithfulness, honour, and stands for dignity.

In bad aspect it influences: vanity, egoism, arrogance, hate, and domination.

Under favourable influence: you can seek employment ... try for a promotion ... ask favours ... gain through personal enterprise and increased responsibilities.

Under unfavourable influence: it is best to avoid seeking favours from persons of wealth and those in superior positions . . . not to divulge your secrets . . . overcome a tendency to be egoistic, over-ambitious, venturesome, over-confident, and domineering. You are apt to suffer financial losses if you speculate or lend money.

The Moon

Ruler of Cancer, is known as the Force of Life and rules the Personality.

In good aspect it influences: idealism, reception, grace, adaptability, domestic and maternal instincts.

In bad aspect it influences: weakness, changeability, inconsistency, laziness, and unreliability.

Under favourable influences: seek changes, journeys by water, new friendships, increased trade, better domestic conditions, and improvement for women.

Under unfavourable influence: women should try to avoid danger of illness, losses and disappointments . . . the planet affects general health conditions, public unpopularity, and possibilities for disagreeable changes as well as sorrow through females.

Mercury

Ruler of Gemini and Virgo, is known as the God of Knowledge and rules the Mind and Memory.

In good aspect it influences: ingenuity, intellect, versatility, and concentration.

In bad aspect it influences: carelessness, artfulness, cunningness, shiftlessness, and shrewdness.

Under favourable influence: good for publishers, editors, reporters, distributors, advertisers, book-keepers, architects, teachers, lawyers, scientists, and young people; correspondence, writing literary work, and all mental pursuits. The mind is keen and thoughts come clearly.

Under unfavourable influence: Be careful when signing contracts . . . watch emotional impulses . . . act with prudence . . . avoid changes or removals . . . guard against friction with relatives, neighbours, or co-workers. Tends to disturb the stomach and nervous system.

Venus

Ruler of Taurus and Libra, is known as the Goddess of Love and Beauty.

In good aspect it influences: peace, happiness, perfection, and harmony.

In bad aspect it influences: love of ease and pleasure, immodesty, self-indulgence, and thoughtlessness.

Under favourable influence: shop for a new wardrobe, jewellery, and luxuries . . . seek opportunities for romance, marriage, entertainment, social activities, and popularity . . . cultivate new friendships with the opposite sex . . . deal with dress-makers, clothiers, artists, singers, actors, musicians . . . make collections. The feelings and emotions are easily aroused and you respond more readily to affection and sympathy.

Under unfavourable influence: use moderation in all dealings with the opposite sex . . . refrain from excesses of all kinds . . . possible liability to disappointments or disagreements in domestic affairs . . . you are more sensitive and easily hurt . . . postpone important social functions . . . do not speculate . . . do business only with those you know can be trusted.

Mars

Ruler of Aries and Scorpio, is known as the God of War and the Centre of Divine Energy.

In good aspect it influences: courage, activity, adventure, fearlessness, and executive ability.

In bad aspect it influences: boldness, audaciousness, destructiveness, and selfishness.

Under favourable influence: deal with builders, engineers, machinists, soldiers, dentists, and surgeons. You are more ambitious, energetic, ardent, and resolute. The tendency is towards more success and progress in business and personal affairs. You can tackle problems that call for aggressive effort, speed, hard work, and common sense.

Under unfavourable influence: keep out of controversial

matters where friends or co-workers are concerned . . . guard against carelessness that may lead to accidents . . . be patient with delays, interruptions, and restrictions . . . watch temperamental displays of indiscretions . . . be cautious when dealing in property or real estate matters.

Jupiter

Ruler of Sagittarius, is known as the God of Fortune, and is the Royal Planet, said to control the Divine Wisdom.

In good aspect it influences: generosity, benevolence, happiness, devotion, philosophy, and security.

In bad aspect it influences: wastefulness, extravagance, impatience, and lawlessness.

Under favourable influence: begin new ventures, buy and sell, speculate, ask favours, proceed with matters pertaining to lawyers, bankers, merchants, brokers, politicians, and physicians. Attend important social functions. It tends to make you more hopeful, generous, and popular.

Under unfavourable influence: shun speculative investment . . . watch out for misplaced confidence, bad judgment, and extravagant urges . . . women should be very careful of all health matters, sign no contracts, and make no promises.

Saturn

Ruler of Capricorn, is known as the God of Time.

In good aspect it influences: steadfastness, vitality, justice, prudence, and action.

In bad aspect it influences: hypocrisy, discontent, deceit, and avariciousness.

Under favourable influences: good for dealings with plumbers, shoemakers, miners, gardeners, farmers and landlords. Seek favours from elderly people. Use tact and diplomacy instead of force. Proceed to finish all matters pertaining to real estate. You can obtain a position of trust and responsibility.

Under unfavourable influence: postpone changes, removals, and long journeys . . . do not start new ventures . . . guard your speech and delay important decisions . . . be careful with elderly people . . . caution must be exercised in buying, selling or making investments . . . unfortunate for marriage . . . watch your health.

Uranus

Ruler of Aquarius, is known as the God of Air. It is a rather eccentric planet that controls all unpredictable activities.

In good aspect it influences: originality, inventions, freedom, individualism.

In bad aspect it influences: peculiarities, unexpected and unforeseen happenings, and obstinacy.

Under favourable influence: you may make changes, investigate new, original, or unique undertakings. Travel for business, work for social reform and humanitarian principles. Deal with electricans, railroads, aeronautical firms, inventors, and scientists.

Under unfavourable influence: use caution around sharp instruments or inflammable objects . . . be careful while travelling . . . avoid changes or removals . . . do not confide in strangers or persons of the opposite sex . . . enter into no partnerships, do not join any clubs or associations . . . practice restraint and avoid unconventional association.

Neptune

Ruler of Pisces, is known as the God of the Waters. It is the Spiritual Awakener and gives Inspiration and Idealism.

In good aspect it influences: inspiration and idealism. Universal intelligence.

In bad aspect it influences: indolence, deceit, disrespect, and shiftlessness.

Under favourable influence: good for business dealings in shipping chemicals or perfumes, activities related to the seas and liquids in general. Favours voyages, artistic endeavours, and matters concerned with secret orders. Conducive to mysterious romantic associations.

Under unfavourable influence: avoid dealings with hospitals, prisons, and other confining institutions ... guard against fraud, deception, and get-rich-quick schemes ... avoid doubtful friendships.

The Planet Pluto: Ruler of the Unknown

Strange as it may seem, it is nevertheless a fact, Pluto was the missing planet. It has been allegorically expressed by Jesus as the Prodigal Son; by Moses as Abel; and by the prophets of the Scandinavian *Edda* as "Ragnarok". In our esoteric system there are ten celestial bodies somewhere: The Sun and nine planets. Until 1933 we had only nine in all. Where, then, was the lost one? The exalted adept alone can solve this problem. Suffice it to say, it symbolizes the missing soul within the human constitution. Pushed out of the line of march by disturbing forces, Pluto became, for a time, the prey of disruptive actions and ultimately lost form, and is now a mass of fragments. The ring of planetoids between the orbits of Mars and Jupiter indicates to us the empty throne of Abel, whom Cain (Mars) slew in his anger. The time ultimately came when this orb was reconstituted. Until that time the missing soul sought its physical mate in vain—except in rare cases.

The old, and now much abused, Chaldean sages were thoroughly acquainted with the planetary influences, and in order to teach these principles to their youth they elaborated beautiful imagery in the form of fables and allegories. They gave the nature and power of each group of organs in the human brain to the character of that planet which they believed controlled its activities, and then worked out the theory into a series of mythical histories of gods and divine personages who incarnated themselves for the benefit of man.

Thus Mars took the character of Vulcan, the god of War; Venus and her son, Cupid, were assigned the character of Love and the sympathetic tendencies of the human heart; while the benevolent Jupiter assumed the position of Father, the kindly, generous parent, good alike to all his offspring.

To continue, the Sun becomes the great archangel Michael, who defeats Satan and tramples upon the head of the Serpent of Matter; the Moon becomes transformed into the angel Gabriel; Mercury becomes the angelic Raphael, the genius of wisdom and art; and Saturn becomes the angel Cassiel, the genius of reflection in the astral light.

Uranus, Neptune and Pluto, of course, were not known to the Chaldeans.

14

THE TWELVE HOUSES

THE MAGNETIC polarity of any given geographical point of our earth's surface is changing every moment. This continual changing in the earth is accompanied by a corresponding change in the electric and more ethereal vital currents of the atmosphere. Both these varying conditions are caused, primarily, by the diurnal motion of the earth upon its axis from west to east, which causes the whole heavens to transit the visible horizon from east to west during the space of one natural day—twenty-four hours. The secondary causes are the various motions and aspects of the Sun, Moon and planets as they relate to the positions of the earth in her annual orbit about the sun. The primary basis, the diurnal motion of the planet, claims our attention first. We will, therefore, briefly examine its nature and philosophy.

The real motions of the earth are the only motions that have any real influence upon the physical organism of its inhabitants. These motions determine the length of the day, measure out to us the proportion of light and darkness, regulate the seasons, and fix with the hand of fate, the exact duration of the year. All these have a manifest influence upon the organism of man.

As our mother Earth revolves upon her axis, the whole of the heavens seem to rise, culminate and set upon every portion of her surface. Though this rising and setting is only an appearance so far as the heavens are concerned, it is absolutely real to the earth's habitants, because the influences, as they transit the earth from east to west, are exactly the same as if the earth was the stationary centre of our solar system, and the heavens were revolving around it.

The varying conditions of the astral and magnetic forces are caused by the various angles at which, in the apparent motions, the stellar influx is reflected to any given point of the earth. For instance, the conditions at sunrise are quite different from the conditions prevailing at noon when the Sun is shining upon the meridian. At sunset we see another wonderful difference manifested, possessing nothing in common with either noon or sunrise. Then, again, we have the midnight state of the earth and the atmosphere in which the conditions are the polar opposite of those in force at noon. These cardinal points of the day indicate the greatest changes, but, as a matter of course, these changes from one to the other are gradual. To measure this gradual angular change the ancient astrologers divided that space of the heavens visable at any moment into six Houses or mansions, as they termed them, and the opposite or invisible arc into the same number, making twelve in all, designated as the diurnal and nocturnal Houses of the heavens. Modern Astrologers follow the same principles, because their influence can be verified in every correctly calculated Horoscope, when the time, day, month, year and place of birth occupied by the native are taken into consideration.

These twelve Houses contain, like the Signs of the Zodiac, 30 degrees of space each, but unlike them their distance is measured by degrees of right ascension, or time, instead of celestrial longitude. This is the only real relation existing between the twelve Houses and the twelve Signs. Each House comprises a department of life, or mode of expression, or type of interest distinct from the other houses.

The First House. Relates to your personality, natural disposition, self-interest and outlook on the world generally. Physical appearance, and constitution and how you will express yourself. The first House also represents matters in health that concern the head and face.

The Second House. Your financial prospects, your skill and conditions that have to do with earning power. Benefits of income from personal possessions, profit or loss. The nose, throat, ears and neck are the parts of the body related to the second House.

The Third House. The logic and memory power you have,

relatives and kindred, short journeys, vehicles of travel, writings, studies, mental inclinations and ability in advertising, publicity and manual skill. The lungs, arms, hands and shoulders are controlled by the third House.

The Fourth House. Conditions at home, environment, real estate, property owned, savings, the father and automobiles. Opposition in your business or career, conditions later in life, agricultural matters and mines. This House represents your digestive system and the breast.

The Fifth House. Love affairs, amusements, personal pleasures, and children are influenced by this House. Also speculations, personal attainments, affairs of showmanship, the theatre and the arts. The outlook for the year also depends upon planetary influences in the fifth House. The parts of the body controlled by this House are the heart and back.

The Sixth House. Your health, sickness arising from worry, servants, fellow workers, service to others, employer relations, food and clothing. Occupation, hygiene, the Army and Navy. Also small animals. The digestive organs and abdomen are represented by this House.

The Seventh House. Your ability to see both sides of a question, the general public, the husband, the wife, contracts, legal partnerships, law suits, open opposition, unions, marriage and divorce are in this House. The kidneys and veins are controlled by the seventh House.

The Eighth House. Legacies and all matters concerned with the dead, taxes and debts. Money and goods of others. Financial affairs of your marriage partner are placed in this House. Also spiritual regeneration and occult studies. This House rules the muscular system, sex organs and bladder.

The Ninth House. This House relates to philosophical and higher education. Universities and the professions, particularly legal, scientific and literary. Long journeys by water or air and interests at a distance. This House controls the nervous system, liver, hips and thighs.

The Tenth House. This House represents matters of government, politics and power, credit, the mother. Also occupational advancement; profession, career. Affects honour and reputation; relations with parents and superiors. Rules the knees.

The Eleventh House. Relates to income from occupation. Fraternities. Influences wishes, desires, friends, as well as fears and apprehensions. Controls the legs and ankles.

The Twelfth House. The House of secrets, troubles, restrictions, sorrows, self-defeat. Secret enemies. Confidential arrangements, relations with confining institutions such as asylums, hospitals, prisons. Also has to do with large animals. Rules the feet and toes.

CONCLUSION

The poet Manilius, celebrated in the days of Caesar Augustus, set forth the Astrology of the Romans in the following beautiful description of the twelve Signs and the constellations:

Now constellations, Muse! and signs rehearse;
In order let them sparkle in thy verse;
First Aries, glorious in his golden wool,
Looks back, and wonders at the mighty Bull,
Whose hind parts first appear, he bending lies,
With threatening head, and calls the Twins to rise;
They clasp for fear, and mutually embrace,
And next the Twins with an unsteady pace,
Bright Cancer rolls; then Leo shakes his mane
And following Virgo calms his rage again.
Then day and night are weighed in Libra's scales,
Equal awhile, at least the night prevails;
And longer grown the heavier scale inclined,
And draws bright Scorpio from the winter signs.
Him Centaur follows with an aiming eye,
His bow full drawn and ready to let fly;
Next narrow horns, the twisted Capricorn shows,
And from Aquarius' urn a flood o'er flows.
Near their lov'd waves cold Pisces takes their seat,
With Aries join, and make the round complete.